"Colonel Palmer has written a comprehensive, objective and highly creditable synthesis of America's involvement in Vietnam. Of all that has been written about that tragic period of our national history, no publication that I have read more accurately addresses the complex and controversial issues involved in our most visible but least understood war. Colonel Palmer has made a significant contribution to the literature, and thus an understanding of what really happened."

W. C. Westmoreland
General, U.S. Army, Retired

"The author's credentials are unimpeachable, based as they are on extensive, varied and prolonged combat service in Vietnam.... The book will add a new and clearer picture of the pluses and minuses; of the faulty and sound decisions at high levels.... But the major points I wish to stress are the excellence, clarity, frankness and readability of this book...a fine contribution to history."

Matthew B. Ridgway
General, U.S. Army, Retired

DAVE RICHARD PALMER

SUMMONS OF THE TRUMPET

A HISTORY OF THE VIETNAM WAR FROM A MILITARY MAN'S VIEWPOINT

BALLANTINE BOOKS • NEW YORK

To the two and a half million Americans who heeded the summons of the trumpet and served their country in Vietnam. Veterans of a woeful crusade, they have not found their country particularly grateful for that service.

CONTENTS

Maps ix
Preface...................................... xi
Acknowledgments   xv

PROLOGUE: The Incomprehensible War...........xvii
PART I   The Advisory Decade, 1954–1964
             Chapter 1   The Lines Are Drawn   3
             Chapter 2   The Drift to War   6
             Chapter 3   The Naive Years   15
             Chapter 4   Realization and Reaction   24
             Chapter 5   Arms and Advice   30
             Chapter 6   The Battle of Ap Bac   37
             Chapter 7   The Downfall of Diem   52
             Chapter 8   Turmoil and
                          Transformation   59
PART II   Stemming the Tide, 1965
             Chapter 9   Season of Decision   79
             Chatper 10   Rolling Thunder   93
             Chapter 11   The New Face of Conflict   102
             Chapter 12   Battle of the Ia Drang   116

PART III	The Search for a Strategy, 1966–1967	
	Chapter 13 "An Escalating Military Stalemate"	135
	Chapter 14 "A Protracted War of Attrition"	147
	Chapter 15 More Rolling Thunder	154
	Chapter 16 The Iron Triangle	168
	Chapter 17 The Phalanx of Fire	177
	Chapter 18 The Search Fails	186
PART IV	The Climactic Year, 1968	
	Chapter 19 The History Teacher	207
	Chapter 20 General Offensive— General Uprising	220
	Chapter 21 Unexpected Callers	232
	Chapter 22 The Battles of *Tet*	240
	Chapter 23 Of Victory and Defeat	255
PART V	The Search for a Peace, 1969–1973	
	Chapter 24 Nixon Takes Command	271
	Chapter 25 Vietnamization	278
	Chapter 26 Cambodian Incursion	290
	Chapter 27 Lam Son 719	302
	Chapter 28 The Test	310
	Chapter 29 Exit America	326
	Chapter 30 An Indecent Interval	332
EPILOGUE:	No More Vietnams	340
	Sources	343
	Index	349

MAPS

Indochina xxiii
South Vietnam xxiv
Battle of Ap Bac 45
Battle of the Ia Drang 124
Landing Zone X-Ray 126
Operation "Cedar Falls" 175
The *Tet* Offensive 239
Operation *Toan Thang 43* 297
Operation *Lam Son 719* 305

PREFACE

This book is the story of America's military involvement in Vietnam—why we entered, what we did, and how we left.

It has been very astutely observed that the United States, with a policy of keeping a soldier in Vietnam only a year, didn't have its army there for twelve years; rather, it was there for one year—a dozen times. As a result, there was no readily comprehensible pattern of continuity. The war was too cut up. My intent has been to provide a broad history of our entire military experience in Vietnam, putting all those years into perspective.

There will be those who claim that history, true history, can't be written so soon after the event. In a sense, of course, they are correct. The definitive version of the Vietnam War will be published decades hence in multiple volumes. But we live now. And we may be compelled to wage another war before those volumes become available. History, if it is to have any real purpose, tells us where we have been and where we are, thus helping to point out the best avenue into the future. Perhaps this work will begin to give shape to some of those vital road signs.

Vietnam, like all our wars, had its full share of errors and shortcomings, as well as triumphs. The reader expecting this book to be a whitewash of our military activities will be disappointed—as will one anticipating a complete condemnation of our efforts there. We went through this longest of American conflicts with both successes and failures; despite the pitfalls inherent in dealing with such an emotion-laden subject, I have attempted to balance the scales.

America's military role in the Vietnam War passed through three distinct phases, each punctuated by a dramatic exclamation point. First was the decade when Americans were advisors only; it ended with U.S. combat troops rushing into the fray in 1965. Next was the period when perplexed military leaders sought solutions to the strategic paradox they found themselves in; it closed with the thunderclap of the *Tet* offensive of 1968. Last was the prolonged search for a way out; it culminated with the massive bombing of North Vietnam at Christmastime in 1972. The five parts of the book parallel this chronological outline.

The book ends with the American withdrawal in the early months of 1973. What happened after the departure of our fighting men is an unhappy and indelible part of the political and moral history of the United States, but it does not belong in the story of our direct military involvement in Vietnam. That involvement ended in 1973. And to make sure it could not begin anew, Congress made further military action in Southeast Asia illegal. Just as the struggle there had flamed for years before America entered, so was it fated to endure after America exited. The American military intervention was one phase of a much longer war—this book is about that phase, not the longer war.

This volume is not a study of campaigns or battles. The focus is at a higher level—the translation of national policies into military strategy and operations. Nevertheless, strategy viewed in isolation from its tactical realities loses meaning, so selected campaigns or battles are woven into the narrative of each of the five parts. Nor is strategy a one-sided matter; the plans and actions of North Vietnam and the Viet Cong receive full treatment.

No war is ever strictly a military affair. Each has political, economic, and psychological ingredients as well. For Vietnam, that was especially true. It may well have been, in fact, that the military ingredient was not even the major one in Vietnam. The literature on the conflict would seem to confirm that—library shelves groan under the weight of all the words on the war, but surprisingly few of them deal with the military aspects of it. "Surprisingly," because it *was* a military conflict; over two-and-a-half million Americans fought there and nearly fifty-thousand of them were killed in action. Therefore, with full recognition that there were other considerations and dimensions, this book is singly devoted to an investigation of America's *military* involvement. Other factors are discussed only as required to provide a backdrop to the story.

Over a period of eleven years I had unusual opportunities to study the war from many angles: from relatively revealing vantage points in Washington and Saigon; from the academic observation post as a college faculty member both in the United States and South Vietnam; from the inquisitive position of a graduate student; from the muddy level of a combat soldier actually fighting the war. My military duties took me from one end of South Vietnam to the other, from the Demilitarized Zone in the north to the Ca Mau Peninsula in the south, from the Cambodian border to the South China Sea. I participated in airmobile assaults in the delta and in armored penetrations of Viet Cong jungle redoubts near Saigon; I accompanied convoys in the Central Highlands and got ambushed in the A Shau Valley; I sipped gin and tonic with reporters in Saigon and played very poor tennis at the Cercle Sportif. I was fortunate to have had such a wide array of experiences—they have perhaps given me some small degree of perspective. They should also indicate that, although I have tried to write as an historian, the book is, in the final analysis, a soldier's view of Vietnam.

# ACKNOWLEDGMENTS

I am most grateful to the many people who have helped me with this work. Some of them I never met, like the helicopter pilots flying through heavy fire to take out a wounded comrade; some I never talked to, like the Viet Cong guerrillas firing from ambush sites along a jungle road. But they and others too numerous to name deeply influenced the writing. I readily admit a debt to them all.

Of those whose advice had a direct impact on the book, I would be remiss not to mention several whose aid was most significant. Thomas E. Griess, head of the History Department at West Point, first set me on the road. His initial prodding and continued encouragement were all-important; had it not been for him, I would never even have begun. Charles MacDonald generously contributed time and experience to assist me in putting the study into publishable form. George Alexander, Richard Craig, and George Pappas provided me the essential ingredients of an environment conducive to writing and the time required to do it; the first two at the Vietnamese National Military Academy in Dalat, and the third at the U.S. Army Military History Institute at Carlisle Barracks. Pappas also assisted by obtaining valuable comments from impartial readers.

Several others enhanced the manuscript by donating material or by candidly critiquing portions of it. Some did both. Alphabetically: Reamer Argo, John Bahnsen, Calvert Benedict, Elwood Cobey, Tom Collier, Clyde Earnest, Curtis

Esposito, Roy Flint, John Galvin, Lorena Glover, Bill Graf, James Grimsley, David Hawley, Richard Hilton, Charles von Luttichau, Jay Luvaas, Harold Moore, Marvin Mucha, Ramon Nadal, Jim Ransone, Theodore Ropp, Lou Schroeder, Norm Schwarzkopf, Charles Sell, Robert Shoemaker, Sidney Smith, Jim Snide, Thai Minh Son, Nguyen Van Su (assassinated in the Central Highlands, 1972), Lam Quang Thi, Jim Torrence (killed in a helicopter crash in the Mekong Delta, 1971), VeLoy Varner, Arthur Wade, William Westmoreland, Jack Woodmansee, Dao Mong Xuan, and Rush Yelverton. Their contributions did more than improve the book—they made it. However, because I did not always agree with them or use their material just as they gave it to me, I still must accept whatever criticism accrues for all mistakes.

Leroy Miller, Ronald Latham, and Nguyen Thi Lien provided professional administrative assistance; Pham Thi Ngoc Loan and Marilyn Kelly combined to prepare the original manuscript, while Alma Brown and Barbara Sides helped with revisions. James Stanton sketched the maps. The careful and devoted attention of all of them was indicative of the pride and high standards they possess in full measure.

Last, and in several ways most important, was my family. Allison and Kersten helped as only they could, while Lu was a mainstay. She uncomplainingly kept things glued together at home while I spent a total of two years in Vietnam and disappeared on several other occasions to do research and writing. Then she lent a hand in refining the final manuscript. To her, critic and helpmate, I owe the most thanks of all.

PROLOGUE:
The Incomprehensible War

Rocky Bleier, a star football player at Notre Dame in the mid-1960s, had planned to play professionally with the Pittsburgh Steelers. But someone goofed. The Steeler management failed to protect Rocky with one of the many loopholes available, and he was drafted. He became the only one of the thousands of America's professional athletes to fight in Vietnam. A grenade blast nearly cost him his legs. His career as an athlete seemed to be over. Later, in an interview, Bleier expressed bitterness at only one aspect of his unhappy experience: no one had ever told him what it was all about. Not in basic training, not en route, not in his unit in Vietnam. "I wanted some reason for doing what I was going to do," he said, "but I never got it."

Millions of Americans fought in Vietnam; few knew why. Like Rocky Bleier, most of them came home unable to comprehend the reasons for their sacrifice of time—or blood. They found family and friends who were similarly perplexed. The inability to understand was not caused by lack of time to grasp the reasons why, for the war dragged on and on, an unpopular, unending conflict in which victory seemed impossible. A generation grew to adulthood in its shadow. Some of the last to die there had not even been born when the United States first became involved.

As a matter of fact, for most Americans the fighting in Vietnam was cast in the murky, unreal light on the other side of the looking glass. In a simpler age, Lewis Carroll had unknowingly but splendidly described the Alice-in-Wonderland quality of our longest war:

> "Well, in our country," said Alice, still panting a little, "you'd generally get to somewhere else—if you ran very fast for a long time as we've been doing."
>
> "A slow sort of country!" said the Queen. "Now here, you see, it takes all the running you can do to keep in the same place. If you want to get somewhere else, you must run at least twice as fast as that!"

It was a war to confound even the experts. In a manner of speaking, it was not a war at all. Other clashes in our recent past had been fought according to rather clear rules, in campaigns which could be followed on a map, against a visible and usually vilified foe, and for a recognizable objective. By those standards, then, the war in Vietnam was a nonwar. Soldiers and civilians alike found it fragmented and frustrating. Although it was the best documented and the most reported in our history, it was paradoxically the least comprehended.

Yet there it sits athwart our history. Years and years of it. Easily our longest war. An indigestible lump leaving in its wake a society divided and, altogether, hundreds of thousands dead. It cannot be allowed to remain incomprehensible. If there are to be no more Vietnams, we must know more of the first Vietnam. We must try to fathom the course and conduct of our military involvement there.

Perhaps the first step toward understanding it is to ponder some of the reasons for misunderstanding. They are many.

To begin with, it was a limited war. The United States did not mobilize. Only a small percentage of our population was engaged in the fighting; at home all but the military services and draft-age young men enjoyed "business as usual." The country sensed no feeling of immediate danger and certainly no spirit of total involvement. It just wasn't like World War II, people were quick to note, when everyone was involved, when conflict was total.

Most wars, it can be argued, have been limited. One can dig way back in history to say that the final Punic War—when Rome defeated Carthage, slaughtered the population, razed the city, plowed under the ruins, and sowed the furrows with salt—was not in any way limited. And Genghis Khan's campaigns were most ruthlessly unlimited. But it is hard to find other examples; in some manner or other a limiting factor was always present. Even in World War II our wish to eradicate the Nazis was limited by our capacity to train men and produce machines in numbers sufficient to do it. Similarly, we were quick to accept a limited peace with Japan rather than be forced to invade their home islands and pay total war's bloody bill.

What made Vietnam so different was that the United States had the strength to do pretty much as it pleased with North Vietnam. Even in the Korean conflict it is doubtful that we had the power to obliterate all of China. In Vietnam, though, for the first time in our history, nothing limited us. We did it to ourselves. To be sure, there may have been overriding political or humanitarian reasons to do so, but the fact remains that artificial restraints were applied. This gave rise to much of the debate and confusion over the war's conduct. Moreover, those self-imposed manacles severely reduced the strategic options available, which in turn led to further questioning of our military policies.

Dissent and dissenters inside America itself did much to discredit the war by spreading doubt and sowing despair. With that in mind, it is pertinent to recall that this nation has never gone to war in all its long history without significant numbers of people predicting doom or crying shame. The United States is not a militaristic nation. Though we have fought our share of wars, we have never been comfortable with them. Vietnam, in this regard, proved to be not unlike our previous clashes. But the limited scope of the war, combined with its unusual length, made things different this time around. In our last three wars before Vietnam something happened to still or mute the dissenters. The Kaiser's unrestricted submarine campaign paved the way for our entry into the First World War, Pearl Harbor provided a rallying cry in World War II, and even Korea had the unifying element of naked, unprovoked aggression. Nothing of the sort ever occurred in Vietnam. Neither resounding victory nor imminent danger ever arose to unite our populace. From first to last the home front remained an arena of conflict, oftentimes as active as the war front.

It is wrong to lump all the dissenters together, for they covered a wide spectrum of society. They were housewives aghast at the televised blood-letting and college students faced by the draft, college professors and retired generals, editors and politicians, plain people and sophisticates. They ranged from the far left to the far right. Some were motivated by patriotism, others by communism; some were moved by opportunity, others by morality. However, most had two things in common: they were highly visible and vocal; and their ranks grew as the war years stretched on and on.

In addition to outside dissent, internal disagreement over policies and practices spilled over into the public arena, further clouding the perception of unfolding events in Vietnam. Debate inside the government fueled the countrywide controversy. From first to last the government was peculiarly inept at projecting a convincing case, but not from any lack of trying. Lumberjacks leveled forests to produce enough paper to hold all the competing arguments. The number of books spawned by the war bid well to exceed the number of battles. In an open society, that is how it should have been, how it must be if we are to benefit from our mistakes. But, while such disagreement may have been unavoidable, and perhaps even laudable, it constantly eroded whatever store of understanding a person might have acquired.

In short, debate and dissent, based on emotion as well as logic, grew apace as the war progressed, serving mightily as major contributors to confusion.

Next, the news media must also bear some responsibility for having muddied issues in the war. Never before had a combat zone been so saturated with newsmen. At any given time they numbered in the hundreds, blanketing that small corner of the globe. One might think, then, that reporting would have been better than ever. But, it now appears that press coverage remained generally below the standards set in past wars.

There were many reasons for this. Most reporters in Vietnam were sincere and professional. Their problems, though, were acute. At best the fighting was hard to cover and difficult to describe. A universally understood vocabulary for such wars has yet to emerge; old terms can be misleading while newly coined words take on widely varying connotations. Moreover, the peculiar physical environment in Vietnam, the on-again-off-again pattern of the fighting, the limited aspect of the war, the newness of television reporting, and the impact of the domestic debate itself were mitigating factors which must be recognized. Too, governmental press agencies were not blameless when it came to presenting an accurate picture of events. Nevertheless, despite all rationalization, the conclusion persists that the American press failed to clarify the war in Vietnam and, not unfairly, can be accused of adding to the public bewilderment.

Technology, too, changed the public perception of combat. Television and communications satellites made it possible for the action to come, live and in color, right into living rooms across America. "War is hell" has always been a commonly accepted adage, but saying it is not as convincing as seeing it. Much of what America—and the world for that matter—thought about Vietnam came from the television tube. One story making the rounds was of a television reporter, new to Vietnam and the realities of war, who found himself suddenly in the thick of a hot action. Watching open-mouthed as jets dropped napalm on enemy positions right to his front, he blurted into the microphone, "My God! It's just like watching television!" Seeing combat through the extremely limited lens of a television camera is a marvel in modern electronics, but not the truest way to learn what is going on.

Perhaps the major factor of all in blocking our attainment of a good grasp of developments in Vietnam was the very nature of the war itself. Or rather the wars. The conflict was not only a military one. Economic, political, and psychological factors at times required equal or greater emphasis than purely military activities. We weren't used to having our wars served up that way. But, as if that weren't confusing enough, there existed side by side in Vietnam at least three distinct kinds of military warfare. What is more, at different times different combinations of the three held sway. And only one of them happened to have fit the mold of recent American experience: the regular war between regular forces of both sides using modern weaponry and conventional tactics. The other two—revolutionary warfare and protracted warfare—spring from the writings of Mao Tse-tung and a few other military philosophers.

Twentieth century Americans had come to consider conflicts as being between like and like, between antagonists with broadly similar doctrine, weaponry, and outlook. But these new forms of warfare resembled more a duel between Roman gladiators, one bearing the traditional round shield and short stabbing sword while his enemy fought with weaving net and pointed trident. We just were not mentally prepared for warfare of that sort.

Finally, no small source of perplexity was the oriental setting itself. Few Americans have achieved an understanding of the Asian, his culture, or his countries. Nuances with deep meaning often pass completely over the head of a Westerner, while unimportant events can be blown out of all proportion in the occidental mind. The so-called cultural gap can and does foment mistrust and misunderstanding.

These are some of the reasons for misunderstanding, some of the factors which made Vietnam so emotional and so contradictory an issue. Perhaps, having at least a general appreciation of the causes of consternation, we can set them aside and turn with some hope of profit to investigate the military history of the Vietnam War.

Time heals all wounds. Rocky Bleier, with time and much determination, overcame the damage to his legs. Precisely two years after America terminated its military involvement in Vietnam, he helped lift the Pittsburgh Steelers to the championship of professional football.

The wounds to our national psyche will fade, too. But the scar tissue is permanent. It is time that we examine dispassionately how we got it. It is time that we try to comprehend what has appeared to be an incomprehensible war.

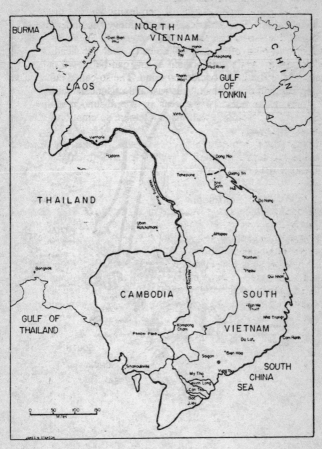

Indochina

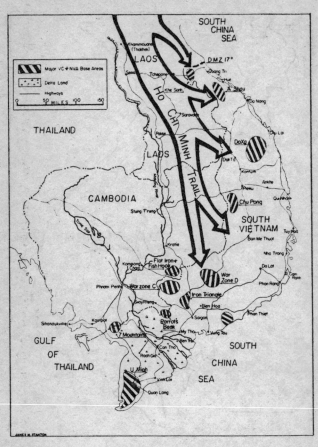

South Vietnam

PART I

THE ADVISORY DECADE

1954–1964

CHAPTER 1

The Lines Are Drawn

January 1961 was one of those memorable months which, in retrospect, was fateful. Events in the United States, the Soviet Union, and Vietnam combined to raise the curtain of a bitter drama fated to endure for the next dozen years.

In the United States the focus of attention was the inauguration of a new president. John Fitzgerald Kennedy took the oath of office on a day marked by bitter cold; Washington lay white underneath an unusually heavy blanket of snow. But the weather didn't dent the spirit of the occasion. A thrill hung in the air. Times were good, the president was young and vigorous, a wave of optimism was breaking over the land. Kennedy put stirring inaugural words to the exuberant mood. "... we shall pay any price, bear any burden, meet any hardship, support any friend, oppose any foe to assure the survival and success of liberty."

In Russia, just a few days earlier, Premier Nikita Khrushchev had belligerently pledged Soviet support to what he termed "wars of national liberation." Conceding that America's nuclear superiority made expansion by conventional means almost out of the question, he offered communists everywhere a far safer

3

route to worldwide ideological domination. Countries emerging from the grasp of colonialism seemed to offer especially promising opportunities. Confidently, and with unusual candor, the premier summoned all followers of Marx to foment and support insurgency warfare:

> There will be liberation wars as long as imperialism exists. Wars of this kind are revolutionary wars. Such wars are not only justified, they are inevitable.... Communists support just wars of this kind wholeheartedly and without reservations and they march in the vanguard of the peoples fighting for liberation.

Ominously, Khrushchev informed the world at large that the prototype for this new kind of conflict was to be the struggle even then being waged for control of South Vietnam.

In North Vietnam, in a broadcast timed to coincide with Khrushchev's bellicose statement, Radio Hanoi announced the formation of the National Liberation Front. The NLF was to be the political apparatus to direct the insurgency in South Vietnam.

President Kennedy's inaugural address constituted a direct response to the communist challenge. "To those new states whom we welcome to the ranks of the free, we pledge our word that one form of colonial control shall not have passed away merely to be replaced by a far more iron tyranny." The lines were drawn. Kennedy saw action to match his words. With the frost of his breath wreathing his face, the new president proclaimed, "Now the trumpet summons us ... to bear the burden of a long twilight struggle ... against the common enemies of man: tyranny, poverty, disease, and war itself."

Optimistic America answered the summons of the trumpet and went to war in Vietnam.

Exactly twelve years later, in January 1973, an agreement signed in Paris would end U.S. military efforts in Vietnam. The trumpet would be silent, the mood sullen. American fighting men would depart with the war unwon. The United States of America would no longer be willing to pay any price.

But all that was in the future. No one in Washington in those brave days of January 1961 saw any reason to doubt the word of the new president or the resolve of the United States.

In South Vietnam, that same January, on some unremembered and unremarkable battlefield, the war claimed the life of the first American soldier to be killed in action.

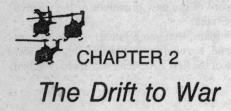

CHAPTER 2

The Drift to War

The Vietnam War began with a whimper, not a bang. American involvement in Southeast Asia was so gradual as to be almost casual, a slowly escalating process all but defying determination of a precise starting point.

The seeds of later entanglement sprang from official Washington's dilemma in September 1945 when France reasserted her old colonial sway over Indochina—Vietnam, Cambodia, and Laos. On one hand, the United States had great empathy for all subjugated nations; on the other, France was a valued ally. Torn, America lamely stood by, assuming a hands-off attitude. Later, when the Vietnamese people rose in rebellion to shake off the French, with communists dominating the leadership of the powerful nationalistic movement, Washington's anxiety heightened. Still, United States aid remained discreetly indirect, taking the form of economic assistance to Paris. Only when shocked by the triumph in China of Mao Tse-tung's Red Army did the administration in Washington begin sending significant amounts of aid directly to Indochina. By 1950, after both Peking and Moscow had extended diplomatic recognition to Ho Chi Minh and his followers, President Harry S. Truman had become thoroughly convinced of the predominantly communist coloring of the Vietnamese insurgency forces, the Viet Minh. When war erupted in Korea that year, the fear of global aggression from an expansion-minded, monolithic communist world seemed confirmed. Truman viewed Vietnam in that overall Red light. Aid increased. An American military mission entered Indochina to oversee the expanded program. Estimates vary widely, but by 1952, the United States was paying something beyond a third of the cost of the French-Indochina war; by 1953 the total surged to half or more. Newly elected President Dwight D. Eisenhower inherited the situation at that point.

Eisenhower's first mission was to conclude hostilities in Korea. This barely accomplished, Vietnam cried sharply for more of his attention. Promptly upon being freed from the costly burden of war in Korea, China had begun a massive shifting of supplies and materials to Indochina. That grand infusion permitted the Viet Minh to escalate from guerrilla to regular warfare throughout much of Vietnam. The French, already reeling, sagged lower yet. Worried, Eisenhower increased shipments of stocks, and unenthusiastically considered intervention. Meanwhile, as officials in Washington debated, the two opposing generals in the field brought the matter to a decision.

The French and the Viet Minh fought the climactic battle at an unimportant and unimposing village high in jungle-covered hills near the Laotian border—Dien Bien Phu. (Memories of that battle would return fourteen years later to haunt and distract American leaders at a crucial moment.) In January 1954, Viet Minh General Vo Nguyen Giap surrounded a large French force at Dien Bien Phu, isolating it from all support except that dropped by parachute. Through February and into March the French held on doggedly. But they were doomed without help—and by March they knew it. Desperately, Paris asked Washington to intervene. An all-out U.S. air campaign might save the beleaguered forces at Dien Bien Phu, while American ground elements might stabilize the overall situation. Or so the French claimed wistfully.

White House advisors argued heatedly in closed sessions. Refusal to act meant a great communist victory, anathema to the young Republican administration. Allies were queried, but showed no interest in a combined campaign. Unilateral intervention carried grave risks and no promise of success. Moreover, having just ended the unpopular Korean War, the country itself had no stomach for another Asian conflict. The President decided against committing American combat forces. As a life-long soldier, he understood only too well the limitations of power—and the full range of implications one accepts in wielding it. The United States would help with money and equipment, Eisenhower informed Paris, but not with men.

On 6 May 1954, General Giap launched his final assault. On the seventh, Dien Bien Phu fell. A day later Indochina was the main topic on the agenda at a peace conference in Geneva. For all intents and purposes, the French involvement in Indochina had ended. Though it was not so apparent at the time, American involvement had begun. Seeds sown in 1945 had led ultimately to a grafting operation in 1954.

Participating in the conference in Geneva were Russia, the United States, France, Great Britain, Red China, Laos, Cambodia, and representatives of the two Vietnamese sides—the communists and the anti-communists. American negotiators apparently had nothing constructive to offer, neither concessions to the communists nor succor to their foes. Russia and China, however, feeling the time was ripe to consolidate gains, urged Ho Chi Minh to accept a divided Vietnam. The final accord, completed on 20 July 1954, provided for separation of Vietnam at the 17th Parallel, giving the northern half to Ho Chi Minh and the southern to Emperor Bao Dai. Elections were scheduled for two years later to determine a government for all Vietnam. Laos was effectively if not formally divided. Only Cambodia came away intact; Prince Norodom Sihanouk spiritedly insisted throughout on autonomy—and got it.

The United States and the anti-communist Vietnamese were so unhappy with the results that they refused to join other delegations in endorsing the accords. President Eisenhower later said that he had personally refused to have an American signature put on any paper which ceded territory to communists. The American delegate, however, issued a declaration signifying that the United States would not attempt to modify the accords and would view any violation with "grave concern." Regardless of misgivings in Washington, the fact of two Vietnams could not be denied.

As the delegations headed home, Vietnamese in both Hanoi and Saigon took stock of their new countries.

Chaos was the final legacy of a narrow and utterly selfish French colonial policy. Under the century-long foreign domination, native Vietnamese had been permitted no more than a nominal participation in their own government. Especially in the South, the French had made no sincere attempt to foster a responsible and able civil service, nor had there been an effort to educate the mass of the people. Exploitation, not improvement, had been Paris' guiding policy. Vietnam had been carefully groomed for perpetual colonialization, not in the least for independence. French law and French citizens had dominated the country. The Vietnamese found themselves completely in charge, but with neither experience nor training for the task.

In the North, Ho Chi Minh at least had the structure of his own party apparatus to build on. But in the South a virtual vacuum of leadership prevailed at every level of government from hamlet, through district and province, right up to the top. A parallel void existed in the administrative bureaucracy, the vital infrastructure of government. Unfortunately, the need for a strong government couldn't have been greater. War losses had been heavy, the economy lay in ruin, bandit gangs ran amok in the absence of effective police, religious sects staked out claims to various areas, displaced persons from the North crowded in by the hundreds of thousands. All in all, the outlook was grim.

Emperor Bao Dai had previously contributed little of value to his country—unless one counts some lovely villas erected in the cool, mountain resort of Dalat where he cavorted with his favorite concubines. In fact, he had waited out the fighting with resplendent disinterest on the French Riviera. Now, from wisdom or sloth, or maybe both, Bao Dai decided to continue running things by remote control from his snugly comfortable niche on the Mediterranean. To do that, he needed a strong prime minister. Faced with a dearth of candidates both capable and conscientious, he turned reluctantly to a political opponent, Ngo Dinh Diem.

Diem, scion of a mandarin family, was then fifty-three years old. His father had occupied an important position in the emperor's court, a connection assuring the best possible education for young Diem. Intelligent and energetic, he rose quickly. At twenty-eight he was a province chief, at thirty-two minister of the interior. About then, however, disgusted with his country's supineness under the heavy French colonial rule, he resigned. For years he roamed, organizing his own followers, working against the French, espousing nationalism, and emphatically rejecting communism. His travels took him around the world. In 1951 he set up headquarters at Maryknoll Seminaries in Ossining, New York, and Lakewood, New Jersey. From there he launched a two-year speaking campaign, travelling from campus to campus preaching a theme of Vietnamese nationalism. But universities were not his only forum; assisted by his brother, a Roman Catholic priest, Diem won the support of Francis Cardinal Spellman. With the cardinal's help, he gained entry into influential Washington offices. Among those whom he favorably impressed was a young senator from Massachusetts, John F. Kennedy.

Diem's formidable problems in raising Vietnam from wreckage were lessened by the fact that the insurgents initially left him alone. Ho Chi Minh never once lost sight of his ultimate objective—to unify both Vietnams under his leadership—but he had difficulties of his own in the North. The backwash of war had been even more severe in the Red River Delta than in the Mekong Delta. And, as the Northern leader saw it, the elections set for 1956 would almost certainly extend his control over the entire nation. He did not need to harry Diem—or so he reasoned.

Diem energetically set about consolidating his hold on South Vietnam. In addition to the obvious necessity for organizing a government and easing the country's severe economic convulsions, he established three goals: erase any vestige of French influence by eliminating their preferred status; dominate or neutralize the then powerful politico-religious sects; secure and strengthen his personal power by removing or weakening potential competitors. Altogether, a Herculean task. Along Saigon's main street, Rue Catinat, cafe philosophers sipped Pernod and reckoned that the odds were about eight to one that Diem would not last a year.

Displaying a surprising shrewdness, and cashing in early on the good will gained by his two years in America, Diem achieved all three aims and got United States commitment to him in the bargain. Eager to help build a strong anti-communist regime in South Vietnam, and perhaps feeling somewhat guilty at his refusal to try to bail out the French at Dien Bien Phu, President Eisenhower permitted the small American mission in Vietnam actively to assist Diem and clandestinely to hamper Ho Chi Minh. That policy led to some minor acts of sabotage in North Vietnam before that country succeeded in closing its borders. Washington also began to funnel aid directly to the Saigon government rather than through the French. That decision, taken in October 1954, undercut the last real lever the French had over the Vietnamese. Replacing French officers, American advisors arrived to train the Vietnamese army, a move which angered that army's commander, General Nguyen Van Hinh. However, when Hinh objected, Diem peremptorily ordered him out of the country. At first he refused to leave. Rumors of a coup circulated. Diem's hold was tenuous. At that critical point President Eisenhower took a hand, dispatching General J. Lawton Collins, a former chief of staff of the U.S. Army, as special ambassador to South Vietnam. Collins let it be known that Washington would not support any leader but Diem. Talk of a coup stopped. Hinh joined Bao Dai on the Riviera, and Diem owned an army, complete with American advisors.

With French influence cut down to size, and Washington firmly behind him, Diem quickly turned on his next target—the religious sects. Those strongly independent, well-organized groups, generally oriented around a splinter religious concept, had defied successfully the Japanese, the Viet Minh, and the French. During the Japanese occupation of World War II, the sects had achieved considerable authority and autonomy. To protect their interests and followers they had organized on a territorial basis, developing ultimately into three quasi-independent "nations," each a curious oriental blend of religious, economic, political, and military factors. Constant strife made them strong, success made them confident. They were indeed exceedingly tough foes for the fledgling Saigon government, but they fell with surprising quickness before Diem's shrewd, swift attacks.

Diem moved rapidly to attain his third goal. On the anniversary of his appointment as premier he called for a national referendum to determine whether Bao Dai would remain as emperor or whether a republic should be formed. When asked about the Vietnam-wide elections scheduled just a year from then, elections required by the Geneva Accords, Diem curtly reminded his questioners that neither his government nor its sponsor, the United States, had signed that agreement. Claiming with some justice that a fair election in a communist country was a contradiction of terms, he flatly refused to participate in elections with Hanoi.

In October 1955 Diem became the first president of the newly formed Republic of South Vietnam. That same month the United States established the Military Advisory and Assistance Group for Vietnam. On Rue Catinat, cafe philosophers sipped Pernod and discussed rubber prices.

The turn of events jolted North Vietnam. Ho Chi Minh was furious. Riding his great popularity as a nationalistic leader, he had succeeded in gaining complete mastery over his northern lands. He was ready to bring the South, too, under his sway. All along it had seemed such a sure thing. The elections of 1956 would obviously have united all Vietnam under his banner. To begin with, there were more people in the North than the South, and, while the North would be certain to get a good turnout and a solid vote, agitators left in South Vietnam in 1954 would see to it that the vote there would be small and splintered. As a matter of fact, Hanoi had not been altogether displeased that Diem had been able to straighten out South Vietnam so well; the communists would have that much less to do after unification. But all those hopes and plans were abruptly shattered when Diem jerked the election rug out from under Ho.

Hanoi refused to accept the *fait accompli*. All Ho's dreams revolved around a unified, communist Vietnam. He resolved to fight. The long war, believed to have been over, had not run its course after all.

The stage was set. North Vietnam, supported by communist powers, stood on one side; South Vietnam backed principally by the United States, on the other. One antagonist sought conquest, the other to defend

13

its territory and its right to self-government. Throughout the ensuing two decades of war, those basic aims never changed.

President Eisenhower had not sought war. He was anything but eager to become embroiled in hostilities on the Asian continent. But the tide ever since 1945 had been pulling that way, and the American policy of containment had been neither forceful enough to deflect the current nor flexible enough to adjust to it. The United States, without quite realizing what was happening, had drifted into war.

CHAPTER 3

The Naive Years

When he scuttled the elections planned for 1956, Diem accurately foresaw bitter conflict with his northern kinfolk. But his vision—and that of his American advisors—was not so clear when it came to seeing the form the war would take.

Not that there hadn't been precedents to examine. When dignitaries had met in 1945 to sign peace documents aboard a battleship in Tokyo Bay, they had signalled the end of grand war and the emergence of small war. The world had changed and so had the ways of warring. Iron Curtain and Cold War, rising nationalism and dying colonialism, super weapons and super powers—all combined confusingly to bring forth a spate of small wars and near-wars, shadowy conflicts remaining limited except in the very number of them. Multiple pinpricks replaced the saber slash. Saigon's soldiers and their American advisors could draw on the vivid lessons learned from conflicts such as those in Greece, the Philippines, and Malaya, and—certainly not least important—from the recently terminated struggle in Vietnam itself. Insurgency wars all.

But, by a line of reasoning which even in retrospect is hard to comprehend, Diem's American advisors chose

15

to take their cue from Korea, the one war of the previous decade that had been an aberration.

It is considered a truism of history that only the vanquished really learns from the last war. A victor is not faced with the loser's agonizing requirement to analyze where he went wrong. The winner of a conflict almost invariably prepares for future fights using methods which brought past successes.

The U.S. Army in 1956 was unprepared to cope with an insurgency; it was no better prepared to so advise another nation. Recent American experiences had been in Korea and World War II, where force opposed force, where maps portrayed a neatly defined battlefront, where ground taken or lost meant something. Thus, despite numerous and unmistakable signs crying out that times and warfare had changed, professional military advisors persisted in viewing any potential invasion of South Vietnam strictly within the blinders of their own background. So, to shield the South from open assault across the 17th Parallel, American advisors and American dollars fashioned an army patterned after those forces which had decisively defeated Germany and Japan, and had later stopped the Red Chinese in the rugged hills of Korea.

Ironically, of all the world's armies, few have had more exposure to guerrilla-type fighting than the U.S. Army. Starting with colonial days, when eastern Indians posed the threat, the history of the American fighting man is largely one of combatting insurgents. In the Revolutionary War he himself fought as a partisan as often as not. Throughout the nineteenth century our forebears struggled to stamp out redskin insurrections from the Florida swamps to the western plains, and the present century opened with Americans waging and winning a bitter counter-insurgency campaign in the Philippines. But all of that was history; and, unfortunately, studying military history had gone out of vogue in the post-World War II U.S. Army. The army's corporate memory was little more than one generation long, stretching back no farther than the experiences of the men in it.

Lieutenant General John O'Daniel became the first chief of the military advisory effort in Vietnam. He had earned an outstanding reputation training Koreans. With assembly line efficiency, he had turned out division after division for the Korean Army—each a carbon copy of the U.S. divisions with which they were designed to fight. In Vietnam, O'Daniel attempted to repeat his Korean success, shaping the Vietnamese Army into "light" divisions of some eight thousand men each. His successor, Lieutenant General Samuel Williams, enlarged the divisions and created corps headquarters. Towards the end of the war, "Vietnamization" would become a key term; at the beginning, though, the operative word was "Americanization."

According to the recollections of Tran Van Don, an officer who participated in the first planning sessions in 1954, the South Vietnamese themselves were more inclined to pattern their army after that of the Viet Minh forces, but their ideas were rejected by the Americans. General O'Daniel and members of his staff insisted that U.S. style organizations were necessary in order for American logistical support to be effective. The Vietnamese, new to the task of building an army, and needing American assistance, acquiesced.

Forthwith, a nifty miniature copy of the U.S. military establishment emerged. It was a scale model replete with American style uniforms, weaponry, and tactics. There was even inculcated a degree of interservice rivalry as air force, navy, marine, and army commanders vied with one another over the painfully limited pool of leadership talent and for a bigger bite of the budget. The army itself consisted of separate units of rangers, paratroopers, special forces, armored troops—to name but a few.

Nevertheless, considering that they had set out to build a force capable of blunting a conventional attack, those early American advisors probably did their work well enough. We can't know because it was never tested. General Giap had not the slightest intention of engaging in open combat. The situation, as he read it, called for insurgency warfare.

The inability to foresee what form the war would take was the first great failure of our military involvement in Vietnam.

For a time, however, it looked as if the South Vietnamese might be on the right track. The insurgency began with those men, maybe six thousand or seven thousand strong, who had remained in South Vietnam after the country had been divided in 1954. They were unable to make much headway. For one thing, not all were overly loyal to a regime in Hanoi that they had never known. Many simply faded from the movement, leaving the others weak in will and numbers. On Hanoi's orders, though, the faithful obediently initiated the first phases of insurgency—mostly political agitation and local organization. But their progress remained imperceptible. So little did they achieve that Saigon went on record in 1957 as believing "that the Viet Minh authorities have disintegrated and been rendered powerless." That claim may have been overly optimistic, but not by much. The Viet Cong—the name by which the insurgents had become known—had indeed floundered badly. A captured document admitted as much, saying, "A mood of skepticism and nonconfidence in the orientation of the struggle began to seep into the party apparatus and among some of the masses."

Undeterred by the slow start, Ho sent cadremen to replace the defectors, bolster the loyal, and reinvigorate the revolution. That first wave from the North, it should be carefully marked, was actually comprised of native Southerners. They were Viet Minh who had gone to or remained in the North when the country had been partitioned. All told, of some one hundred thousand who originally went north, perhaps sixty-five thousand eventually returned clandestinely to commit violence in the name of unification. For over two years these men had lived and trained and waited in North Vietnam for the day when they would return to their homeland as liberators. Steeped in insurgency strategy, full of faith in their cause, they fairly burned with revolutionary fervor. They had families and friends in a countryside known to them intimately from childhood. They would be a very, very tough enemy.

By mid-1957 most of them were in place and functioning. Insurgency activities took a dramatic swing upward. Reorganized and revitalized, the Viet Cong began an aggressive recruiting campaign. Their ranks swelled. At every opportunity they harangued the people, pointing out miserable conditions—which were all too real—as proof of Saigon's indifference to the plight of the countryside. Despite a great deal of obvious progress, South Vietnam was hardly a cohesive country. Diem was unable to correct every fault at once, and unwilling to correct some at all. Peasants endured poverty, landlordism, endemic disease, harsh taxation; in return there was little they could see that the government did for them. Officials were distant and often corrupt. The Viet Cong found fertile ground for the seeds of insurgency. Magnifying the adverse situation, Saigon bureaucrats saw no need to vie for the loyalty of the peasantry—an aloof attitude playing directly into Viet Cong hands. In an insurgency, the people themselves are the ultimate objective. The battle is for their hearts and minds, for their loyalty and support. In failing to recognize that, Diem forfeited many of his earlier gains. In time, more and more villagers responded to the lure of Viet Cong promises and the realities of governmental unconcern and exploitation. The revolutionary movement accelerated.

Terror has been aptly defined as the propaganda of the dead. Gaining momentum, Viet Cong agents turned increasingly to this grisly method of persuasion. Murdering selected officials or natural leaders, they simultaneously reduced the amount of influence the government could wield and struck fear into undecided peasants. Sabotage, too, became increasingly common. Roads, bridges, power stations, rail lines, and other vulnerable objects suffered repeated damage or destruction. Security outside the major urban areas all but disappeared.

Viet Cong sway inexorably expanded, spreading out from safe bases to bite off village after village. The weaknesses of the central government, coupled with Saigon's simply astounding ignorance of the extent and nature of the threat, permitted the guerrillas to proceed virtually unmolested. Finally, by about the end of 1958, the malignancy had eaten so deeply into the rice-roots level of the countryside that it could advance to more overt levels of warfare in several provinces. Orders from Hanoi reached the Viet Cong in December, directing them "to open a new stage of the Struggle." Recognizing the need for increasing the level of support to the insurgents, Hanoi's high command also formed the 559th Transportation Group (the number indicating its activation date: the fifth month of 1959) to establish an infiltration net along South Vietnam's unpopulated and vulnerable western flank. The 559th did its work well, opening the network of trails soon to be known as the Ho Chi Minh Trail.

Still the Saigon regime failed to react adequately to the danger. Beset by economic frustrations, suffering the throes of organizing a government in a nation of severely limited administrative talent, and essentially apathetic to the problems of peasants, President Diem concentrated ever more power in his own hands—or in the hands of his family. He just could not conceive of the success of any movement which relied upon the masses for support. The incredible naivete of South Vietnamese and Americans alike can perhaps best be expressed in the words of officials on the scene. In

April 1959, a major general, the second ranking American military man in Vietnam, told a committee of the U.S. Senate that the Viet Cong had been "gradually nibbled away until they ceased to be a major menace." A few months later the American ambassador in Saigon reported that South Vietnam's internal security was "in no serious danger." These and similar remarks came even as guerrillas were escalating the insurgency across the land!

American slowness to grasp the true essence of the situation is all the more remarkable considering Washington's deep interest in Southeast Asia. The importance of events there was underlined in 1959 by President Eisenhower:

> Strategically, South Vietnam's capture by the Communists would bring their power several hundred miles into a hitherto free region. The remaining countries of Southeast Asia would be menaced by a great flanking movement. The loss of South Vietnam would set in motion a crumbling process which could, as it progresses, have grave consequences for the forces of freedom.

That belief, dubbed the "Domino Theory," clearly marked South Vietnam as an area considered crucial to American interests. The country was rotting away, therefore, not from a lack of will to defend it, but because officials remained mesmerized by the naive notion that Hanoi would one day launch a standard invasion.

Another great influx of cadremen slipped in from North Vietnam as the Viet Cong upped the level of fighting again in 1959. Emboldened by their splendid successes that year, they redoubled all efforts in 1960. A total of around 250 officials died at the hands of assassins in 1959; a year later the number leaped to about 1,400. Also, guerrilla units began to attack large formations of South Vietnam's regulars. They overran district and provincial capitals, decimated whole battalions, ambushed convoys—and always faded away before the inevitably cumbersome counterattack rumbled up.

At long last, some American advisors and a few of their Vietnamese counterparts began to lose their overweening sense of complacency. They became increasingly uneasy as 1960 faded. The overt invasion for which they had so long prepared had never come. Moreover, the previously placid countryside seemed to be growing ever more agitated. Efforts to stamp out the guerrillas had obviously failed.

Slowly, official policy shifted to take cognizance of the real situation. In the summer of 1960, five full years after the insurgency began, American planners started working on a counter-insurgency program. South Vietnamese units belatedly altered their training to include antiguerrilla tactics. Gradually, Saigon reoriented itself to defend against the now obvious internal menace.

Even at that point, though, the fundamental character of the problem remained but dimly recognized. The insurgency, although finally seen as a very real emergency, was still thought of by most, soldiers and civilians alike, as a sort of military nuisance which could be stopped simply by the application of appropriate military measures. The very terms that were coined indicated a failure to perceive the essential nature of the war: to defeat *insurgency*, Americans turned to *counter-insurgency* with its connotation of combatting the symptoms of revolution rather than the causes. A better word might have been *resurgency*. Lessons learned by other nations recently faced with uprisings were largely ignored. Full realization had not yet dawned.

Nevertheless, a turning point had been reached. The war had entered a new period. When Lieutenant General Lionel C. McGarr replaced General Williams in the late summer of 1960, he gained approval for American advisors to accompany Vietnamese units on combat operations.

In the United States, John F. Kennedy and Richard M. Nixon were jousting for the presidency. It was to be the last presidential race for a long while in which the Vietnamese War would not be a major issue.

CHAPTER 4

Realization and Reaction

Throughout the Eisenhower years, American interest in Vietnam remained rather keen, although actual involvement was relatively limited. Military personnel assigned there never numbered more than about seven hundred. Ike, himself an old soldier, valued the advice of his military chiefs, and they adamantly and consistently counselled against committing American troops to a ground war in Asia. Just helping the Saigon regime at all was a gamble, he knew, but so long as potential losses in event of defeat remained small, involvement was an acceptable risk. In other words, by holding down on his commitment, Eisenhower incurred only limited risks. Or, in Pentagon jargon, he accepted a "limited-risk gamble."

But, in the waning months of the general's second term, ominous drumbeats signalled a changing scene. Laos lay in shambles, Cambodia grew daily more hostile, Indonesia glowered in outright antagonism. Other countries, not yet involved but still inclined to resist communism, were wondering whether they had chosen the wrong side after all. To cap it all, South Vietnam, long rotting from within, had suddenly erupted in exposed and running sores. Something had to be done.

That was the problem confronting the new administration coming into office in January 1961.

The echoes of his inaugural address were hardly still before Kennedy began a far-reaching review of the dismal situation in Southeast Asia, a review lasting nearly a year and resulting in both a sobering realization of the imminence of a communist triumph there and a hasty American reaction to forestall it.

With Laos crumbling and South Vietnam obviously tottering, with earlier optimistic reports vanished in the smoke of Viet Cong victories, Kennedy had to act quickly. No sooner was he settled in the Oval Office than he ordered clandestine operations to be conducted in both Laos and North Vietnam. He directed his secretary of defense to study what measures were necessary "to hold Southeast Asia outside the Communist sphere," and he shipped five hundred more men to South Vietnam. He even came close to moving combat forces into Laos and the Central Highlands of South Vietnam. Four months after taking office, he sent Vice President Lyndon B. Johnson out to Saigon for a first-hand look.

The vice president, who could not have begun to guess how large a shadow Vietnam would cast over his own future, returned with a strident call for more help:

> The battle against Communism must be joined in Southeast Asia with strength and determination to achieve success there—or the United States, inevitably, must surrender the Pacific and take up our defenses on our own shores . . . The struggle is far from lost in Southeast Asia and it is by no means inevitable that it must be lost . . . There is no alternative to United States leadership in Southeast Asia . . .

Nevertheless, Johnson advised Kennedy against sending American combat troops. The Texan said that dispatching U.S. ground units "is not only not required, it is not desirable."

Eisenhower's objective in Vietnam—to maintain a

non-communist government in Saigon—continued to be the objective of the Kennedy administration, as, indeed, it remained the American objective throughout the war. Gradually, though, President Kennedy concluded that there were four reasons warranting unusual U.S. exertions to preclude a take-over by Hanoi. First, America had already committed itself to resist communist expansion, and the facts of aggression were quite clear. The International Control Commission, a body set up to supervise the Geneva Accords of 1954, had found North Vietnam guilty of "subversion and covert aggression against South Vietnam." Hanoi, while not forthrightly admitting its complicity, ingenuously called the North "The Great Rear" and the South "The Great Frontline." No one seriously doubted that North Vietnam initiated, nurtured, and directed the war. Thus, South Vietnam was seen by Kennedy in the same cold war light as Berlin and Korea; one more place where Red aggression had to be thwarted. The second reason was Washington's fear of losing all Southeast Asia, and perhaps more, should South Vietnam fall. Already Cambodia was wavering, while Laos was locked in a three-way internecine struggle between nationalists, communists, and neutralists. Some doubts as to the validity of the domino theory were beginning to crop up, but its foreboding thesis made it a theory best not put to the test. Significantly, too, the dominoes themselves believed unreservedly that the fall of Southeast Asia would endanger them. Nations in the regional arc from New Zealand to Australia to Thailand put intense collective pressure on Washington to retain a presence. Up to this point, Kennedy's logic for involvement was lifted almost unchanged from Eisenhower's. But two new concepts confronted the new president.

Vitally concerned with the prestige of America, with Washington's image abroad, and anxious to foster credibility as leader of the non-communist world, President Kennedy blanched at the thought of the strongest nation on the globe being outdone by a ragged band of insurgents. After having openly aided Saigon ever since 1954, Washington, in Kennedy's view, simply could not swallow defeat. No matter that America's commitment during those seven years had been modest—a "limited-risk gamble"—failure was failure. It was unthinkable that the United States should refuse to honor its pledges or make good its threats. Ironically, loss of face, usually thought of as an oriental concept, thus became the third motive for involvement.

Finally, and perhaps of most consequence in the long run, Vietnam loomed as the testing ground for Khrushchev's wars of national liberation. General Giap stated the challenge squarely when he said, "South Vietnam is the model of the national liberation movement of our time. If the special warfare that the United States imperialists are testing in South Vietnam is overcome, then it can be defeated anywhere in the world." It was obviously the Soviet Union's hope that Hanoi's campaign in South Vietnam, by demonstrating the surefire success of insurgency warfare, would become the inspiration for a wave of similar conflicts around the world. It was as clearly the American aim to prevent such a wave by proving that insurgencies could be defeated. As General Maxwell D. Taylor, the president's personal military advisor in 1961, explained, "We had to cope with it to burst the myth of invincibility."

Meanwhile, through summer and into the autumn of 1961, the situation in Vietnam steadily worsened. Murder squads slaughtered officials at ever increasing rates. Sabotage teams rampaged unchecked, spreading still more horror and destruction. Viet Cong units grew stronger and waxed bolder, mounting in September alone three separate attacks with forces totalling over one thousand men. In one of those assaults, storm troops overran Phuoc Vinh, a provincial capital only forty miles north of Saigon. Leaving a gruesome reminder of their visit, they decapitated many of the defenders and stuck their heads on long rows of sharpened poles. Diem declared a state of emergency.

Washington, alarmed at how rapidly South Vietnam seemed to be sinking, decided to increase American aid. Official observers and special study groups practically inundated Saigon's facilities for handling them. The question was not *whether* to help; it was *how* to help. Kennedy sent General Taylor to probe the situation. He returned with wide-ranging recommendations for political and economic reforms—and an appeal for a massive military increase, to include several thousand troops. In an ironic afterthought, the general cautioned that the consequences of his recommendations might include larger commitments later, consequences which were to be subsequently realized after he became ambassador to South Vietnam. The build-up, he warned President Kennedy, "should not be undertaken unless we are prepared to deal with any escalation the communists might choose to impose." He could not have found more prophetic words.

Those escalatory recommendations hit official Washington hard. Resistance to taking so drastic a plunge ran deep and strong. For fifteen years, ever since World War II, it had been a cliche to say that America should never become involved in a land war in Asia. Korea had seemed to be a bloody case in point. What is more, reinforcing the reluctance, intelligence estimates portrayed gloomy prospects for success even with increased aid. Yet, for the four reasons enumerated earlier, President Kennedy felt compelled to act. South Vietnam would succumb if he didn't, a prospect he could not accept.

Moreover, there was now a fifth factor involved in the equation—domestic politics. Kennedy had already suffered a humiliating setback at the Bay of Pigs and had failed to prevent the construction of the Berlin Wall. His image as a dynamic leader had not fared well. A third fiasco in his first year in the White House could well prove politically fatal. Accordingly, the young president resolved in November 1961 to escalate the U.S. commitment in an effort to stave off the defeat he could not afford. It is not clear whether he concerned himself overly much with General Taylor's warning about enemy escalation.

The Pentagon reacted swiftly. By year's end, American strength had burgeoned to around 3,200 men; helicopter units were at work; a Marine air element had flown ashore; aircraft for combat and logistical support were on the way in; comptrollers had found funds to support an enlarged South Vietnamese Army. On 8 February 1962 a new U.S. military headquarters opened its doors in Saigon. The Military Assistance Command, Vietnam (MACV), headed by General Paul D. Harkins, had the job of coordinating and directing the enlarged American commitment. In the words of General Taylor, the creation of MACV had shifted the American military commitment "from an advisory group to something nearer—but not quite—an operational headquarters in a theater of war."

Realization had come, albeit years late. It was now to be seen if the belated reaction was in time and strength enough to reverse the communist current.

CHAPTER 5

Arms and Advice

All in all, 1962—the Year of the Tiger—was one which the South Vietnamese and their American advisors would remember with pride. At the lunar new year holidays that winter, Hanoi's forces appeared well nigh unstoppable—but just twelve months later it would be Saigon's troops who would have good cause for a jubilant celebration. The insurgency was beaten down that year, if not to its knees at least sufficiently to allow Diem and Kennedy to sense the first stirrings toward eventual victory.

But it was touch and go at first. The year did not begin well. Continuing the momentum they had gained in 1961, Viet Cong leaders increased the frequency and ferocity of their attacks in the opening months of the new year. More and more the insurgent pattern changed from hit-and-run, ambush, and terror to outright assault on regular South Vietnamese units. Outposts were picked off with frightening regularity. Much of the countryside was openly controlled by a National Liberation Front government which levied taxes, regulated trade, drafted men, and punished criminals. The output of rudimentary arms factories supplemented with equipment infiltrated from North Vietnam and with weapons captured in battle, made possible an increase in both quantity and quality of Viet Cong firepower. The insurgency was not far from moving into the final phases foreshadowing victory.

Not all the woe was communist instigated. A foolish strafing and bombing attack by two disgruntled South Vietnamese fighter pilots against Diem's palace in February did little damage to persons or property, but seriously harmed American attempts to forge a more cohesive military machine. That affront, coming just over a year after an abortive coup attempt by airborne forces, sealed forever Diem's mistrust of the military. He intentionally fragmented his army's chain of command, gathering still more power unto himself. For the remainder of his rule, combat operations would be severely hobbled by overcentralized control, administrative restraints, and flimsy cooperation between officials at all levels. In many cases junior officers, especially province chiefs, had a hot line to the palace, bypassing all intermediate channels. Such a system might serve to consolidate power at the top, but it is hardly likely to bring about the level of military efficiency needed to preserve that power. And, beyond all doubt, it bedeviled American advisors unremittingly, causing untold consternation and frustration.

There were plenty of Americans to be bedeviled. They surged by the thousands into South Vietnam as the early weeks of 1962 rolled by; more than fifteen thousand would be on hand before the year's end. It was a veritable invasion of advisors. Washington seemed obsessed with the notion that sheer numbers would instill a sense of urgency and a spirit of aggressiveness into Saigon's operations. Americans came to advise at practically every level and in virtually every aspect of Vietnamese life, bringing new arms and new ideas and new vigor—and new problems. The military was there, of course, but so were political and economic and social agencies. As their numbers proliferated, their influence became increasingly pervasive. That in itself led to complications.

For one thing, Vietnamese officials had somehow to cope with the massive injection of new programs and program managers. One story which made the rounds in Vietnam about that time compellingly portrays the ubiquitous reach of American efforts as well as the Vietnamese reaction to many of our well-meaning if ill-conceived actions. It seems that a farming expert determined that a good thoroughbred bull or two would in short order improve the scrawny breed of cattle found in Vietnam. Straightway, he procured and presented to a particular province a huge and proven bull. The expert boasted ecstatically about the benefits his experiment would bring. It was soon learned, however, that the bull was too massive to service the small cows; they buckled under his weight. Not discouraged, the province chief and his advisor built a special platform to support the bull's weight. But the bull didn't hanker to the idea and refused to cooperate. Artificial insemination was out of the question for lack of facilities. Completely balked, the province chief ruefully turned the bull out to pasture with the other animals. There it mingled and ate, but, of course, accomplished nothing. Eventually the farming expert returned to check on his pet project. He asked the province chief how things stood. Glancing resignedly at the great beast devouring grass in a nearby field, the province chief replied, "I think the bull he is just another American advisor."

Another difficulty encountered in the rapid build-up was that Americans themselves were unsure of precisely what was needed. Though it may seem utterly unbelievable, it is nonetheless true that the Pentagon had to order a crash, army-wide campaign to reeducate its officers. Steeped in conventional theory and oriented towards an atomic war in Europe, many professional officers did not even recognize the term "counter-insurgency," much less were they prepared to practice it. Nor were the policy makers themselves sure of how to go about defeating insurgents. Lacking a base of doctrine or experience, and evidently spurning most of the ready lessons of history, administrators and bureaucrats in Washington spawned a terminology which passed for a philosophy. With biting insight, military analyst Hanson W. Baldwin decried "the muddy verbosity and the pompous profundity that are beginning to mask the whole subject of counter-insurgency and guerrilla war." Bernard Fall further lamented that "too many amateur counter-insurgency cooks have had their hands at stirring the revolutionary warfare broth." Given such a climate at the top, it was foreordained that great gaffes would occur. A typical example is the manner in which special forces, the Green Berets, went to war. Trained to operate behind enemy lines to *coordinate* partisan activities, special forces teams were sent to Vietnam to *counter* partisan activities. Instead of prowling around in the enemy rear—which would have been North Vietnam—they dotted the South Vietnamese countryside with fortified base camps. Trained to fight stealthily, they fought statically. Groping for doctrine as they went along, Americans in 1961 and 1962 quite often had to adopt a shotgun approach. Naturally, not all the blasts were effective. But so many pellets were sent zinging that at least a few struck true.

New equipment was one such area. Modern arms had an astonishing initial impact—the spirit and effectiveness of Saigon's soldiers rose noticeably. Retrained to operate from helicopters and to fight mounted in amphibious armored personnel carriers, they had the edge over Viet Cong regulars. At first contact with helicopters, the guerrillas broke and ran in blind panic. Government units ran up a string of first-rate successes before the shock and surprise wore off. Armored vehicles, especially the highly mobile M-113, similarly struck terror among the insurgents. "The enemy's M-113s raided our controlled area which caused us a lot of trouble," one Viet Cong commander reported. "These M-113s are more difficult to evade than tanks...they have a formidable speed." In the flat stretches of the Mekong Delta, drivers found they could run down fleeing Viet Cong soldiers like hounds after rabbits.

The U.S. military build-up was itself a tonic to the Army of the Republic of South Vietnam (ARVN). Morale soared as it became obvious that America intended to remain. Victories in the field bolstered confidence, while the new arms provided a high degree of mobility—both factors being primary requisites for defeating guerrillas. Problems there were, and plenty of them. Desertions continued to plague commanders, for instance. And apathy never quite disappeared. Leaders were inexperienced and the pool of talent from which to select officers was woefully inadequate. Political maneuvering too often came easier to the generals than military maneuvering. And a lingering veneer of previous "big war" training still hampered "small war" capability. Even so, the ARVN improved tremendously during 1962. What's more, shortcomings notwithstanding, by year's end they had snatched the military initiative from the Viet Cong.

It may well be, however, that the most important step forward was not a military one at all. It was the awareness, at long last, that purely military solutions could never defeat the insurgency. Diem and his advisors came to realize that they were fighting a political war as well as a military one. Saigon finally saw that the populace had to be separated from the insurgents and that real social reform was necessary to counter the enemy's appeal. That was a basic lesson. Furthermore, it was one that had already been demonstrated several times. It is the history of man, though, that he is slow to learn from past experience.

Early in 1962, South Vietnam launched an exceedingly ambitious strategy of denial, called the Strategic Hamlet program. The idea may have sprung in part from modest but rather successful French experiments years before, but the primary pattern came from a similar and hugely successful program used in Malaya by the British. The Strategic Hamlet program was designed to secure the peasants by drawing them together into central, defensible hamlets. Each hamlet was to have moats, barbed wire, and trained defenders. Unhappily, the program was destined to fail, but perhaps more through the fault of execution than of concept. When the first hamlets were immediately successful, and when officials recognized that President Diem himself was personally pushing the program, competition ran rampant. Province chiefs vied with one another to construct the most, to "secure" more people. Statistical progress, boosted by eager U.S. advisors, became overly emphasized to the detriment of real progress. In the rush to do too much too soon, the entire program grew unwieldy and eventually collapsed of its own weight. However, the crash was to come later; in 1962 strategic hamlets held real promise.

As the year progressed, the insurgency was slowed, then halted, and finally reduced. Advised by Americans urging them to "close with and kill" the enemy, granted superior mobility by armored vehicles and helicopters, ARVN units gradually gained the upper hand. Unable to come up with a counter for the newfound mobility and firepower of government forces, guerrillas took a bloody mauling. They still could, and did, give as good or better than they got on occasions. But those occasions were growing farther apart. Most significantly, Hanoi was no longer able to replace losses with Southern-born cadremen—the supply of those men was all but exhausted by late 1962. Rocked by the unexpected influx of Americans and shocked by the revitalized South Vietnamese army, insurgents began to lose heart. According to several who left the movement then or later, even stalwart Party members became demoralized by the sudden reversal of their fortunes, experiencing "severe cases of doubt and indecision."

Not that the war was won. Far from it. No realist could foresee anything but more blood and much sweat down the road ahead. Imminent defeat had been prevented, but ultimate victory remained a long way off. Nonetheless, at least a cautious expectation of eventual success seemed justified. When Secretary of Defense Robert McNamara and General Maxwell Taylor returned from a fact-finding trip to Saigon in the autumn of 1962, they were sincere in believing that "the major part of the United States military task can be completed by the end of 1965." The insurgency tide had been turned—the problem was to keep it flowing the right way.

CHAPTER 6

The Battle of Ap Bac

There was once a time when the American army needed foreign advisors. Dreadfully short on discipline and know-how, George Washington's amateurish Continentals straggled into battle quite ill-prepared to face any sort of organized foe. They were indeed pitiable, soldiers only by virtue of having received the title and musket. Willing they may have been; able they were not. Having neither a nucleus of professionals nor a backstop of military tradition to draw on, Congress turned with scant hope to Europe for trained officers. They came. Lafayette, Steuben, Kosciusko, de Kalb, Pulaski, Duportail—just to mention a few of the better known names is to evoke an image of the vitally important role they played in the winning of our War of Independence.

Those advisors tackled an awesome task: molding an army from raw material in a backward country in the midst of war. A strange and often inhospitable environment seriously complicated their job, not to mention problems created by the barriers of language and other cultural differences. Then too, buffeted by puzzling and sometimes petty crosscurrents of political and personal jealousies, and meeting more than occasional resentment from the fiercely independent Patriot officers themselves, the foreigners often suffered acute frustration and actual bitterness. Nonetheless, they persevered. They taught tradesmen and farmers and backwoodsmen how to erect fortifications, to march, to form line from column, to use the bayonet— and they imparted confidence. Ultimately, they forged from rabble a competent and capable American army. To them, more than history has admitted, we owe our independence. Usually unsung and often unloved, they nevertheless performed their advisory duties with the distinctive mark of the professional. The victory at Yorktown stands as a monument to their success.

One can find many parallels between that long-ago advisory effort and our own in Vietnam. More than a few of the problems of advising are universal and timeless. An obvious—and, ironically, often overlooked— problem is the basic fact that an advisor must work with an imperfect organization. An army requiring advisors is not one without faults. If it could operate effectively on its own it would do so; no fighting force tolerates foreigners in its midst unless it really needs them. The Army of South Vietnam (ARVN) needed assistance. Just as Americans in 1776 had to start from scratch, so did South Vietnamese in 1954.

Another unchanging reality of advising is the more or less constant cocoon of frustration enveloping the advisor. Adjusting to advising is a greater individual challenge than can be easily imagined by anyone who has not tried it. For the soldier, who is conditioned to obeying and being obeyed, the ambiguities and subtleties of vicarious leadership form a sharp departure from the norm. America's Revolutionary War European advisors agonized over unprofessional performances just as did South Vietnam's American advisors. Across the centuries they shared common bonds of frustration, of diligent and professional application, and of eventual success. By the end of the Revolutionary War, Washington led a proud and battle-ready band; by the end of the Vietnamese War, South Vietnam had units that were as good as many in the U.S. Army.

But it was not easy. Nor was it quick. Many road-blocks had to be overcome. There were failures aplenty among the successes. Along that littered route to success, the Battle of Ap Bac looms as a notable and notorious landmark.

Actually, any of a hundred battles could have been selected to illustrate the fighting during the years when Americans served only as advisors. Many clearly portray the tactics employed as well as the relationship between commander and advisor. Of all of them, though, the Battle of Ap Bac became the most famous—or infamous, depending upon one's point of view. Newspapers in the United States gave it headline treatment. Writers described it as "the bloodiest single battle of South Vietnam's four-year war against the Communist Viet Cong," and "one of the most costly and humiliating defeats of the South Vietnamese army and its United States military advisors." On the other hand, General Harkins claimed stoutly that, although it might appear to have been a defeat, it was not. MACV Headquarters made no secret of its belief that less-than-objective reporting had blown the battle out of all proportion, creating unnecessarily a cause célèbre. Be that as it may, the result was that the Battle of Ap Bac became a case in point, a symbol to illustrate the manifest disappointments and difficulties encountered by advisors.

Skill in advising is a reflection of one's ability to influence other individuals. Results spring from the interplay of personalities between advisor and advised, from the alternate clash and cohesion of wills. To understand the Battle of Ap Bac, then, it is first necessary to know the main characters. There were three: Lieutenant Colonel John Paul Vann, Colonel Bui Dinh Dam, and Major General Huynh Van Cao.

Vann, blond and balding, was a short, energetic, ambitious, highly intense career soldier. He evoked strong reactions in all who met him. His voice had an irritating, sandpaper quality which was accentuated by its high pitch. A subordinate, striving to form a word profile of him, came up with: tough, smart, irritable, brave, tactless, blunt, responsible, abrasive, responsive, sensitive. Another officer, a student of psychology, thought Vann was a prime example of a person suffering a "runt complex." Certainly there was in his makeup a driving restlessness never permitting him to be still. He participated personally in every operation he could, oftentimes carrying a rifle in the lead squad. Courageous to a fault, he never missed a chance to prove it. Between combat operations, he remained active; travelling, cajoling his counterpart, organizing athletic events, dropping propaganda leaflets, experimenting with hand grenades (he determined that a grenade dropped from 200 feet would explode approximately head high), talking avidly with reporters, gathering material for a book—and doing all his paper work at night. In superb physical condition, he delighted in doing a back flip from a standing position and then chiding others because they couldn't. The volleyball games he organized daily in the American compound at My Tho in the Delta stressed physical contact and aggressiveness above skill and technique. He drove himself and subordinates mercilessly. Those who didn't know him well detested him.

However, for his own men, there was nothing Vann would not do. Time and again, when the situation was hottest, he would show up. The advisor on a combat operation had total faith that, in an emergency, "John P." would be there personally with all the support he could muster. He was odd, his men readily admitted, and unusually headstrong, but, withal, "a damn fine soldier." He earned the respect of those under him, a grudging respect which soon turned to admiration, and finally to outright devotion.

His complex character would probably have made John Paul Vann an outstanding commander in combat; it did not suit him so well for the role of advisor. But that is what he was during the Battle of Ap Bac—senior advisor to the ARVN 7th Infantry Division.

Colonel Dam was the new commander of the 7th Division. Ap Bac was his first battle. The epitome of the French concept of a chief of staff, Dam in fact had been chief of staff of the 7th until his elevation to command it. Educated but not highly intelligent, he was intensely loyal to his superiors and quite demanding of those under him. At a time when many senior officers were politically motivated, Dam remained dedicated to his profession as a soldier. Americans liked him for his pleasant personality and keen sense of humor, and for the plain fact that he did his job well. They typed him as a competent administrator, but not a commander. As chief of staff he was seldom involved in the details of planning or supervising a battle; administration was his forte as well as his responsibility. Therefore, when he became the division commander, he was untested and unschooled in coping with the intense pressures of leadership in combat, nor was he practiced in making decisions. His greenness would be a major factor in the upcoming Battle of Ap Bac.

The third key player was General Cao. Short, and chunky in a tough sort of way, Cao was a fine soldier. Until just before Ap Bac he had been commander of the 7th Division. He left that post when he was promoted to the position of IV Corps commander, a job giving him responsibility for all of the part of Vietnam south of Saigon. While commanding the 7th during the halcyon days of 1962, Cao had been hugely successful. He knew his area and his enemy. Launching a series of brilliant operations, he had played a large part in the great advances made throughout South Vietnam that year. His division had cut deeply into Viet Cong strength, striking hard at both the enemy infrastructure and regular forces. The fame of the 7th grew and honors accumulated, culminating with a special parade in Saigon. Immensely proud, Cao likened himself to Napoleon.

But if Cao was an outstanding general, he was an even better politician. (In fact, a few years later, he resigned from the army and pursued an outright political career, serving as one of his country's first senators.) His every action was carefully tempered by the impact it would have on his superiors. He was smart and successful—and very much the product of his country and his time. Through the spring and summer of 1962, officials in Saigon wanted battlefield success. Cao gave it to them. Then, imperceptibly, as the tide turned against the Viet Cong, President Diem's attitude shifted. Cao sensed the shift. Abruptly, he ceased his effective operations and initiated a series of futile sweeps accomplishing nothing much except to anger his already irascible advisor. Vann and other Americans railed at the loss of momentum, but Cao replied obliquely, "It does not pay to be too successful, for you then become a threat."

In October 1962, a ranger company assaulted a Viet Cong unit in a prepared position, suffering about 30 percent casualties. The rangers had properly boxed the guerrillas in before closing for the kill, leaving them no options but to fight their way out or surrender. Never before had any of General Cao's units lost so many men while attacking the enemy. Combat victories notwithstanding, Saigon officialdom was frowning increasingly on commanders who took casualties. A day after the bloody fight President Diem summoned Cao to Saigon. The general cooled his heels all day outside Diem's office. At 8:00 P.M. he went in. What was said has never been revealed, but the results were immediately evident. The 7th Division virtually stood down. Those few operations that were launched invariably left the enemy a route of escape. Candidly, Cao explained, "It is not prudent to corner the rat." Soon he moved up to become Corps commander, vindicating his political acumen if not his military integrity. Not unexpectedly, by the time he departed the relationship between Cao and advisor Vann, who had been simply flabbergasted by the whole negative turn of events, had deteriorated beyond repair.

Perhaps Vann did not recall or had not read the admonition of Rudyard Kipling:

> Now it is not good for the Christian's health
> to hustle the Asian Brown;
> For the Christian riles, and the Asian smiles,
> and he weareth the Christian down,
>
> And the end of the fight is a tombstone white
> with the name of the late deceased,
> And the epitaph drear: "A fool lies here
> who tried to hustle the East."*

When Dam replaced Cao, much of the tenseness that had been generated between the Americans and the Vietnamese quickly dissipated. Dam was easier to work with and more receptive to ideas. What's more, he appeared eager to fight. He and Vann agreed that a carefully planned and well executed operation should be conducted as soon as possible to set the tone for Dam's tenure of command. In short order, on 2 January 1963, elements of the division jumped off on the operation which resulted in the Battle of Ap Bac.

From the start, the Battle of Ap Bac, if not a mistake, was a misnomer. It was supposed to have been fought around the village of Ap Tan Thoi, not Ap Bac. Government intelligence had pinpointed the presence of a major enemy headquarters at Ap Tan Thoi. Intelligence officers estimated that a reinforced company stood guard over the headquarters. To both Vann and Dam it looked like a perfect objective for the new commander's first operation—the enemy was not strong and with any luck at all the 7th Division could destroy both the headquarters and the security detachment, thereby gaining a resounding victory.

The initial plan was good, except for the unclear

*This passage is a chapter heading from Kipling's "Naulahka." Some versions use the word "Aryan" in place of "Asian."

command relationship among participating elements. The scheme of maneuver called for the 11th Infantry Regiment to be inserted by helicopter to the west, north and east of Ap Tan Thoi. Once the infantrymen were in place, a light regiment of civil guards (later to be called regional forces), commanded by the province chief and supported by a mechanized troop mounted in M-113 armored personnel carriers, would slam the door shut on the south side. Two infantry companies were set aside as a reserve. Artillery support was available and, in an emergency, so was tactical air. All told, a weighty force to smite a single company. Victory seemed assured, defeat out of the question.

But the intelligence officers had been wrong. The enemy was not in Ap Tan Thoi; he was in Ap Bac. And he was there in strength. A reinforced Viet Cong battalion, the fierce 514th, had deployed some five hundred men in carefully prepared defenses along the canals from Ap Tan Thoi to Ap Bac, with the center of mass nearer to Ap Bac. The insurgents knew a fight was imminent, although their agents had been unable to obtain precise details. Therefore, they prepared alternate plans to cope with the various likely possibilities. Communications, command, security, and logistical arrangements were at least adequate, probably good. Morale was up because they were primed to do battle. They fully intended to stand and fight.

Having been rocked back on their heels by the government's mopping-up operations in 1962, Viet Cong tacticians had devised "counter-mopping-up-operations." A primary element in the new tactics was an effort to neutralize the impact of helicopters and armored vehicles. In the forthcoming battle, the Viet Cong commander was set especially to counter the helicopters; he had at least two .50 caliber machine guns and assorted other automatic weapons, all manned by individuals carefully trained in anti-aircraft techniques. Whereas Colonel Dam hoped to swoop in and surprise a small force, the enemy commander anticipated a heavy engagement and he was actually eager for it. It was not the Viet Cong who had a surprise coming.

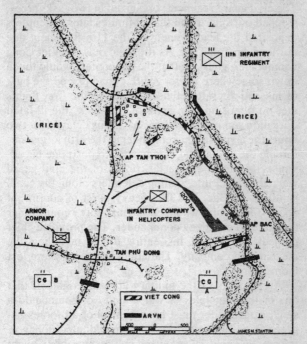

Battle of Ap Bac

Villages in that part of the Mekong Delta stand out as sparsely wooded islands in a vast sea of paddy land. Virtually the only usable routes of travel follow the tree-lined canals. Those canals, with their steep banks and heavy fringe of vegetation, are normally the only significant terrain features in an otherwise open and monotonously flat countryside. The canal lines formed natural defensive positions, affording protection and concealment to the defender while permitting perfect observation and murderous fields of fire out over the shimmering rice paddies. In those tree lines lurked the well-armed 514th.

Just after dawn on 2 January 1963, the battle began. The civil guard regiment, organized in two task forces, stepped out smartly on time. Minutes later helicopters deposited the lead element of the 11th Regiment due north of Ap Tan Thoi. As it turned out, the Viet Cong commander, guessing that the helicopters would touch down somewhere nearer Ap Bac, had placed the bulk of his anti-aircraft defenses there, so the first flights met no opposition. In spite of that luck, the ill-fated operation soon began falling apart. Fog delayed for two hours the arrival of the remainder of the 11th Regiment, forcing the regimental commander to postpone his advance. Meanwhile, one task force of the civil guard walked straight into waiting defenders along the canal south of Ap Bac. The first heavy burst of gunfire, at about 0730 hours, wounded the task force commander and killed a company commander. The province chief immediately halted his entire force, including the mechanized company. The attackers everywhere lost momentum.

All students of the military art learn right off that one of the principles of war is unity of command—a single commander must have control of all forces engaged in an operation. Diem's premeditated policy of fragmenting military command and responsibility might have been politically expedient, but it was militarily indefensible. This battle presents a perfect example of what can happen if unity of command is not guaranteed. The province chief was wholly independent of the 7th Division commander, while the mechanized troop answered directly to neither. Thus three separate commanders reacted each in his own way when the initial plan proved unworkable. A concerted team effort would be next to impossible to achieve in those circumstances. Actually, long before the operation had begun, the 7th Division's very capable artillery commander, Captain Nguyen Van Su, had warned Dam and Vann that the splintered command arrangement would make it impossible for him to coordinate supporting fires should the situation become fluid. Su, a completely professional officer, had attended the advanced artillery course at Fort Sill, Oklahoma. From training as well as from experience, he knew the vital necessity for unity of command. Unfortunately, neither Colonel Dam nor Lieutenant Colonel Vann had listened to the earnest young captain. Or else they had rejected out of hand the idea that their plan could break down.

Knowing that the 11th Regiment was just getting organized north of Ap Tan Thoi and was drawing sporadic fire from the village, seeing one task force pinned down, and learning that the other task force and the mechanized troop had halted a mile west of Ap Bac, Colonel Dam decided to commit one company of his reserve in the vicinity of Ap Bac in order to get things moving again. He still thought the enemy's main point of resistance would be nearer Ap Tan Thoi.

Vann, circling over the area in a light airplane, agreed with the decision to commit the reserve, but he did not like Dam's choice of site. The two argued until Dam permitted his advisor to search for another one. For more than half an hour all action on the ground marked time while three aircraft—Vann's, the helicopter unit's control ship, and a South Vietnamese observation airplane—made repeated passes low over the area, their occupants discussing and debating over the radio and in the clear where best to land. They finally chose a spot in the angle between Ap Bac and the enemy-held canal—right in the center of the Viet Cong position! Not surprisingly, when the ten lumbering troop helicopters—old CH-21 "flying bananas"—touched down at 1020 hours, enemy gunners were ready.

A withering, converging fire from both Ap Bac and the treeline ripped into the helpless, hovering choppers, knocking one out immediately and damaging several others. While troops frantically scurried out of the stationary craft, five supporting gunships—smaller helicopters with weapons hung on their sides—blasted enemy positions along the canal, but with negligible effect. One helicopter flew toward the stricken ship in an effort to pick up the crew; Viet Cong fire promptly brought it down. A third tried to rescue both crews and was also shot out of the sky. Within minutes four helicopters fell victim to the intense ground fire. Guerrilla gunners downed a fifth before noon. All told, only a single helicopter escaped being hit. The insurgents definitely succeeded in answering the challenge of the chopper that day.

By noon utter turmoil prevailed in the 7th Division command post. Captain Su, seeing his worst fears realized, struggled vainly to bring order to a fire support coordination center which would more aptly have been described as a fire support consternation center. Dam, the fine chief of staff who had not yet made the transition to commander, appeared lost in the hubbub. As the crisis mounted, he became subdued and withdrawn, hesitating to make decisions and failing to push subordinates. He sorely needed a calm, strong advisor. But Vann merely added to the commotion and confusion. Highly impassioned by the excitement and emotion of battle, he became even more aggressive and abrasive than usual. First pacing restlessly around the command post, then racing to his airplane for a topside look at the battlefield; at one moment angrily demanding that the civil guard attack, the next berating the mechanized company, meantime trying to adjust artillery, or rushing back to push for action by the reserve, he was a dervish stirring a situation that needed settling. He was not likely to get much out of a haggard Colonel Dam.

As the day progressed, word of the battle spread rapidly. Soon the command post was crowded with reporters and high ranking visitors—including General Cao. In a trice that shrewd officer grasped the situation. Much to Colonel Dam's relief, Cao took charge.

After restoring calm in the headquarters, he cautiously analyzed the progress and status of the battle.

What he saw was not all bleak. Despite their initial losses, South Vietnamese forces actually stood in a rather good position. To the north, the 11th Regiment, which had been reinforced with a ranger company that had come in by boat, was holding down those enemy elements around Ap Tan Thoi. That left the Viet Cong troops near Ap Bac isolated and vulnerable, because nearby waited the two civil guard task forces, the reserve company which had flown in, and the mechanized troop with its heavy firepower and armored mobility. Above orbited gunships ready to pounce on retreating enemy troopers. A determined push could crush the defenders around Ap Bac. That done, those in Ap Tan Thoi would be encircled and the entire hostile battalion could be annihilated. Vann and his subordinate advisors, eager for the kill, urged their counterparts to attack.

Their pleas fell on deaf ears. Cao remembered only too starkly his standing instructions to avoid casualties. Having been willing to let the 7th Division take on a company, he most emphatically was not prepared to accept the losses which would have been entailed in coming to grips with a battalion. Under Diem's ground rules, relief from command was the reward for aggressive but bloody battles. While his advisors chafed at his timidity and gnashed their teeth at the lost opportunity, Cao calmly called in air and artillery and requested reinforcements.

(Although it is getting ahead of the story, it must in fairness be recorded here that those cautious tactics were, in spite of the very sincere exhortations of the U.S. advisors, precisely the same that any American commander would have used after U.S. troops were committed in 1965. Moreover, the American's fate for accepting human losses in lieu of calling for firepower to do the job would have been the same as that of the South Vietnamese commander—removal from command. It is always the commander, not his advisor, who shoulders the actual responsibility for making decisions. What one might urge as an advisor, he might not do as a commander.)

Higher headquarters responded to Cao's plea for help by sending an airborne battalion which parachuted into the battle area as dusk fell. However, instead of dropping east of Ap Bac to complete the encirclement, they came in west of the combat area. "It is not prudent to corner the rat," Cao had said. Scattered in the dark, the paratroopers were unable even to assemble until midmorning the next day. That night the Viet Cong broke contact and drifted away eastward. Attempts to head them off after daylight proved futile. The Battle of Ap Bac was over, except for the recriminations which shortly followed.

Viet Cong losses had been 36 captured, an unknown number wounded, and perhaps 50 or more killed. Saigon's casualties were 66 dead, including 3 Americans, and 115 wounded, of whom 6 were American. By those terms the battle had been a draw, another of a long series of indecisive clashes. But raw numbers are relatively unimportant. It was a fight the Viet Cong had wanted. And the results were what they had hoped for. Though they could not justly claim outright victory, they could take smug comfort in the severe damage they had inflicted on U.S. helicopters and in the undeniable fact that they had held off so powerful a force. It was *not* a fight the South Vietnamese had wanted. Though they could rightly invoke even less of a claim to victory than could the Viet Cong, their whole purpose once the situation became clear was to disengage, to terminate the battle. When Cao had accomplished that, he and his subordinates preferred to forget the unfortunate encounter as soon as possible. Unable to reveal their actual political shackles, South Vietnamese officers simply had to endure in silence the biting gibes of the press. For the Viet Cong, though, Ap Bac brought waves of delight. Far and wide they broadcast a tale of smashing victory, of triumph over Saigon's men and Washington's machines. For the rest of the war, Ap Bac remained a landmark of Viet Cong progress. As long as they lived, survivors wore a round, red medal showing a proud warrior in front of a rising sun with the words "AP BAC" inscribed in an arc below the sun. In terms of psychological impact—which may well be more meaningful than military results in an insurgency war—Ap Bac was a decided victory for the Viet Cong and an ignoble drubbing for the 7th Division and its American advisors.

Actually, claims of victory or defeat miss the crucial point. Soldiers on the field generally performed well the things they were told to do. The real difference lay in the realm of higher policies, particularly those emanating from the palace in Saigon preventing unity of command and refusing to acknowledge that gains required expenditures. Hanoi was willing to buy victory with blood; Saigon was not. It was that simple.

In the end, the battle and the ensuing public uproar served to underscore emphatically that South Vietnam's army was not yet a fully professional force endowed with able leaders. More training for officers and men alike was required before the ARVN could operate effectively on its own. Building an army is an excrutiatingly slow process, as George Washington's advisors had also learned.

CHAPTER 7

The Downfall of Diem

Despite setbacks such as the one at Ap Bac, South Vietnam's prospects for victory loomed increasingly larger and brighter as the early months of 1963 marched by. Insurgent incidents, having peaked early in 1962, had steadily declined ever since; there were about half as many in March 1963 as in the same month a year earlier. Outwardly the Strategic Hamlet program appeared to be making great gains, although it was exhibiting certain worrisome signs of splitting at the seams. On the battlefield ARVN units held the upper hand, largely because American advice and equipment were more effective, the former as a result of experience gained and the latter as a result of industrial adaptation to the peculiar needs of warfare in Southeast Asia. On balance, things were looking up.

Those factors were reflected by the dejected mood within the insurgency movement itself. Disenchantment racked the ranks. Having had a quick win wrested from their grasp in 1962, the Viet Cong reluctantly but realistically retrenched for the long haul. Ruefully, they contemplated the starkly diminished status of their insurgency. Something had to be done to regain the initiative, the leaders knew, but in light of their curtailed options they were at a loss to say what that something should be. Not for some five or six years had days dawned so bleak and unpromising for the Viet Cong. Then, at that low point, help swept in gratuitously from an unexpected quarter.

Swarming out of pagodas in Hue, on Buddha's birthday in May, came flocks of militant monks fervently intent on righting what they claimed was a religious imbalance of power. Roman Catholics, a distinct minority in the country, held most high positions in the South Vietnamese government. Buddhists noted that Catholics, beginning with President Diem and his family, received preferential treatment, garnering the lion's share of influential or lucrative positions. By taking their protest to the streets, the yellow-robed dissenters set in motion shock waves of protest which eventually swamped the Diem administration.

The solution for the Saigon government, if there was a solution, lay in discovering the perfect balance between strength and suppleness. It was a task to try Solomon—and Diem was not a Solomon. Predictably, his response to the demonstrations was harsh and uncompromising. Buddhist leaders refused to yield in the face of that intransigence. They escalated the confrontation. In a carefully staged suicide, a monk sat down cross-legged on a Saigon street, had friends douse him with gasoline, and stoically struck a match to his dripping robes. Photographs of that ultimate act of protest shocked Western nations, particularly the United States, focusing attention on Vietnam as no other single event had. Having thereby gained a forum, Buddhists angrily charged Diem and his family with religious repression. Rioting broke out in Saigon.

Diem, against American advice, insisted on dealing severely with the rioters to suppress what he considered to be base treason in the midst of war. Once before, in suppressing the sects, he had been successful by remaining firm in the face of all opposition. He had been right then. But times had changed. Buddhists continued to burn themselves to death; Diem's troops, directed by his widely hated brother, Ngo Dinh Nhu, continued to treat agitators harshly. Sympathy and support for the South Vietnamese president dwindled.

Meanwhile, the Viet Cong were quick to take advantage of the opportunity thrown their way. They regained the initiative as Saigon's counter-insurgency campaign wandered fitfully, largely neglected as the Buddhist revolt consumed the interest and resources of newsmen and officials alike.

Another factor aiding the insurgency just then was the formal partitioning of Laos in July of 1962, granting Ho Chi Minh the unhindered use of the network of infiltration trails bearing his name. Supplies sped southward just in time to cascade into South Vietnam when Saigon's army, preoccupied with the Buddhist crisis, was looking the other way. That massive injection of equipment spurred the insurgency onward. But the upsurge went unnoticed. All eyes that summer were fixed on the religious drama in Saigon.

August was the climactic month. After seventeen thousand Buddhists demonstrated in the capital, Diem declared martial law over all the land. At about that time, President Kennedy began seriously to consider dumping the Vietnamese president. Henry Cabot Lodge, the 1960 Republican vice presidential nominee, replaced Ambassador Frederic E. Nolting in a move widely interpreted as a hardening of the U.S. line. Cambodia, reflecting the spreading disenchantment with Saigon, severed diplomatic relations with South Vietnam. That same fateful month, guerrillas overran and put to the torch the original strategic hamlet, Ben Tuong, the showplace of the entire program, a bold stroke sounding the death knell of Diem's much advertised and broadly acclaimed technique for ending the insurgency.

It had been bound to happen sooner or later. The program had been too ambitious—it quite overreached Saigon's ability to implement it. If not doomed from the outset, it had at least been destined to suffer severe setbacks along the way. American advisors, some more intent on statistics than stability, must share the blame for having let things get out of hand. For instance, reports from the field indicated that 875 new hamlets had been completed in August 1963. In a month when government control was crumbling everywhere, such figures were patently preposterous. At any rate, the resounding and reverberating crash of the Strategic Hamlet program served forcefully to augment the cacophony of voices clamoring for Diem's hide.

Watching from the wings stood South Vietnam's generals. For years they had chafed under Diem's overcentralized control and had grudgingly swallowed disasters like Ap Bac. Now, seeing all their recent gains against the Viet Cong being washed away in the churning rapids of the religious strife, they began secretly plotting to overthrow the president. Diem himself had created a climate conducive to such treacherous thoughts by his evident and long-standing disdain and distrust of his military men. To assure loyalty and safety, he had surrounded himself with family members and specially equipped and trained guard units. To prevent collusion, he had erected an elaborate command system with many nominally junior officers having direct access to the palace. Field commanders often got the impression, and rightly so, that someone from Saigon was constantly peering over their shoulders. Cooperation in combat by units answering to different bosses was a sometime thing; Diem's policy of divide and rule was hardly the best policy for a new army striving to lift itself into efficiency. Distrust bred frustration, frustration generated discontent, discontent led to disloyalty. The generals needed only opportunity and excuse to depose Diem. The Buddhist crisis brought both.

Compounding the rapidly deteriorating situation, Madame Nhu, Diem's sister-in-law, made an intemperate and ill-timed trip to the United States. While she travelled and talked, Buddhists continued to commit suicide by flame. Her husband, Ngo Dinh Nhu, increased his already sinister reputation by unnecessarily ham-handed treatment of demonstrators and by mysterious contacts with elements of the communist enemy. Beautiful, sharp-tongued, fiery, inevitably dubbed "The Dragon Lady," Madame Nhu attracted large audiences and page one coverage. Far from aiding Diem's cause, though, she helped bury it. Typical of her insensitivity to public opinion was her offhand remark concerning the blazing suicides: she was, she said, so delighted that monks thus removed themselves from opposition to Diem that she would clap her hands at every such street "barbecue."

As events closed in on him, Ngo Dinh Diem became even more stubborn. Force alone was ever his answer, not force and compromise. In the eyes of many influential Americans, including President Kennedy, democracy in South Vietnam had become Diemocracy.

Kennedy, the first Roman Catholic president of the United States, was particularly sensitive to charges that he supported a Catholic dictatorship in a Buddhist country. He inclined increasingly to the view of those urging him to oust Diem. Kennedy's advisors differed. Some had become vehemently anti-Diem, others remained convinced that, for all his faults, he was better than any potential replacement. In Saigon, General Harkins lined up behind the South Vietnamese leader while Ambassador Lodge concluded that the controversial president had to go. That split strained relations between the two top Americans. But, as conditions constantly worsened, sentiment drifted inexorably closer to ouster. A military revolt had been thwarted in 1954 by General Collins' blunt warning to the generals that the United States would not tolerate it. Washington issued no such warning in 1963. Indeed, a group of generals headed by Duong Van "Big" Minh, Tran Van Don, and Le Van Kim, actively plotting a coup d'etat, received unofficial assurances as early as August that there would be no American opposition to their plot.

The key member of the coup group was Tran Van Don, who at this time was acting Chief of the General Staff. He apparently served as the intermediary between Ambassador Lodge and the other generals, operating with an ever present CIA agent.

On 1 November fighting erupted in Saigon between units led by a group of conspirators and those soldiers remaining loyal to President Diem. The generals had planned their stroke carefully and in tight secrecy. It was then boldly and bravely carried out. After a brief, fierce encounter the palace fell to troops led by Colonel Nguyen Van Thieu, a young officer himself destined later to become president of South Vietnam.

Diem and brother Nhu fled, escaping to Cholon, the Chinese suburb of Saigon, where they found refuge in a Catholic church. From there Diem telephoned Ambassador Lodge to ascertain the American position. Lodge offered nothing more than concern for the president's personal safety, telling him, "You have certainly done your duty. As I told you only this morning, I admire your courage and your great contributions to your country. No one can take away from you the credit for all you have done. Now I am worried about your personal safety. I have a report that those in charge of the current activity offer you and your brother safe conduct out of the country if you resign." Deciding that he had no other alternative, Diem contacted the rebel generals and accepted their demand that he go into exile. He and Nhu prepared to leave the country as an armored column rumbled over to the church in Cholon to escort them to the airport.

But the generals had second thoughts. Diem still possessed extraordinary influence. The coupmakers feared him alive. Should he somehow return to power, they knew, their own lives would be forfeit. The soldiers—at least some of them—decreed that Diem must die. They directed an aide of "Big" Minh's, a Captain Nhung, to kill the president. Not only was Nhung trustworthy, he was a counter-intelligence officer, hardened to the chilling chore of assassination. When Diem and Nhu entered one of the two M-113 armored vehicles sent for them, for what they supposed would be a safe ride to Tan Son Nhut Airport to a waiting airplane, Captain Nhung tied their arms to their sides and blew their brains out. Nhung himself later died in mysterious circumstances, carrying to his grave the whole story of the murders.

Within a fortnight, President Kennedy, too, was shot to death, and Lyndon B. Johnson inherited the shambles of Vietnam.

CHAPTER 8

Turmoil and Transformation

No period during the entire war was more bewildering, either at the moment or in retrospect, than the months following Diem's death. That the war had come to a major crossroads would become apparent later, but at the time no one was sure what was happening. Not in Saigon, not in Hanoi, not in Washington. It was a turning point stretching out over one complete, excruciating, perplexing year. It was a time of change, of decision, of crisis. A year of turmoil and transformation. It was a time when no one knew the answers and only a rare few even knew what questions to ask. When it ended, the Viet Cong insurgency had given way to outright invasion from the North, and the American advisory effort stood at the threshold of becoming an American expeditionary force.

The year started on a high note for the South Vietnamese. A wave of relief washed over the land in the wake of Diem's demise. Ecstatic citizens danced in the streets. They tossed flowers at grinning soldiers, happily applauded the generals, and smashed everything they could lay hands on that reminded them of the Ngo family. They even toppled a column holding statues of the Trung sisters—revered national heroines who led a revolt against Chinese conquerors in the year 40 A.D.—because someone noticed that the statues had bustlines more like the despised but well-built Madame Nhu than of the ordinary Vietnamese woman. Released from their autocratic ruler, the Vietnamese people looked forward expectantly to a rosy future. Unhappily, it was not to be.

Quite often appearances lag behind reality, which was the case at that moment. The bright afterglow of the coup against Diem distorted Saigon's assessment of the situation. South Vietnam was actually as close to defeat in the seesawing struggle with the Viet Cong as it would ever be. The insurgents were on the verge of victory. Douglas Pike, America's foremost expert on the Viet Cong, wrote in retrospect: "[The insurgency] came perilously close to success in the anarchical situation that developed during and after the last days of the Diem government. The NLF stood at the shore of victory, but slowly the tide ebbed." One reason for the ebbing, Pike believes, is that previously dormant political factions arose to steal some of the Viet Cong thunder.

That is probably a correct observation, but it is one that could be made only after the event. At the time, the political situation appeared to be utterly disastrous. The generals had the strength to destroy but not the unity to build. General Duong Van "Big" Minh established a provisional military government, which quickly demonstrated its utter ineffectiveness. Minh himself, though enjoying wide popularity, was a distinct disappointment. Unable to reconcile differences among his squabbling generals, he lethargically drifted from day to day, failing to gain more than nominal control of the framework of government. He lasted not three months before being booted by Major General Nguyen Khanh, a goateed, moonfaced officer who had been educated at the U.S. Army's Command and General Staff College at Fort Leavenworth, Kansas. Ambassador Lodge, hoping the energetic, 33-year old Khanh would make a better leader than Minh, tendered immediate recognition to the new regime.

Khanh initially displayed some promise, but evil floodgates had been opened. A gaggle of generals and a colonel here and there suddenly discovered their own previously latent talent and desire for the nation's highest office. A series of coups, attempted coups, and counter-coups plagued Saigon throughout 1964.

Khanh started by sacking three of the four corps commanders and five of the nine division commanders, actions consolidating his position but worsening the already devastating turbulence in the administrative machinery of government. For in wartorn South Vietnam, corps and sometimes division commanders served as territorial governors, almost as legal war lords. In addition, virtually every province chief and district chief was also a military officer. Hence, every time the soldiers played musical chairs it shook the country's governing apparatus through and through. Each successive change cheapened the central government's credibility and diminished its strength. Still the jousting generals persisted in their political maneuvering.

That summer Khanh set himself up as president, but the political rungs remained too slippery to hold. After just ten days he was obliged to step down and form a triumvirate of generals. Three heads ruled no better than one, however, so in September the trio surrendered authority to a committee of fifteen, with Khanh staying on as premier. That arrangement in turn gave way in October to a constitutional government boasting a civilian premier, Tran Van Huong. Huong served, however, at the whim of the military, which was still headed by the irrepressible Khanh.

Bickering erupted again in December. After delicate maneuvering, Khanh and the air force commander, Air Vice Marshal Nguyen Cao Ky, dissolved the short-lived civilian government. Ambassador Maxwell Taylor, with what he later termed "calculated asperity," called in the group responsible, which included Ky and

General (future president) Nguyen Van Thieu. "Do all of you understand English?" the irate Taylor demanded. "I told you all clearly...we Americans were tired of coups. Apparently I wasted my words...Now you have made a real mess." He dismissed them saying, "You people have broken a lot of dishes and now we have to see how we can straighten out this mess."

Diem had been dead for fourteen months; most observers had lost count of the number of governments Saigon had seen in that time.

At long last even the most chuckleheaded officer came to realize that the coup route led to a political dead end. The generals finally reached a consensus: General Khanh reluctantly left the country one year after he had first seized power, and a civilian government headed by Dr. Phan Huy Quat took over. That was to be Saigon's final involuntary change of leadership. During an emergency period a few months later, the civilians asked the military to resume control, thus, in a manner of speaking, overthrowing themselves. Marshal Ky then became premier and General Thieu took over as chief of state. National elections in 1967 made Thieu president, a position he would hold until the sudden collapse of the South more than two years after Americans withdrew from the war.

Not all the political turmoil of that tumultuous year was caused by intramural battles within the army. Montagnards in the Central Highlands rose in insurrection. The mountain folk had long simmered under Saigon's rule. The age-old differences between Vietnamese and Montagnards were essentially racial and ethnical, with each looking down on the other. Now the Montagnards saw Saigon's preoccupation with its inveterate coupmakers as a heaven-sent opportunity to break free. Under a united front, tribal troops took important persons hostage, occupied several key locations, and demanded independence. American special forces officers, who had trained the Montagnard soldiers in the first place, and therefore had a close working relationship with them, intervened. Their efforts to negotiate helped calm the rebels, and a daring helicopter rescue of the hostages effectively ended the serious if brief rebellion.

All told, between coup attempts, racial antagonism, religious unrest, and economic disruption, any government however stable would have had its hands full that chaotic year. And that witches' brew of difficulties was over and above the communist insurgency itself— which had expanded dramatically while Saigon was busy sorting out its political differences.

Having swept back into contention during the time of trouble in 1963, the Viet Cong gleefully greeted Diem's overthrow and the subsequent political disorder. Hanoi recognized its golden opportunity and acted with dispatch to take advantage of it. For ten days in December 1963, the Central Committee of the Vietnam Workers' party discussed the options newly opened. Revolutionary warfare theorist Truong Chinh presented the committee's conclusions in a top secret session. "The key point at the present time," he said, "is to make outstanding efforts to rapidly strengthen our military forces to change the balance of forces between the enemy and us in South Vietnam." Every exertion was to be made to continue the momentum gained. "It is time," Chinh said, "for the North to increase aid to the South; the North must bring into fuller play its role as the revolutionary base for the whole nation." Hanoi knew that Saigon stood on the thin edge of anarchy and dissolution—a stiff shove could end the war abruptly. General Giap received the order to provide the shove by beefing up the Viet Cong.

Among his various methods of escalating the military effort in the South, Giap took three steps which were to bear heavily on the future progress of the war: rearming the Viet Cong; sending native Northerners to the South; and directing terrorist activities against United States advisors and installations.

Up to this point Viet Cong fighters had been armed

with whatever booty they could obtain—weapons from both world wars, surplus French and American guns, Chinese imports, arms captured in battle, homemade devices, even ancient muzzle-loading flintlocks. However, as the number of insurgents increased, problems inherent in resupplying and maintaining so polyglot an inventory became acute. Standardization was the obvious answer. Consequently the high command in Hanoi began a progressive conversion to a standard family of small arms using a single caliber of ammunition. Foremost among the new weapons was the excellent Soviet assault rifle, the AK-47, firing a 7.62mm round. Along with hand weapons came a more modern lot of supporting arms. Machine guns using the same 7.62mm ammunition, a highly effective rocket launcher, 82mm mortars, and recoilless rifles were the foremost items in the new inventory. Most were Chinese copies of Russian models.

By the end of 1964, the infusion of new weaponry was nearly completed. All regular Viet Cong units had them. The insurgents then boasted a clear firepower advantage over the ARVN, which was still armed with antiquated American small arms. However, the Viet Cong's increased effectiveness and reduced resupply problems were partially offset by a new worry—a logistical tail. No longer could insurgents resupply themselves simply by knocking over a government supply dump; the rapid firing Russian weapons devoured tons of Russian or Chinese ammunition, all of which had to be transshipped from Hanoi. Thus Giap had made a most crucial decison; for the duration of the war his forces in South Vietnam would be reliant on the long infiltration route through Laos and Cambodia, or on shipments by sea.

Accordingly, oceangoing vessels, laden with arms and ammunition, began nosing out to sea to rendezvous with Viet Cong supply agents on deserted beaches along South Vietnam's lengthy and largely unwatched coast. Others set a course for Cambodia's major port, Sihanoukville (later renamed Kampong Som), from where the supplies could be slipped into South Vietnam via the Mekong's many waterways. At the same time, North Vietnamese labor battalions began improving the network of trails snaking southward through the Laotian Panhandle. They did their work well. Soon, General Giap's overland supply routes ran, turnpike style, along South Vietnam's entire western flank. Collectively, that system of trails, way-stations, stockage areas, repair facilities, and defensive points was known as the Ho Chi Minh Trail, a monument to the man responsible for the insurgency.

Giap's second critical decision was to send native Northerners southward. Quite likely the Hanoi high command considered that step long and soberly before taking it. Recruiting in the South was going well enough in terms of numbers, but an insurgency requires trained and dedicated leadership. Previous leaders had been Southerners trained in the North and infiltrated back. Those were men to be reckoned with while they lasted, but death, disease, and desertion had more than decimated their ranks. After all, it had been ten long years since they had initiated the struggle. To replace the fallen and to fill the leadership ranks of newly raised units, policy makers in Hanoi were reluctantly forced to turn to men of the North.

These new leaders could not be as effective as the ones they replaced. The old knew the countryside; the new found it strange—even their speech was poorly understood by the Southern peasant. The old always had relatives close at hand to shelter and supply them; the new had left their families a journey of weeks or months away. Graves for the old would be in the land of their ancestors; for the new who fell, unmarked plots in a remote jungle far from the home village. Should the old win they would rule the land they fought over; should victory crown the efforts of the new they would most likely return to the North rather than reap the spoils in the South. However motivated and dedicated the Northerners might have been, there was no way they could do as well as their predecessors. Still, for the number of leaders Hanoi needed, there was no alternative. Northerners went south. Around twelve thousand of them during 1964. By midyear perhaps 40 to 50 percent of all insurgency cadres in the South were men born and raised in the North. The Viet Cong therefore realized gains in terms of increased strength, but they unavoidably forfeited a good degree of individual and group effectiveness.

One of Giap's worst errors, as it turned out, was authorizing his field commanders to strike directly at Americans. His policy was probably designed to discourage any further spread in the scope or size of the U.S. advisory effort, but it ran the grave risk of provoking even greater intervention. That is in fact what ultimately happened, though not in 1964.

On 3 February 1964, enemy forces struck a U.S. compound in Kontum, opening a sustained, countrywide campaign against American advisors. The campaign included a series of bombing attacks in Saigon, peaking spectacularly in May when frogmen sank a U.S. Navy ship at berth in the capital city. Later, guerrillas mortared American air bases and terrorists blew up structures housing advisors. Altogether, American losses were light, but over the months, unable to retaliate, obliged to endure the bombing passively, military men began to reach the outer limits of frustration. They fairly itched to strike back.

Other actions taken by insurgents within South Vietnam could also be faulted. Going all out for victory, the Viet Cong began to forfeit popular support; in fact, they took steps virtually guaranteeing the alienation of a large segment of the population. Coincident with their terrorist campaign against Americans came indiscriminate bombing of civilian buses, market places, hotels, and other public gathering places. In discussing his December decison, Truong Chinh had stated that communist methods should include actions to "properly punish a number of reactionaries and tyrants who owe blood debts to the people." In a word, terrorism. Guerrillas also raised their already onerous taxes and began forcibly impressing unwilling recruits into their ranks. These were serious steps because ultimate revolutionary strength is inseparable from public support. Whether all this was the doing of Northern cademen who were not especially sensitive to the fate or feelings of the local people, or whether it was premeditated policy, the result was the same: growing public antipathy for the Viet Cong.

Nonetheless, despite those questionable decisions, the revolutionary movement continued to escalate ominously, particularly militarily. Throughout the year Viet Cong forces waged a series of blood battles with ARVN units, winning some and losing some, but always coming back for more. Increasingly daring, they became easier to find and harder to destroy. Casualties were heavy, but still the guerrillas managed to recover and increase. General Maxwell Taylor was openly amazed: "Not only do the Viet Cong units have the recuperative powers of the phoenix, but they have an amazing ability to maintain morale." Insurgents gradually enlarged their base areas, grabbing virtual control in several localities. In Binh Dinh Province, for example, the Viet Cong flag flew everywhere except over a few district towns and in the city of Qui Nhon. In Tay Ninh Province, farther south, Viet Cong officials were all satisfied with their political and military status in forty-six of the province's forty-eight villages. Overall, American estimates placed the amount of land under hostile sway at 40 percent or higher.

Finally, at year's end, insurgents grouped the 271st and 272nd Regiments to form their first division-sized unit, the Viet Cong 9th Division. Fully equipped and freshly trained with the new family of Soviet weapons, the 9th Division entered battle on 28 December at Binh Gia, a Catholic village forty miles east of Saigon. The 9th chewed up the outgunned and unsuspecting 33rd

Ranger Battalion and 4th Marine Battalion before ARVN commanders realized what they were up against. Then, in a bold gesture of defiance, the 9th held its position on the field for four days before retiring.

Unquestionably the Viet Cong had grown alarmingly strong and aggressive. The year had been one of impressive qualitative and quantitative improvement. But the armed forces of South Vietnam had not been stagnant.

Saigon's forces also made steady progress during 1964, though their improvement was not as remarkable as that of the Viet Cong. In raw numbers South Vietnamese armed strength rose by more than one hundred thousand, to a total of over half a million men. The quality of many units understandably declined during the rapid expansion, for the limited reservoir of capable leadership did not permit officer development to keep pace with force development. By and large, airborne and marine troops, armored units, and a few ranger elements acquitted themselves commendably. They were elite outfits to begin with, however, blessed with carefully chosen commanders and a tradition of élan. The rest of the army, not so fortunate, wrestled with the agonizing problem of molding high-quality leaders from low-quality clay. As for the common soldier, he was never a worry. Given training and leadership, he was able and willing to do everything asked of him. Generally, units of poor commanders were easy to pick out because they invariably lacked spirit and aggressiveness. Eventually, though, the combination of American advice, better schooling, attrition of unfit officers, and experience itself worked a slow transformation, inching the quality of leadership upward. The process was exceedingly slow, to be sure, but there was progress nonetheless.

At first the exhilarating involvement in politics had lifted morale in the army, but that quickly dissipated in the disappointing welter of senseless intrigue. And, naturally, making a coup or defending against one took troops away from the more important mission of fighting Viet Cong guerrillas. However, except in the high command, the series of coups had less of an impact on the military than one might suppose. After the first few instances, most middle level officers came to realize the folly of continuing the internecine bickering. If they didn't, American advisors at all levels constantly harped on the subject, urging their counterparts to get on with the war. The message soaked in. In one example, not at all atypical, an armored force commander received orders via radio to join his commander for a coup attempt in Saigon. At first he was visibly shaken. Orders are orders; outright disobedience is a serious matter. But the young officer knew that political dissension was ripping his country apart, that coups were wrong. He pondered his predicament for a moment, then broke out in a broad grin. After explaining to his advisor what was happening, he calmly spoke into the microphone, telling his boss that he "did not hear" the last transmission because of excessive static. Then, after quickly switching off every radio in his unit, he proceeded on the last instructions he had acknowledged—which were to march *away* from Saigon. By autumn of 1964, rocks thrown in the presidential pool in Saigon caused worrisome but not overwhelming ripples among administrators in the field. Still, officers had to keep a wary eye over their shoulder—which was one eye they couldn't keep on the Viet Cong.

South Vietnamese and Americans had gleaned sad lessons concerning pacification from the wreckage of the Strategic Hamlet program. It was seen that a successor scheme had to be more methodical and less ambitious. In the summer of 1964, when the spreading insurgency seriously threatened Saigon itself, officials contrived a new plan entitled *Hop Tac*, a Vietnamese phrase meaning cooperation. Four concentric zones were drawn around the city with the innermost initially receiving greatest emphasis in resources needed to rebuild both confidence and community spirit. Meanwhile military forces concentrated on clearing the outer belts of Viet Cong. When the first zone was declared secured the whole operation was moved out one ring and repeated. In theory, the pacified area would spread from the center like an oil spot. In actuality, the program did not produce as expected; it was just too big a step for a government in turmoil to take. Nevertheless, the experience educated officials for the next try—and it did at least succeed in loosening the insurgent squeeze on Saigon.

In comparison to its status at the beginning of 1964, South Vietnam's army ended the year stronger in manpower and experience, weaker in terms of relative strength with its adversary, wiser in politics, and better versed in pacification. It had a long way to go, but barring an unforeseen disaster it was equal to the task of deflecting the military thrust of the Viet Cong. More, at that point, could hardly have been expected.

Perhaps most encouraging of all the trends and currents of 1964 was the steadily solidifying assistance from outside nations. The United States, of course, carried the bulk of the load, but other countries rallied to the cause. Australia had been assisting South Vietnam ever since 1962. The continent down under increased its commitment and was joined by other Asian states, notably New Zealand, Thailand, Korea, Malaya, and the Philippines. Each nation contributed in a different way—for example, Malaya trained policemen while New Zealand sent a combat engineer detachment—but the significant point was that they had tangibly joined the fight.

President Lyndon B. Johnson upped America's stakes. He sent more ships and planes, increased the number of advisors, and replaced the top level of leadership in all major agencies in the country—political, military, economic, and psychological.

At the top of the list of those replaced was Ambassador Lodge. To begin with, Lodge was an influential

Republican politician, and 1964 was an election year. Stateside politics were an evident distraction. At one point Richard Nixon, then an attorney for the Pepsi-Cola Company, visited Saigon. After the running mates of 1960 had conferred, eager newspapermen asked Nixon if he and Lodge had talked about politics. "We had a very interesting discussion and actually we made a deal," Nixon quipped. "He is going to put a Pepsi-Cola cooler in the embassy in Saigon." Neither Nixon nor Lodge got the nod that year—Barry Goldwater stormed the Republican convention—but Lodge left in June to have a try.

There were other reasons for the ambassador's departure. Notably, he had been unsuccessful in uniting all elements of the United States mission. The country team was simply not functioning. Secretary McNamara reported bluntly to President Johnson that Ambassador Lodge and General Harkins were at loggerheads, and that, as a result, the entire American effort was something short of efficient. In a double switch in June, General Maxwell Taylor replaced Lodge and General William C. Westmoreland succeeded Harkins. Taylor and Westmoreland had worked together before, they were professionally compatible and personally close, and Taylor, as a past army chief of staff, was clearly the senior. Cooperation seemed assured.

Westmoreland had arrived in Vietnam in January 1964 just a few days before General Nguyen Khanh overthrew General Minh. That bloodless but abrupt change of leaders served notice to the American general that he was in a situation unlike any for which he had been trained or conditioned. Graduating with highest military honors from West Point in 1936, he had served with the horse artillery in Oklahoma and Hawaii before World War II. During that war he commanded an artillery battalion in Africa and fought from Normandy to Germany with the 9th Infantry Division. Becoming a paratrooper afterwards, he led an airborne regiment in Korea. As a brigadier general he attended

Harvard Business School in 1954—the year the United States began its military involvement in Vietnam. As the army's youngest major general, he next commanded the 101st Airborne Division at Fort Campbell, Kentucky. From 1960 to 1963 he served as superintendent at West Point. Only forty-nine years old when he reached Saigon, Westmoreland had a distinguished record and was an inside bet to become chief of staff, the highest position in the army. For all that, however, he was hardly prepared for his new job. Experience in World War II and Korea was not necessarily the best grooming for coping with insurgency warfare. But neither was anyone else in the Pentagon's stable of generals really ready for Vietnam.

Prior to leaving the United States for Vietnam, Westmoreland visited General Douglas MacArthur. Perhaps recalling his own unhappy episode in Korea, the ailing old soldier cautioned General Westmoreland to take care. "Your assignment there," he said, "will be ripe with opportunity, but fraught with danger."

Early in August, not long after both Westmoreland and Taylor were settled into their new jobs, North Vietnamese torpedo boats attacked the U.S. Navy destroyer, *Maddox*, while it was patrolling international waters in the Gulf of Tonkin. Hanoi's navy, showing more audacity than reason, repeated the raid two nights later, this time taking on both the *Maddox* and a sister destroyer, *Turner Joy*. Angrily, American carrier-based jets retaliated by blasting the raiders' ports and fuel depots in North Vietnam. Shocked by the affair, the United States Senate, in a near unanimous vote, passed the Gulf of Tonkin Resolution, signifying its acquiescence in the use of American power in Southeast Asia and reaffirming the importance of South Vietnam to interests the United States held vital. Those actions, publicly proclaiming American resolve and symbolically returning the war to its source in the North, were a grand bolster to morale in the South.

Actually, though neither the general public in South

Vietnam nor the United States knew it, President Johnson had months previously initiated clandestine raids against Ho Chi Minh's territory. Indeed, it was probably one of those raids that had goaded the North Vietnamese torpedo boats into sallying out of their harbors. Under the code name "34-A," actions against the North included seaborne raids, airborne drops, psychological operations, reconnaissance flights, and sabotage. Overall, the effort was modest and achieved no more than modest results. Its greatest value was psychological—the South Vietnamese, after years of passively enduring a conflict caused by their Northern kinfolk, could at last strike back at their tormentors.

Among the most notable indicators of American resolve was the continued rise in the manpower being committed. Later, in reflecting on the vicissitudes of 1964, General Earle Wheeler, Chairman of the Joint Chiefs of Staff, stated that the Americans were probably what kept South Vietnam from crumbling. "We had inserted advisors at all unit levels down to and including battalions," he said. "They were like the steel reinforcing rods in concrete."

Special forces strength, especially, mushroomed during 1964. The 5th Special Forces Group—thirteen hundred strong—deployed to Vietnam to recruit and train irregular units to screen border areas. At the beginning of the year there were twenty-five remote border camps standing astride infiltration routes along South Vietnam's sieve-like western border with Cambodia and Laos. By year's end the number of camps had doubled. The special forces teams in charge of those mud and barbed-wire forts were officially advisors, but unavoidably they were fighters, too. Out on the end of the line, they either fought or perished. The first Medal of Honor of the war was awarded to a captain for his heroic defense in July 1964 of one of the isolated base camps.

In addition to people, injections of equipment bolstered the effort. Some eighty helicopters and nearly one hundred airplanes arrived to raise the total number of U.S. aircraft to around six hundred. Among them were reconnaissance jets, air defense interceptors, and medium bombers. By December some 23,000 military men were based in South Vietnam. Other thousands served aboard ships cruising the South China Sea and at air fields in Thailand.

This evidence of an increasing American commitment was matched by a growing confidence in the ultimate ability of South Vietnam, with American help, to defeat the insurgency. Not everyone agreed with that appraisal, for in the summer of 1964 the situation looked far worse than it actually was. As at the start of the year, there was a gap between what was read and what was real. Although the specter of defeat had receded somewhat, many observers, having only just recognized its presence, could not judge its distance. Forecasts of impending doom were not rare.

But the worst was over. Both Americans and South Vietnamese had learned much in the decade since 1954. A great deal of it, unfortunately, had been by trial and error, but the lessons had been absorbed nonetheless. They applied that knowledge vigorously in 1964. Slowly, officials picked up the pieces of previous programs. New ones were begun. A fresh crop of district and province chiefs ("new brooms" wielded during the time of coups did at least sweep away a certain amount of dead wood) started grappling with the monumental task of providing security and gaining the confidence of the people. Despite the debilitating inner turmoil, ARVN elements stood off an aggressive enemy who had grown stronger and bolder. Without question, slippage was great; all too many officials kept an eye cocked on the smoldering situation in Saigon. Generals, having come to their positions on the wings of a coup, were naturally rather sensitive to the shifting political winds. But, on balance, South Vietnam experienced forward movement. Tortuous though it was, progress was made.

By late summer or early fall, officials could once

again see—by squinting—what they described as light at the end of the tunnel. (They would later regret ever having used that phrase.) They were cautious; hope had been dashed before and most informed participants recognized how very, very long that tunnel was. However, they reckoned hedgingly that victory would come *if* the favorable trends continued and *if* the Vietnamese didn't inflict another coup on themselves and *if* the religious issues remained muted and *if* the American public would be patient. Only one "if" was not considered—and it was the one circumstance that would occur.

Nowhere in their analysis of the situation did Vietnamese or American staffs seriously consider an overt intervention by North Vietnam. Then, in the waning months of 1964, intelligence officers pieced together a picture of entire units of the North Vietnamese army (NVA) infiltrating southward. Three regular regiments—the 32, 95th, and 101st—had left their home posts in the North and were known to be working their way down the Ho Chi Minh Trail. That information cast a sinister shadow over New Year's Eve celebrations in both Saigon and Washington. It looked as if the invasion that advisors had expected a decade before was on the way at last. That dim speck of light at the far end of the tunnel winked abruptly out.

PART II

STEMMING THE TIDE

1965

CHAPTER 9

Season of Decision

Hanoi sweltered under the prickly blanket of a humid summer day. A languid sultriness choked the Northern capital. Pedicab drivers, more interested in shade than fares, hunkered down in the shadows of buildings, dozing in that squatting position of rest which few but the Oriental can comfortably assume. Subdued by the oppressive heat, storekeepers and occasional shoppers engaged but half-heartedly in their ritualistic haggling. Policemen stood somnolently at corner posts. The casual visitor on that torpid day saw no outward evidence indicating that a momentous decision was in the making. However, unlike the sleepy city, the conference room near Ho Chi Minh's office was highly charged with tension. The men of the Lao Dong Politiburo, the top rung of the ruling hierarchy, sat around a wide, cloth-covered table, and carefully presented their ideas and recommendations. The group had split into two roughly equal sides on the matter. Debate had been hard. All eyes now rested on "Uncle Ho." He would make the decision. Ho Chi Minh, the thin, aging leader of Vietnam's communists, sat silently stroking his wispy grey beard. Several long minutes flickered past. Finally he looked across to his plump defense minister, General Vo Nguyen Giap.

"Are you absolutely certain we can support such an effort?"

"Yes," was the firm reply from the Tiger of Dien Bien Phu.

"Then it is decided," Ho informed his ministers. "We will commit our army to the war of liberation in the South."

That scene, or one very similar to it, took place in Hanoi in the late summer of 1964, probably in August. The fateful results of Ho's decision became evident in late autumn and early winter when surprised American and South Vietnamese intelligence officers discovered the presence of regular North Vietnamese Army (NVA) units in South Vietnam. At first they detected only individuals and small units, but soon regiments were confirmed and entire divisions of the NVA were suspected.

By committing its regular forces to a cause which had previously been cloaked in the guise of an internal war, Hanoi dramatically altered the entire thrust and scope of the conflict. It was a key command decision. Indeed, it may well have been *the* key command decision of the war.

Ho Chi Minh did far more than merely move hostilities up a notch in intensity—he changed the very nature of the war by switching from moral and logistical support of the Viet Cong to military intervention in South Vietnam. In effect—and the point is highly significant—he shifted from an insurgency war to something akin to a protracted war. Insurgency warfare is a method used by *internal* revolutionaries to oust their own government; protracted warfare, on the other hand, is employed by a weak nation to repel a powerful foreign invader.

How, one might ask, could Hanoi look upon the South Vietnamese as foreign invaders in South Vietnam, their own nation? A good question. The answer lies in Ho Chi Minh's view of all Vietnam as an entity

80

which should rightfully have been his. Theorist Truong Chinh, enunciating a politburo policy in December 1963, some eight or nine months before the August decision to invade, had said, "The war waged by the people in South Vietnam is a protracted one because we are a small people having to fight an imperialist ringleader which is the U.S.A." In other words, by a convenient warping of logic, the United States could be considered the powerful foreign invader and the Saigon government nothing more than "lackeys and running dogs" of the Americans. "It also has the characteristic of an internal war," Chinh admitted, "but the purpose of either war, the aggressive war or internal war, is to serve the U.S.'s political purposes." However it was explained, the fact remains that Hanoi's high command knowingly changed forms of warfare.

That deliberate and puzzling scrambling of dogma is what made Ho's decision so momentous. Communist warfare, like communism itself, is doctrinaire by definition. A life-long communist like Ho Chi Minh does not lightly tinker with doctrine.

In his policy statement, speaking for the politburo in Hanoi, Truong Chinh had also announced, "On one hand we must thoroughly understand the guideline for a protracted struggle, but on the other hand we must also seize the opportunities to win victories in a not too long period of time... There is no contradiction in the concept of a protracted war and the concept of taking advantage of opportunities to gain victories in a short time." The giants of communism, Russia and Red China, thought Chinh daft. And they as much as said so. Mao Tse-tung had long ago written his classic warning to impatient revolutionaries: "The rash advocates of a quick victory, lacking the stamina of an arduous, long, drawn-out war and bent upon a speedy conclusion, clamour for strategic decisive engagements the moment the situation takes a slightly favorable turn. To act on their advice would be the worst mistake imaginable..." More recently, Nikita Khrushchev, while proclaiming the merits of wars of national liberation, had pointedly cautioned that those wars "must not be identified with wars among states..." Moscow and Peking were noticeably cool to the tampering with doctrine. Hanoi, for all intents and purposes, had moved the fighting in Vietnam from a war of national liberation to one among states. Apparently not satisfied with continuing a war fought by proxy in another land, Ho Chi Minh not only risked attracting destruction to his own carefully nurtured country, he chanced losing the test case for wars of national liberation.

Why, if the insurgency were really going so well, did the North Vietnamese leader gamble with unforeseen consequences by abandoning a successful strategy? If, to the contrary, he had sensed that the trends were running against the Viet Cong, why had he not obeyed insurgency dogma which demands rolling with the punch, requires fading from strength? Why, indeed, did he order his troops southward at all? We may never know for sure, but there are three different hypotheses, one of which must contain most if not all of the answer.

The most commonly accepted theory is that Hanoi saw 1964 as the beginning of the end for Saigon. According to this line of reasoning, communist leaders believed the South Vietnamese were vulnerable for a knockout blow which could be administered in the winter and spring of 1965 by Viet Cong regulars if they were reinforced by North Vietnamese forces. NVA troops could tip the balance and win the war at once. General Westmoreland himself inclined to this reasoning. In his published report on the war he wrote, "Capitalizing on the political disorder which afflicted the Saigon government, upon the weakness of government administration throughout the country, and upon deteriorating morale in the Vietnamese armed forces, the North Vietnamese and their southern affiliates were moving in for the kill." Left unanswered by that analysis, however, is the vital question: if victory was within grasp, why switch strategies for the sake merely of attaining it a few months earlier? It doesn't add up. Ho Chi Minh's quest for ultimate triumph had already consumed two decades; time was the least important factor in his equation of victory.

To Americans, raised in a free, competitive, capitalistic society, time is a precious commodity. It is the one thing that cannot be bought or built. We can't bear wasting it. A moment lost is never regained. It is money; a business can increase its productivity by saving time, hence enlarging its profit. To Asians, steeped in Confucian concepts, time is an endless stream flowing from an infinitely regenerating source. It is precious enough, a commodity to be valued, but because it is of unlimited abundance one can hardly use too much of it. Thus, that which we husband the most carefully they expend the most liberally. We even picture it differently. Western cultures depict time graphically in linear symbols; our calendars have starting and stopping points and run horizontally along a page. The oriental calendar is in the form of a wheel, a graphic symbol with neither beginning nor end, a continuum. A quick victory is strictly a Western concept. In war our attitudes and expectations lead us to seek the lightning stroke of victory, to shun the indecisiveness of stalemate. To accuse Ho Chi Minh of running unnecessary risks and defying his own dogma simply for the sake of a quicker win—particularly with victory only a matter of months away—seems to assume he would have used our values in making his judgments. That is a most doubtful assumption.

Some thoughtful observers have offered a second motivation for Hanoi's surprising move. It could have been, they say, that the power of the Viet Cong had become so strong in late 1963 and early 1964 that Hanoi feared an eclipse of its own influence. According to this view, Viet Cong leaders, enjoying a steadily growing position of power, were displaying some reluctance to continue playing a role wholly subservient to the

North. Since Ho Chi Minh's goal was to unite Vietnam, not to foster a second communist nation, he could be expected to look with disfavor on any signs of NLF independence. Therefore, to counteract that separatist trend and to reassert complete dominance, Hanoi had to be in on the final victory. Maybe. Over the years differences were bound to develop between Hanoi and the NLF. But, given the extent to which Northerners had taken over positions of leadership within the Viet Cong movement, less drastic cures could most likely have been found.

Those first two reasons share a prime assumption; they presume that the Viet Cong were riding an unstoppable, victorious tide. A third possible reason for the politburo's decision springs from the conjecture that the communists were actually losing the war in mid-1964—and knew it. If the Northern leaders had concluded that they were no longer winning the fight in South Vietnam, the only interpretation one can give to their decision to intervene directly is that they were willing to gamble on a quick victory rather than follow their own text by phasing back into a lower level of intensity. That, in turn, means they saw trends in the South which were leading to a permanent rather than a temporary setback. By this logic, the Northern invasion of South Vietnam is seen as a desperate move to retrieve a losing cause, not as a coup de grace following a victorious insurgency campaign. This last reason is as plausible—perhaps more plausible—than the other two.

To understand Ho's reasoning, we must consider events in South Vietnam during 1964 from the perspective of Hanoi. Conditioned to observing from the vantage point of Saigon or Washington, one can overlook the obvious if he isn't careful. It is useful occasionally to look on the other side of the hill.

Before reaching any conclusions, the North Vietnamese president had first to consider five separate groupings of people. To begin with, of course, would be the communist community itself, which was of no real concern. Ho had North Vietnam firmly under his thumb, and he was not afraid of being abandoned by other communist nations, whatever his course. Therefore, he could concentrate on analyzing the other four. They were: the Viet Cong; those nations aiding Saigon; the government and armed forces of South Vietnam; and, not least, the people of South Vietnam. As covered in the previous chapter, Ho would have gleaned mixed readings from his analyses.

Although experiencing a bounding resurgency during 1963 and early in 1964, the Viet Cong seemed to be in trouble by mid-1964. The most telling evidence was in the expanding presence of ethnic North Vietnamese among the cadre. Those Northerners were not well suited to the exacting requirements of leading an insurgency in the South. To a degree, their presence actually hindered the movement. In the United States, as everyone knows, a clipped Yankee accent in Dixieland grates painfully on Southern ears—Vietnam is not so different. Another revealing observation was that Viet Cong guerrillas, despite better weapons and higher morale and the advantage of the initiative, had been singularly unsuccessful in defeating a demoralized and disoriented South Vietnamese army. They had more or less fought each other to a standoff. If the Viet Cong at their peak could not overpower the ARVN at its weakest, insurgency leaders indeed had some cause for concern. Moreover, the great effort had boomeranged. The cumulative effect of means such as kidnapping, assassination, terrorism, taxation, and impressment was to move the end farther from reach. The insurgents had lost, perhaps forever, their aura of being the army of the people. All in all, Hanoi could not view with optimism the future of its arm in the South.

With respect to "third country" forces the outlook was especially dismal to the Northern rulers. True enough, Americans had made mistakes aplenty and had from time to time seemed to waver in resoluteness, but by August of 1964 they were at least more experienced and did appear finally to be wholly in earnest. The quick military reaction after the Gulf of Tonkin incident spoke eloquently on that subject—and the Congress in Washington had rallied to give the American president an overwhelming vote of confidence. What's more, a new and dynamic general was in charge of MACV, a famous war leader occupied the top desk in the embassy, and each of the major civilian agencies had fresh bosses. Advisors now served at district levels (the rice-roots), and more Americans advised ARVN units in the field. Along with the influx of advisors had come money and equipment in large measure. To make matters worse, the United States was not alone. Noncommunist Asian nations were lining up on the side of South Vietnam. Their aid was not yet significant on the battlefield, but in this kind of war psychological factors are every bit as important as military ones. And, undeniably, outside assistance was a major morale boost for Saigon. Furthermore, the movement to support South Vietnam was spreading. Clearly, the involvement of other countries was anything but encouraging.

At first glance it would seem that Ho would have been totally pleased with the shaky government in Saigon. On the whole he was, but even there he could discern disconcerting trends. After half a year of coup and countercoup, the outlook for stability in Saigon was not good in the summer of 1964. But that was at the top level. At the critical lower reaches of the governmental hierarchy—provinces, districts, villages, police, civil servants—a modicum of stability managed to survive as the months rolled by. Purges following the coup against Diem had indeed severely shaken the entrenched bureaucratic echelons of government. But then, by and large, the generals restructured the various layers to assure that men serving in subordinate positions remained loyal to the central government, not to an individual. Each succeeding coup thus had a diminishing impact on affairs outside the capital. Soon a change of personalities in the presidential palace caused hardly a tremor in the actual operation of government in the provinces. In that light, the men in Hanoi could only surmise that the passage of time might work to strengthen rather than weaken the South Vietnamese government.

Definitely discouraging when gauged in Hanoi was the sputtering but improving army of South Vietnam. Even though thousands of soldiers deserted ARVN units yearly, peasant youths were defecting just as readily from conscripted service with the Viet Cong. More significantly, South Vietnamese officers did not quit, while communist cadre quite frequently did so. More and better equipment, improved training, the experience of years of combat against insurgents, and a deepening hatred of the Viet Cong were a few of the factors making the ARVN a more potent force. That it would continue to improve was the sole prediction a practical General Giap could make.

The last group to whom communists could hopefully look was the populace—the bulwark of previous successes, the "sea" which provided sustenance to the guerrilla "fish." Unhappily, as Ho Chi Minh saw it, even the previously dependable peasants revealed disturbing indications of turning against the insurgents. Terrorism, the final arbiter of the revolutionary, was having adverse feedback. After ten years and thousands of terrorist executions, hardly a family in all the South had been left untouched by this brutal communist tactic. The reservoir of resentment welled over in 1964. Large numbers of refugees from Viet Cong-dominated regions streamed into safer areas. Voting with their feet, those peasants emphatically rejected the insurgents. In that year also, a previously rare phenomenon began to occur more and more often: the people began voluntarily supplying the government with information of Viet Cong activities and locations.

87

This movement of the people away from his cherished cause could well have been the bitterest pill for Ho to swallow.

As the pendulum swings, the Republic of South Vietnam was no longer at the bottom of the arc. Neither was it at the top, but the movement up had begun—the low point was passed. To the leaders in Hanoi the omens spelled a clear message: The Viet Cong were losing effectiveness, outside nations were rallying to the Saigon regime, South Vietnamese forces were developing daily, the population was tending to cast off its identity with and support of the guerrillas. The trends ran unmistakably against North Vietnam. Giap's maximum effort to win in 1964 with orthodox revolutionary warfare had fizzled. Somehow, Hanoi felt, the pendulum had to be stopped short.

Ho's solution was embodied in his radical decision to retrieve his fading chances by sending regular troops southward. A major victory—such as capturing a provincial capital, destroying a large South Vietnamese force, or slicing the South in half—might create defeatism in Saigon, consternation in Washington, and panic in the South. Memories of Dien Bien Phu still loomed large. Giap believed that a smashing success in that pattern could precipitate collapse in Saigon and just might bring total victory. At the very least it should halt the unpromising tide of events, and with a minimum of luck could even reverse it.

But what of the risks of U.S. intervention? Might not Washington commit combat troops? Several of Ho's close counsellors raised that crucial point. Nor was the disquieting question being asked for the first time. Months earlier, when Hanoi had opted to make the all-out effort to win the Viet Cong, the politburo had evaluated the probabilities of an American reaction. The members had calculated it to be a slight risk well worth taking. In his December 1963 report, Truong Chinh had reasoned that the chances of American intervention were "only remote possibilities because the U.S.

cannot evaluate all the disastrous consequences she might bear if she wages the war on a larger scale. She realizes that if she is bogged down in a large-scale and protracted war, she will be thrown into a very passive position in the world." The Pentagon, obsessed with Secretary McNamara's notions that cost-effectiveness and systems analysis would provide a quantifiable answer to every challenge, of course realized no such thing. The North Vietnamese could not have known how often and how seriously Washington had considered committing combat troops ever since 1961. Nevertheless, the United States had not sent soldiers previously, a fact seeming to vindicate the politburo's judgment.

Thus, four primary assumptions formed the basis of Hanoi's belief that it would win the war with Northern forces in 1965:

a. The United States would not commit ground forces to a land war in Asia.

b. ARVN, stretched taut by its counter-insurgency campaign against the Viet Cong, would be unable to cope also with regular formations of NVA troops.

c. A major North Vietnamese victory would precipitate a collapse of resistance throughout South Vietnam (the Dien Bien Phu syndrome).

d. The United States, fearing involvement with Red China, would continue to restrict its air operations to areas south of the Demilitarized Zone at the 17th Parallel.

Policy makers in Hanoi were quite correct in surmising that the South Vietnamese were unable to handle an enlarged threat, and their belief that a stunning victory would have decisive psychological impact was not at all farfetched. They were, of course, dead wrong in believing Washington would neither carry the air war into North Vietnam nor inject ground forces into the South. At the time, though, those were not bad assumptions, especially if one recalls that the Oriental also has trouble penetrating and comprehending the inscrutable Western mind. After all, as Ho read it, Americans, including military leaders, had been for years proclaiming the folly of engaging in a land war on the Asian continent. Indeed, many Americans themselves had been convinced by political statements promising that the United States would not get enmeshed on the ground in Vietnam. That very August, as a matter of fact, President Johnson had announced publicly that he would not consider bombing North Vietnam or "committing American boys to fighting a war that I think ought to be fought by the boys of Asia to help protect their own land."

Just as the North Koreans, listening to American pronouncements in 1950, had become convinced that the United States would not make a stand for Korea, so was North Vietnam convinced fourteen years later that America would not fight for Vietnam. Of such miscalculations are wars made.

President Lyndon B. Johnson had fewer options than President Ho Chi Minh. Hanoi had grabbed the initiative with its decision to invade, leaving Washington a choice of intervening or accepting defeat. Accepting defeat was never for a moment considered, which left intervention. That in turn led to another question: what kind of intervention?

Alarm spread rapidly in the high councils of government in Washington and Saigon as General Giap's regiments began entering the battle in the South. And with that alarm developed a major debate over what to do to halt the invasion. To do too little was tantamount to surrendering South Vietnam to the invader. Too much would risk war with Red China and could conceivably lead to World War III. There, in stark relief, was the infinitely complex problem which must be faced by any power wishing to wage a limited war— the definition of limits. How much is enough? And will enough be too much?

While debate in Washington intensified, fighting in Vietnam did likewise. Emboldened by Northern reinforcements, Viet Cong commanders became more and more aggressive. On the anniversary of Diem's assassination they mortared the sprawling airbase at Bien Hoa and soon afterwards sent their newly organized 9th Division raging into battle at Binh Gia. It became apparent in Saigon that something must be done to retrieve the rapidly deteriorating situation—and soon. One solution proposed was to retaliate with an air campaign against North Vietnam. Another was to dispatch American combat troops to protect U.S. bases. Those were not steps to be taken lightly, however. President Johnson postponed his decision.

"Know your enemy" is a cardinal precept in any competitive endeavor, in none more so than in war. Decision makers in Hanoi were quite right in figuring that neither the public nor the leaders of the United States *wanted* to fight in Southeast Asia. Confusing desire with determination, however, they erred in thinking Americans *would* not fight there. Compounding the error, they unwittingly took steps to pave the way for American involvement by their terrorist campaign against U.S. personnel and installations.

The American people like their politics plain and simple—Machiavelli just does not sell in Middle America. Therefore, a subtle war, a war of shadows, is quite beyond the grasp of most of us and, as several presidents have discovered much to their chagrin, it is difficult in the extreme to convince or enthuse us to resist one. But naked force—Pearl Harbor, for instance—is something else again. By the foolish torpedo attacks against American destroyers in August 1964 (at the very moment when Ho was deciding to invade South Vietnam) North Vietnam caused Congress to endorse President Johnson's use of force in Southeast Asia. At the same time Hanoi's action created a climate for political acceptance of air strikes against the source of aggression. That should have warned the men in Hanoi. A closer reading of American history would also have warned them. But the lessons were missed.

On 7 February 1965, Viet Cong sappers struck the American advisors' compound at Pleiku. That attack turned out to be the final straw. To force the other guy to desist, said President Johnson, we must "apply the maximum deterrent till he sobers up and unloads his pistol." He promptly ordered air strikes against North Vietnam. Americans naturally backed their president because he seemed to be righting a glaring wrong—an overt attack on U.S. servicemen. A month later two U.S. Marine battalions waded ashore near Da Nang and a new war was on. Americans would continue to advise and support, but thenceforth they would fight as well. Westmoreland evacuated U.S. families to clear the decks for the grim struggle ahead.

CHAPTER 10

Rolling Thunder

Stephen Crane, describing a Civil War cannonade in his book, *The Red Badge of Courage*, wrote, "The battle roar settled to a rolling thunder, which was a single, long explosion." Civil War cannonades spewed forth a great deal of sound and smoke, but their results were usually disappointing.

Shortly after midnight on 7 February 1965, a Sunday, a barrage of mortar rounds crashed without warning into Camp Holloway and a nearby airfield in Pleiku in the Central Highlands. Startled advisors and aviators, straining to gather their bearings after the rude awakening, sprinted in underwear and steel helmets for defensive bunkers. As flares and tracers lighted the sky, Viet Cong demolition teams slithered quickly through barbed wire obstacles to plant satchel charges against buildings and under parked aircraft. In the tumult of explosions they withdrew. The well planned, lightning raid left eight Americans dead, 109 wounded, and 20 aircraft destroyed or damaged.

It was the final affront. Not even the presence in Hanoi of Soviet Premier Alexei N. Kosygin deterred the angered American president. Just hours after the attack a message flashed from the Pentagon, ordering

Admiral U.S.G. Sharp, commander of all U.S. forces in the Pacific, to retaliate against bases in the North. Admiral Sharp directed aircraft carriers in the South China Sea to execute "Flaming Dart," a contingency plan long before prepared. In early afternoon that same day forty-five attack aircraft from the carriers *Hancock* and *Coral Sea* roared in low over the coastline to blast North Vietnamese army barracks and port facilities at Dong Hoi, just beyond the Demilitarized Zone. Another thirty-four planes rose from the *Ranger* but were forced back by bad weather. A day later South Vietnamese pilots, flying twenty-four bomb-laden, propeller-driven aircraft under a covering umbrella of U.S. jets, exultantly pounded the Chap Le Barracks, some fifteen miles deep into North Vietnam. Air Vice Marshal Nguyen Cao Ky, the flamboyant Air Force commander, personally led the strike.

On the tenth, Viet Cong sappers blew up a U.S. hotel in Qui Nhon, killing twenty-three Americans as they slept. "Flaming Dart II" promptly took to wing over North Vietnam, with U.S. Navy bombers ripping apart the Chanh Hoa Barracks while South Vietnamese planes attacked a military compound at Vit Thu Lu. With that, President Johnson gave the green light to begin a sustained bombing campaign against North Vietnam. After a few false starts caused by the uneasy political situation in Saigon, the first strikes of the series hit Ho Chi Minh's supply and naval facilities on 2 March 1965. Washington code-named the campaign "Rolling Thunder." Hanoi called it "The War of Destruction." In varying degrees of intensity the bombings of the North were to last for three and a half years.

In addition to the obvious psychological satisfaction derived from striking back at one's tormentor, the Rolling Thunder campaign had two other objectives. As enunciated later in 1965 by General J.P. McConnell, U.S. Air Force chief of staff, one was "strategic persuasion." He explained that phrase by saying the aerial strategy was designed "to apply a measured amount of strategic airpower in order to persuade the North Vietnamese leaders to cease their aggressive actions and to accede to President Johnson's offer of negotiating a peaceful settlement of the conflict." It was a far cry from "bombing them back to the stone age"—more like trying to bomb them into the Age of Reason. The third objective, McConnell added, was "helping to impede the flow of reinforcements and supplies to the Viet Cong in South Vietnam."

The decision to bomb had not been made lightly or precipitately. In one form or another advisors had for years been urging the president to consent to an air campaign beyond the 17th Parallel. Infiltration and frustration were their twin reasons. General Maxwell Taylor had first broached the subject way back in 1961 when he told President Kennedy, "NVN is extremely vulnerable to conventional bombing, a weakness which should be exploited diplomatically in convincing Hanoi to lay off SVN." Shortly after Kennedy was assassinated, the Joint Chiefs of Staff recommended to Secretary of Defense McNamara that the United States must make ready to "conduct aerial bombing of key North Vietnam targets, using U.S. resources under Vietnamese cover, and with the Vietnamese openly assuming responsibility for the actions." In March 1964 McNamara outlined some "retaliatory actions" in a memorandum to President Johnson, including bombing of the North "on a tit-for-tat basis" as well as aerial mining of Northern ports. Finally, in August 1964, in a precedent setting move, President Johnson ordered bombers over North Vietnam in retaliation for torpedo boat attacks against American warships in the Gulf of Tonkin. From that moment onward the pressure to bomb increased inexorably until it was looked upon as a virtual necessity to stave off defeat in South Vietnam.

Ambassador Taylor and General Westmoreland agreed, in a cable to the State Department on 18 August, that "a carefully orchestrated bombing attack on NVN" might convince Hanoi to cease and desist its aggression. The Joint Chiefs of Staff went on record again as recommending "air strikes and other operations against appropriate targets in [North Vietnam]." A survey of courses of action drawn up in September by Assistant Secretary of State for Far Eastern Affairs, William P. Bundy, listed the need to employ air strikes in the North in retaliation for communist actions in the South. Through the autumn months the clamor to bomb increased—and so did enemy provocations. However, President Johnson was locked in an election race with Senator Barry Goldwater, a "super-hawk" who openly advocated the bombing of North Vietnam. Johnson, running as the peace and reason candidate, turned a deaf ear to all advice on Vietnam until the campaign was over and he was roundly elected. Then he promptly approved a secret, two-phase air campaign against Laos and North Vietnam.

Hanoi, however, had anticipated the possibility of air attacks. In November of that election year Premier Pham Van Dong had journeyed to Moscow to request materiel and technical assistance in building a modern anti-aircraft system. He asked for jet interceptors, surface-to-air missiles, and a sophisticated radar control system. The Russians were receptive. Technicians soon arrived to establish the toughest air defense complex seen in any nation since World War II. The longer the United States delayed bombing the costlier it was likely to become, pilots noted nervously.

During the first phase of Johnson's surreptitious campaign, warplanes would concentrate on interdicting infiltration routes in the Laotian Panhandle. Fliers kicked off that operation, called "Barrel Roll," on 14 December 1964. The second phase, expected to last from two to six months, was to be an air war against North Vietnam itself. President Johnson and his planners optimistically expected General Giap to fold his tents within that time frame. The president insisted, however, on firm proof of progress toward stabilizing Saigon's turbulent political environment before he would authorize any bombing of the North. Ambassador Taylor carefully briefed Premier Tran Van Huong and General Khanh, impressing upon them the urgent need for governmental stability. Much as they wanted to see an air campaign against the North, though, the generals just could not restrain themselves; Khanh and Ky ousted Huong that December, earning Taylor's blistering upbraiding and postponing the implementation of the bombing campaign. There matters stood until the sneak attack on Camp Holloway made up the president's mind.

Within the larger framework of the debate over *whether* to bomb had raged an argument over *how* to go about it. Perhaps recalling Theodore Roosevelt's famous dictum, "speak softly and carry a big stick," civilian planners wanted to start out softly and gradually increase the pressure by precise increments which could be unmistakably recognized in Hanoi. Ho Chi Minh would see the tightening pattern, the theory went, and would sensibly stop the war against South Vietnam in time to avoid devastation of his homeland. Assistant Secretary of Defense John T. McNaughton dubbed the strategy "slow squeeze" and explained it in musical terms—an orchestration of activities which would proceed in crescendo fashion toward a finale. "The scenario," he wrote, "would be designed to give the United States the option at any point to proceed or not, to escalate or not, and to quicken the pace or not."

The Joint Chiefs of Staff did not like McNaughton's tune. The generals argued that if force were to be used at all it should be applied hard and fast to obtain maximum impact with minimum loss. To start lightly and escalate slowly, they held, would be like pulling a tooth bit by bit rather than all at once and getting it over with. If the purpose were to affect Hanoi's will, the Joint Chiefs said, the United States would have to hit hard at vital points and demonstrate a willingness to apply unlimited force. If bomb we must, they wrote in a counter-recommendation, then let us destroy all of the North's major airfields and petroleum reserves in the first three days. In short, let us strike in strength with a knockout punch rather than fool around with a jabbing attack which gives the other fellow a chance to cover up—and which in any case he can probably withstand.

The intelligence community—a panel comprising members of the C.I.A., the Defense Intelligence Agency, and State's Bureau of Intelligence—entered the debate strongly on the side of the military. The panel took exception to both of the underlying assumptions on which the civilian strategists had based their theory. First of all, they thought it folly to attempt to program the enemy's mind like a digital computer. He just might not react in what a Westerner would consider a rational manner. Next the panel tried to strike down the prevailing belief that North Vietnam could be brought to heel by air action alone, particularly by a "wrist-slapping" form of aerial bombardment. "North Vietnam's economy is overwhelmingly agricultural and, to a large extent, decentralized in a myriad of more or less economically self-sufficient villages." Bombing would cripple Hanoi's industry and hamper its support of the Viet Cong, the intelligence experts conceded, but we "do not believe that such actions would have a crucial effect on the daily lives of the overwhelming majority of the North Vietnam population." In other words, the enemy's will would not be broken by bombs.

President Johnson overrode the objections of his intelligence and military advisors. Indeed, it is not at all clear whether Secretary McNamara ever even bothered to convey their arguments to him. Ambassador Taylor, still addressed as "General," had given his blessings to the theory, approval which apparently cancelled the objections of the Joint Chiefs of Staff. Thus was born the strategy of "graduated response."

Dreamed up by well-intentioned but naive policy advisors as a sort of compromise between the extreme options of withdrawal from South Vietnam or invasion of North Vietnam, the strategy had a couple of beneficial points and a plethora of shortcomings. First, the good points. America, worried about world opinion, could in this fashion demonstrate its restraint for all to see, especially Red China. And North Vietnam would not be backed in.o a corner as were the Axis powers by the World War II policy of unconditional surrender. In concept the strategy may have been good but, as it actually turned out, not much else good could be claimed for it. Initiative went by forfeit to the enemy, for he could set the pace of hostilities and force the fight on terms of his own choosing. Escalation was a built-in hazard; and the point past which the foe would dare not step might very well turn out to be further than Washington would be willing to carry the conflict. Besides, it was altogether possible that Hanoi could adapt and adjust to punishment gradually inflicted faster than such chastisement could be dealt out. But, for all that, gradualism was the grand strategy pursued in Vietnam.

An argument countering the concept of gradualism in war was succinctly advanced in a statement made in 1905 by British naval reformer, Admiral Sir John Fisher: "The essence of war is violence. Moderation in war is imbecility. Hit first! Hit hard! and hit anywhere!"

Admiral Fisher would have been dismayed at the American policy, but he would have been absolutely aghast at the overcentralized direction and skin-tight control exercised by Washington. Policy makers on the Potomac seemed to do everything but actually fly the aircraft. Secretary McNamara, with considerable help from the White House, selected the targets, specified the strike day, chose the number of airplanes, and stipulated the size of bombs to be dropped. All headquarters between the Pentagon and the cockpit became mere message passers. Washington also imposed severe ground rules: nothing flew north of the 19th Parallel; South Vietnamese planes had to be involved some way in each strike; unexpended ordnance went wasting into the South China Sea rather than being used on targets of opportunity; reconnaissance of a site before a strike was strictly taboo, and was limited even after the attack: pilots who could not manage to line up their target the first time around could not recycle; and so forth.

After the first few raids a chorus of voices raised objections to the ineffective application of power. Ambassador Taylor was clearly disenchanted with the way things were going. On 8 March he cabled his annoyance, reportedly rebuking McNamara for the "unnecessarily timid and ambivalent" way he was conducting the air war. The Joint Chiefs of Staff had not liked the concept; they liked the reality even less. They tried mightily if unsuccessfully to revise or remove the political restrictions. The subject became extremely touchy. At one point when McNamara chided the Joint Chiefs for not achieving enough damage on the raids, General Earle G. Wheeler, the chairman, retorted testily that the best way to improve the cost-effectiveness of the bombing would be for Washington to help the field commanders less.

Air force jets based in Thailand and South Vietnam joined navy carrier planes in conducting the strikes. Chafing quietly under what they deemed to be unnatural restrictions, pilots dodged heavy flak to attack their designated targets, marvelling all the while at rules obliging them to ignore more conspicuous and remunerative and vulnerable targets. By and large, they struck only transportation facilities, such as bridges and tunnels, and military installations like barracks and storage dumps. As a result of restrictive policies, attack aircraft inflicted precious little damage in the opening weeks of the air war. All told, hundreds of airplanes managed to drop only some two hundred tons of ordnance per week—which figures out to very few bombs at five hundred or seven hundred fifty pounds apiece. But that was the strategy, after all—to hit the

North softly as an initial warning. Whether they agreed or not, the players had to adhere to the coach's game plan.

One month after the bombing had begun, John A. McCone, director of the Central Intelligence Agency, turned in a pessimistic analysis of results. "The strikes to date have not caused a change in the North Vietnamese policy of directing Viet Cong insurgency, infiltrating cadres and supplying material. If anything, the strikes to date have hardened their attitude." McCone then urged acceptance of a more rigorous policy. "We must hit them harder, more frequently, and inflict greater damage. Instead of avoiding the [enemy jet fighters], we must go in and take them out. A bridge here and there will not do the job. We must strike their airfields, their petroleum resources, power stations and their military compounds." With the passage of time some of the earlier shackles were in fact eased, but never to the extent McCone and the military thought necessary.

Two months and ten days into the campaign, Washington suspended Rolling Thunder raids for a five-day period. In a confidential message President Johnson wrote, "My purpose in this plan is to begin to clear a path either toward restoration of peace or toward increased military action, depending upon the reaction of the communists." Expectantly, the Pentagon waited for a signal that Ho Chi Minh would accept the hard facts of life and begin backing down. The Northern leader flatly rejected the invitation. Instead, he took advantage of the lull to rush more supplies southward. Graduated response had failed its first test. On 18 May Admiral Sharp resumed Rolling Thunder at a slightly higher level of intensity.

Unlike Stephen Crane's original "rolling thunder," the battle roar would not settle into a single, long explosion. Fits and starts were more its mark.

CHAPTER 11

The New Face of Conflict

General Westmoreland, while closely monitoring the debate over whether or not to use air power against the North, had his own problems on the ground in the South. By the end of 1964 he had sensed that North Vietnamese and Viet Cong combat divisions were "moving in for the kill." Any lingering doubts which MACV intelligence officers might have had disappeared during the early days of 1965 in the dust of Giap's campaign—insurgency was no longer the main threat. South Vietnam was being invaded by conventional forces, if not in a conventional manner. A worried Westmoreland saw victory or defeat hanging in the balance, but he had no reserve of ground combat elements to counter the assault; the South Vietnamese were stretched to their limit, and there was not time to raise, equip, and train new units. Air was his only recourse. In late January he asked for and got authority to employ U.S. air power in close support of ARVN troops in emergency situations. That authority, and the General's willingness to use it, held the invaders at arm's length for the next few critical months.

The first strikes by American jets inside South Vietnam were conducted on 19 February near Binh Gia, the area east of Saigon where the Viet Cong 9th Division had recently mauled several ARVN units. Less than a week later enemy forces trapped a column of Saigon's troops near Mang Yang Pass on Route 19 between Pleiku and Qui Nhon. That wild area had been the slaughter ground for French Group Mobile 100 in 1954. In a classic and famous ambush, Viet Minh forces had cut off and wiped out an entire French armored brigade. Now, eleven years later, the Viet Cong were attempting the same maneuver in the same spot. But this time there was a crucial difference—American air power. Westmoreland reacted immediately, launching relays of jet fighters and bombers and sending in troop-carrying helicopters protected by armed choppers. In a demonstration of air mobility, helicopters evacuated the trapped men without the loss of a single soldier, while the aerial pounding inflicted considerable casualties on the Viet Cong. From that day on U.S. fliers found themselves supporting ARVN ground elements on a nearly routine basis. General Westmoreland's judicious juggling of his rather meager aerial assets provided the moral and material edge needed to let South Vietnam hang on in the unequal contest against Viet Cong and North Vietnamese units.

But air power alone is not enough. At best, an air effort can do no more than stave off defeat; ground victory is attainable only by ground forces. A few days after Rolling Thunder began, U.S. Marines landed on beaches near Da Nang to secure the large air base there. Later that same month a military police battalion arrived in Saigon to provide security to American installations in the teeming city. The arrival of those troops gave the South Vietnamese a sorely needed shot of inspiration. By taking over security chores the Americans also freed some ARVN units for employment against the enemy. However, even as those first forces were arriving, General Westmoreland and the Joint Chiefs of Staff pressed for a larger commitment to forestall an ultimate defeat.

Sensing that the symbolic aerial bombardment of North Vietnam was unlikely to bend Hanoi's will to continue, and seeing that air alone could not plug the South Vietnam dike indefinitely, the professional soldiers wanted enough strength on the ground to hold off the enemy while South Vietnam regirded itself for the new war. They asked for two American divisions and one from South Korea, which would raise the total number of foreign troops to over one hundred thousand men. Again Ambassador Taylor disagreed with the military requests, basing his argument on grounds that so many foreigners would be counterproductive in an insurgency war. On that score alone he was probably correct, but he had not yet recognized the new face of conflict in Vietnam. The war was no longer solely an insurgency. It had taken American officials in Saigon years to perceive that the original threat was insurgency not invasion; long to take root, the idea died almost as hard, not being fully accepted until long after invasion was an open reality. Be that as it may, President Johnson denied the military's request for so large a force. He did, however, authorize two more marine battalions and an increase of about twenty thousand support forces.

Those support troops had the mission of paving the way for a possible larger build-up later. It was high time some thought went to logistics. Despite the years of United States presence in South Vietnam, there existed insufficient ports, airfields, or storage areas to support a major American war effort in Southeast Asia. Although militarily necessary—and repeatedly recommended by military planners—construction of a base complex in South Vietnam had been spurned by Washington officials myopically concerned more with cost effectiveness than with operational capability. The limited and antiquated French-built facilities had been deemed adequate to support the counter-insurgency campaign and to permit a modest introduction of outside forces. Now, at long last, with the possibility of a major ground campaign lurking just around the corner, logistics staff officers began making preparations to support it.

As it happened they were too late. Events overtook them. Before they could do much more than begin, their plans were dwarfed by new and startling requirements. The war sharply escalated to dizzying heights not envisioned by even the most prescient observer. Instead of the one hundred thousand troops Westmoreland had wanted in March, in June he urgently asked for well over two hundred thousand to stabilize the deteriorating situation. He added ominously that the number would go even higher "if the U.S. is to seize the initiative from the enemy." As if to second his own warning, he told Secretary McNamara in July that a further increment of one hundred thousand men—a total of three hundred thousand—would be necessary by the beginning of 1966 in order to regain the initiative.

The sudden change in his estimate of the situation was brought about by a series of battles fought in May and June portending imminent disaster for South Vietnam. General Giap had staggered the South Vietnamese by infiltrating and committing to battle far greater forces than Allied intelligence officers had thought possible. Set back initially in February and March by the unexpected involvement of U.S. airpower and the even more unexpected arrival of American ground forces, Giap had reassessed his chances. They still looked reasonably good. He swiftly reinforced in an effort to topple the tottering Saigon regime before it could regain equilibrium. By May the impetus of his revitalized campaign carried his forces within sight of victory. In that month Saigon was losing the equivalent of a battalion a week, and the Viet Cong were capturing at least one district capital every six or seven days. Typical of the ferocity of the fighting was an attack conducted by the tough 9th Division, now operating with three regiments. It destroyed in one swift stroke an ARVN infantry battalion and a supporting airborne battalion, killing and wounding a total of 650 men.

Faced with a military emergency of major proportions, civilian Premier Quat decided to return the reins of government to the military. General Nguyen Van Thieu became chief of state and Air Vice Marshal Ky assumed responsibilities as premier. That arrangement would endure, ending the long, debilitating period of political turmoil. Just then, however, it represented one more damaging change at a most crucial moment. The immediate impact was to improve Hanoi's odds for a quick win. But ARVN forces always showed a stubborn streak which seemed to grow strongest just when the going got roughest. Helped by the few American combat units and the full force of U.S. firepower, South Vietnam somehow survived those bitter battles of May and June. It was that desperate, back-to-the-wall fighting which prompted Westmoreland to ask for heavy reinforcements right away.

The general's appeal shocked Washington. The crunch point had been reached. The United States had to admit defeat or send in sizable numbers of combat troops. Defeat was unthinkable; by the end of June, Westmoreland had permission to use B-52 bombers, promises of the reinforcements he wanted, and authority to commit his maneuver battalions to offensive combat. The 173d Airborne Brigade, which had flown in from Okinawa in May, had already been blooded. Other combat units began arriving and fighting in July.

The war had lurched upward to reach an entirely new level of intensity and scope which neither Hanoi nor Washington had really wanted or foreseen. A Ukrainian proverb states, "When the banner is unfurled, all reason is in the trumpet." War has a way of creating its own momentum. Ho Chi Minh had erred in believing America would not go all the way to support South Vietnam; Lyndon Johnson had erred in forfeiting the initiative to North Vietnam. The result of their errors was wider war.

Having been at least partially convinced by the oft

repeated American statement that the war in Vietnam must be waged by Vietnamese, the leaders in Hanoi were dumbstruck by Washington's reaction. Consternation and disbelief were their initial reactions. Aspirations for early victory dimmed as U.S. units streamed ashore. Then, after the surprise wore off, General Giap saw yet one more chance to wrest victory. His basic premise, he reasoned, was still valid. A major defeat— such as cutting South Vietnam in half or overrunning a complete province or annihilating a large army unit— would cause collapse of the shaky regime in Saigon. The Americans could not arrive in strength until late summer at the very earliest. Even then, Giap knew, their belatedly begun logistical system would not be functioning adequately. Furthermore, monsoon rains would last until November—drenching, daily rains which would reduce American and South Vietnamese mechanized mobility by a much greater degree than they would hamper the foot mobility of his own army. It was worth a chance. Giap ordered his units inside South Vietnam to regroup while fresh divisions in the North prepared for the long trek southward over the Ho Chi Minh Trail.

By early July, General Westmoreland realized that he had for the moment beaten off the enemy onslaught by the narrowest of margins. As both sides caught their breath, the U.S. commander also recognized the great danger should Giap be able to build up his strength faster than the Americans could get ready. On the surface a lull settled in over the countryside, but underneath a frenzied race developed as each side strove to mass its forces before the other could. This was the point where Westmoreland asked for an Allied strength of over three hundred thousand. He believed defeat would be the probable penalty for losing the build-up race.

The North Vietnamese had the tough task of moving men and materiel in the face of a foe blessed with total air superiority. For great stretches supplies had to be hand carried, often over rudimentary jungle roads and trails. A story, apocryphal but nonetheless illustrative, was told of a North Vietnamese soldier who defected. When asked why, he simply related his tale of travail. Impressed from a farm in North Vietnam, he was assigned as an ammunition carrier. Loaded down with a couple of large mortar rounds, he trudged for two months along the Ho Chi Minh Trail, hiding from airplanes, catching malaria, staying soaked and chilled, sleeping fitfully, always afraid. After weeks of steady plodding and constant danger he finally arrived at a firing site on the border of South Vietnam. He placed his two rounds proudly on the ground by the mortar—and watched in amazement as the gun crew promptly popped them into their tube, firing both in just seconds. A clerk walked over, checked his name off a list and said, "OK. Go back and get two more."

In addition to the difficulties of moving equipment down the jungle trails, Hanoi was experiencing rising problems in putting supplies over the beach, a previously major means of running in guns and ammunition. In February 1965 an alert American aviator had spotted a suspiciously camouflaged ship at anchor in Vung Ro Bay. The report of his sighting led to the sinking of the 100-ton North Vietnamese trawler in the act of unloading a large shipment of arms and supplies. That incident led directly to the establishment of "Market Time," an American coastal interdiction program. U.S. Coast Guard and Navy ships promptly began closing the coast; in May of that year American sailors made their first capture of infiltrators. For the most part, infiltration by sea ceased.

On the other hand, Hanoi's logisticians had a lot going for them. Sihanoukville, the major seaport of Cambodia, was opened by a complaisant Prince Sihanouk to ships of ostensibly neutral nations. Thousands of tons of supplies poured into and through Cambodia while officials in that country carefully looked the other way. Most effective, though, was the old, reliable Ho Chi Minh trail. The inland road complex was well organized and had long been funneling goods southward. The problem was to speed up a functioning system rather than to implement a new one. Besides, sanctuaries in Laos and Cambodia provided free security to stockage points right on the edge of the combat zone. The proximity of North Vietnam itself was a major plus, while the relatively simple Northern combat organizations required a minimum of support, mostly ammunition. Last, but quite significantly, Giap's forces enjoyed both a headstart and the comforting knowlege that Americans constantly underrated their skill at infiltration. Hanoi's ability to send increasing numbers of reinforcements southward against all logical odds was from first to last greater than American analysts ever figured. It was that constant underestimation which left U.S. planners so often one step behind their enemy.

The American line of communications stretched halfway around the world, depending entirely on sea and air lanes. Seaports and airports in Vietnam were therefore an absolute necessity. To wage the war, Westmoreland had requested the immediate employment of a minimum of forty-four U.S. maneuver battalions, a commitment which would require heavy logistical support. He also had to provide for the rising number of Allied battalions as well as for the expanding South Vietnamese army itself. All those new forces had to have base camps, supply and storage areas, ammunition dumps, forward airstrips, heliports, jet airfields, hospitals, supply roads, equipment depots, deepsea ports, fuel centers—the list could go on and on. Westmoreland, intensely aware that "there was no logistic system in being and no development of secure logistic bases," set his engineers working day and night on a crash base development program. Nor could he afford to await completion of the gigantic task before bringing in troops. "In the face of the grave tactical situation," he later wrote, "I decided to accept combat troops as rapidly as they could be made available and to improvise their logistic support."

South Vietnam possessed but a single deep-water port where ocean-going vessels could tie up and unload cargo onto wharves. That one was in Saigon, several miles from the sea up a tortuously winding river which was periodically interdicted by Viet Cong patrols. All other ports were too shallow to berth a deep-draft ship. Sea captains anchored offshore and tediously unloaded using lighters. The fact that we began the immense build-up with but a single harbor is one more sad example of the lack of foresight with which the United States has traditionally gone to war. Why, after a decade of involvement, another anchorage had not been developed is a question hard to answer and harder to justify. True enough, construction of a new port would have been expensive and would have required an ability of officials to see its future need, a clairvoyance apparently greater than they possessed. Also there was the political danger that it would have appeared to be evidence of deeper American encroachment in Southeast Asia. Nonetheless, having committed itself to support a war with equipment and supplies—not to mention advisors and combat support elements—the United States should have recognized the possible need for an alternate port. Moreover, no one should have assumed that a greater commitment was out of the question—escalation is a two-edged blade which the enemy can swing also—and a contingency plan for that larger undertaking should have envisioned the requirement for another port. Such foresight is expected from staff planners in a professional defense establishment. But a niggardly concern for economy precluded any sort of wise contingency preparations.

Not that Westmoreland was unaware of his need. Within weeks of his arrival in 1964 he had determined that there were two undeveloped bays capable of sheltering the largest ships in deep, calm waters: Vung Po

Bay and Cam Ranh Bay. Cam Ranh, indeed, was the finest natural harbor in all Southeast Asia. The ill-fated Russian fleet had used it for a coaling anchorage in 1905 before going on to its doom in the Russo-Japanese War. In World War II, the Japanese navy had established a refueling and refitting station there; the battered hulk of a French cruiser, captured by the Japanese and sunk in 1945 by American warplanes, still stands silent guard over the entrance. When he received authority to build in 1965, the American commander already knew where his major base would be.

On 7 May the first military construction unit arrived. A navy seabee battalion came over the beach at Chu Lai and immediately began laying a jet airfield. To handle jets, airfields have to be nearly two miles long. South Vietnam had only three fields that large: Tan Son Nhut and Bien Hoa near Saigon, and Da Nang far to the north. Airfield construction, like seaport development, was an imperative. A month later the army's 35th Engineer Group landed at Cam Ranh Bay to develop a port, an air base, and extensive depot facilities for all classes of supplies. At the same time an army engineer battalion began constructing a similar base at Qui Nhon. A civilian contract firm known as RMK (Raymond-Morrison-Knudsen) had been operating in South Vietnam since 1962. When the build-up began, RMK's original projects were nearly done. In the emergency Westmoreland drafted the firm and put it to work alongside seabees and engineers. RMK responded, increasing its civilian work force from four thousand in January 1965 to over twenty-five thousand at year's end. The construction challenge was huge, but it was joined; the race against time was on. With the frantic pace of men who knew full well that the job should have been begun months or years before, military and civilian engineers leaped to the task. When all the final accounting is made it may well be concluded that the single most important branch in Vietnam was not the infantry or the artillery or the air force, but the grimy builders of roads and ports and bridges and airfields— the Corps of Engineers.

Just twenty-three days after seabees landed at Chu Lai, marine close support aircraft flew combat missions from a new field. The runway was only thirty-five hundred feet long, requiring the pilots to use special techniques, but it was operational. By 3 July the strip was eight thousand feet long and fully operational. Meanwhile, back at the bay, RMK was installing another airfield adjacent to the rising Cam Ranh port facilities. Instead of digging at the sand with scrapers, the contractor flooded the area with sea water to level a runway quickly. After 150 days of frenetic labor he turned over to the air force a ten thousand foot airfield. Soon, new airfields were under construction at Da Nang, Phan Rang, and Tuy Hoa. Plants in the United States strained their capacity to the breaking point to provide enough aluminum matting to keep up with the hard-working engineers.

The great bulk of all supplies arrived in Vietnam in ships. Once turned on and combined with the Allied maritime services, America's industrial cornucopia sent across the Pacific a flood of equipment and supplies so munificent it proved embarrassing. Ships soon found themselves waiting longer and longer at anchor before they could unload. Eventually the average waiting period stretched out to nearly two months—one vessel stood at anchor 110 days to establish a dubious record. It was not uncommon to count one hundred freighters awaiting discharge. At a daily demurrage cost of four to five thousand dollars per ship, the monetary loss alone was staggering. But more importantly, in those holds were stacked the stores needed to continue the base development program and the supplies needed by maneuver units to fight. While the monumental bottleneck lasted, progress ashore languished.

More and bigger piers were the first order of business. In Charleston, South Carolina, there was a floating steel pier named after its inventor, DeLong. Towing it from Charleston, through the Panama Canal, and across the Pacific, the army brought that first DeLong pier to Cam Ranh Bay. Within weeks after arrival it was in operation, proving to be better than engineers had dared hope. Contracting agents quickly placed orders with firms in Japan to build more of them. MACV made plans to construct completely from scratch a new port near Saigon, but away from the insuperable congestion. It was aptly named Newport.

For all that amazing expenditure of energy and initiative, port construction remained a frustratingly slow process; supply ships continued to stack up while combat troops existed from day to day on austere allotments. Airfield construction went somewhat faster, but air elements were always ready to fight before they had fields from which to fly. All told, the summer and fall of 1965 were dreadful months of sheer bedlam for construction planners and operators. Everything seemed to have an "immediate" tag on it. There were neither equipment nor men enough to do the work as fast as it was needed. As a matter of fact, there was so much to be done that few people could even visualize how enormous the task actually was. Combat troops helped with unloading and lent a hand anywhere else they could. Engineers shuttled back and forth in a fire brigade role. By year's end fifteen construction battalions—ten army, four navy, and one air force—were toiling away in South Vietnam, but they were far too few. President Johnson adamantly refused to call up reserves—which included eighteen seabee and thirty army construction battalions—so RMK filled the breach. The giant construction firm worked under lucrative cost-plus-fee contracts, but in the hectic days of 1965 it earned every penny.

While engineers labored around the clock to complete a logistics complex, and ships by the score stacked up offshore, combat troops streamed into South Vietnam. More marines came, and Australians. The 1st

Infantry Division landed and a brigade of the 101st Airborne came in. A new type division, untested in combat, joined in September—the 1st Cavalry Division (Airmobile). Other American elements were on the way. In October the Korean Capital Division arrived, partial payment from that country for the outside help it had received in turning back another communist invasion fifteen years earlier.

General Westmoreland set a three stage strategy for his increasing forces. In stage I, expected to endure through the rest of 1965, combat forces were told to establish secure enclaves in order to shield vital installations and from which to attack later. The losing trend would hopefully be stopped in this first phase. During stage II, beginning in the early months of 1966, the general envisioned launching spoiling attacks to upset the enemy timetable while the friendly build-up continued. Finally, in stage III, with the build-up complete, he would go after the enemy main forces to defeat them in the field. He anticipated victory from a year to a year and a half after stage III began.

It was not to work quite that way. In spite of superhuman efforts from all concerned, the Americans were doomed to lose the logistics race. General Giap's three key advantages—a shorter line of communications, an already functioning logistical system, and a jump of several months—were too much to overcome. By late September it became evident that Northern forces would be ready to launch their offensive long before the Allies could complete their build-up. Once again Giap's uncanny ability to infiltrate men and supplies had decisively outstripped U.S. estimates.

Recognizing the disheartening fact that he had lost the race for leverage, General Westmoreland faced the most crucial decision he was to make in the entire war. If he waited until his support base was complete before committing his forces, he would hand full initiative to General Giap. With the advantage of the initiative, Giap might very well stage a grand victory which would cause the abrupt collapse of South Vietnam. On the other hand, if Westmoreland started his fight prematurely, gambling on a logistical shoestring, he would be risking a calamity of major proportions. A fiasco like Dien Bien Phu—or even in the style of General Custer's—would provide the adverse psychological shock Giap sought. "An American defeat would have been disastrous to South Vietnamese morale," Westmoreland later said, "undermining South Vietnamese confidence in our ability to defeat the Viet Cong." It was basically a choice between two principles of war, whether to employ the spirit of the offensive or to heed the requirement for security. Westmoreland elected the bolder course, to hit the enemy first.

CHAPTER 12

Battle of the Ia Drang

Ia means river in the dialect of South Vietnam's mountain tribes, the Montagnards. The River Drang rises in a gritty watershed near Pleiku in the Central Highlands. Gathering strength, it flows southwestwardly for twenty-five miles or so through remote stretches of jungle and past occasional patches of elephant grass to strike a sturdy massif of mountains known as Chu Pong. At the point of collision the stream deflects sharply northward to meander around the craggy hills and enter nearby Cambodia. Eventually the waters, combining with other remote streams, make their way to the Mekong River where they roll past Phnom Penh and through the fertile delta south of Saigon to the sea. It is one of the world's more insignificant rivers. But, for two thunderous days in 1965, the Ia Drang had its moment in history.

General Giap intended to gain a spectacular victory—a Southern Dien Bien Phu with all the trimmings—by slicing South Vietnam in half on a line from Pleiku through An Khe to Qui Nhon. Between October 1965 and April of 1966 he planned to commit three full North Vietnamese divisions along that axis. The large attack arrow on his battle map culminated in Binh Dinh

Province, for years a notorious hotbed of communist sympathizers. The steep, jungle-covered mountains in that area would limit the effectiveness of American airpower and virtually preclude operations by mechanized forces. Moreover, as Giap analyzed the situation, his three divisions, jumping off from secure bases in Cambodia and closely supported by Viet Cong units native to the area being invaded, would be superior to any countering force the Americans and South Vietnamese could employ. Strong holding attacks in the vicinity of Saigon and against populated areas near the Demilitarized Zone would tie down reserves, while the tough terrain itself would limit the employment of such reaction forces as Saigon could muster. That was the grand strategy for Hanoi's heralded *Dong Xuan* (Winter-Spring) campaign. Its primary aim was to conquer and secure the Central Highlands which would in turn sever the South and, hopefully, trigger a countrywide collapse of resistance. It was a valid plan, simple, plausible, and with a good probability for success. (Indeed, that is almost precisely what would happen a decade later to win the war for Hanoi.) Giap was justified in being optimistic.

Allied intelligence officers accurately predicted the objective and timing of the offensive, so where and when to meet the threat was no problem to decide. The question was, how? What force or combination of forces would be most effective against the invaders in the terrain they themselves had selected? Both Giap and Westmoreland recognized that mobility was the key to victory in the vast Central Highlands; the North Vietnamese commander counted on his troops' foot mobility while the American general was wed to technological mobility. Looking over the list of incoming divisions, Westmoreland's eyes fastened on the 1st Cavalry Division, an organization built specifically around the concept of mobility—in this case, air mobility.

The 1st Cavalry travelled on wings and rotors rather

than legs and wheels. It had nearly 450 helicopters, five times as many as were found in a normal infantry division. It was an infantry-artillery-cavalry-aviation organization which went to war on the wind. Everything hinged on the helicopter: firepower, maneuver, command and control, reconnaissance, logistics, even administration. Jungles and mountains were not serious obstacles to it, nor were wide rivers or great expanses or a dearth of roads. For those reasons it appeared to be the ideal force to blunt North Vietnamese plans in the Central Highlands where distances are great, terrain rugged, and roads almost non-existent.

When the division arrived in September, it went straight into a base hacked out of jungle at An Khe, midway between Pleiku and Qui Nhon astride strategic Highway 19. There it was close enough to the coast to be supplied and far enough forward to reach areas of expected combat—and stood smack in the path of the projected North Vietnamese avenue to the ocean. Major General Harry W.O. Kinnard, the tough Texan who had commanded the novel organization ever since its stateside tests, began probing for the enemy as soon as his base was established.

So the stage was set for a swirling, month-long campaign which would mark a high point in the history of American arms and would provide a turning point in the Vietnam War. Between 23 October and 26 November 1965, the 1st Cavalry Division, hardly even acclimated to the tropical environment after just a month in Vietnam, would win one of the war's rare decisive battles.

North Vietnamese commanders watched closely as the base at An Khe filled up with men and helicopters. The unforeseen arrival of the American division complicated matters, but, according to their calculations, it was too far away to play a decisive role in the early battles. They decided to stick with their original plan. That was a serious error. The unleashing of a concept new to warfare—an entire division which was airmobile—gave the Americans the benefit of surprise.

By the first part of October, two complete North Vietnamese Army (NVA) regiments roamed the mountainous area west of Pleiku and a third was on its way to join them. Operating under the direction of a field front headquarters (equivalent to an American divisional headquarters), the regiments were bolstered by numerous hard-core Viet Cong units. The 32nd NVA Regiment had been in South Vietnam ever since February, the 33rd had arrived about the same time as had the 1st Cavalry Division, and the 66th was strung out along the Ho Chi Minh Trail in Laos, moving by forced marches to arrive in time to participate in the coming campaign. The front's ambitious scheme—a part of Giap's overall three-division strategy—was to launch a coordinated, step-by-step offensive aimed at achieving a resounding local victory over South Vietnamese and American units around Pleiku. First, to weaken the foe and tempt him to commit reserves, the front commander—General Chu Huy Man—planned to overrun outposts and then ambush relief columns. An old gambit. Then, reinforced by the fresh 66th NVA Regiment, he would pounce on and destroy whatever units had been drawn into a vulnerable situation, or capture such key towns as might be left momentarily unguarded. Having thus won control of the Pleiku plateau, he would combine with the other two divisions for the final phase, the push to the sea.

The curtain raiser was to be at Plei Me, a special forces border camp twenty-five miles southwest of Pleiku. While the 33rd Regiment laid siege to the camp, the 32nd would maneuver to ambush the expected rescue column which would have to come from Pleiku. Having destroyed the relief force, the 32nd would return to unite with the 33rd to wipe out the Plei Me post.

In quick-fading twilight on 19 October the ordeal of Plei Me's garrison began. Heavy and steady shelling hammered the small camp. The defenders were well dug in, but casualties slowly mounted under the constant bombardment. In Pleiku the Vietnamese II Corps commander, Major General Vinh Loc, readied a relief column, but prudently awaited developments. Aware of the recent, ominous buildup of NVA units in the vicinity of Plei Me, he suspected a trap. As hours passed with no major assault being launched, his suspicions seemed confirmed—the North Vietnamese must in reality be aiming either for the reaction force or for weakly defended Pleiku once the column departed. He did not have strength enough to defend Pleiku and to relieve Plei Me at the same time. He waited.

Days passed. There was no lessening of the pounding of Plei Me. The defenders, battered and dazed but grimly hanging on, sorely needed resupply, reinforcements, and medical assistance. The incessant bombardment had beaten their camp almost beyond recognition. Some aerial support could be given at grave risk to crews and aircraft, but it was not nearly enough. The siege had to be lifted. General Vinh Loc coordinated with the senior American in the area, Lieutenant General Stanley (Swede) Larson, who airlifted a battalion of the 1st Cavalry to cover Pleiku while Vinh Loc ordered ARVN forces to rescue the survivors of Plei Me.

On 23 October a strong ARVN column, spearheaded by armor, set out to link up with Plei Me. Fully expecting to be hit en route, the relief column was ready when at dusk it entered the NVA ambush some five miles from Plei Me. In the ensuing fierce engagement, South Vietnamese troops stoutly beat off the 32nd NVA Regiment, inflicting heavy losses. Crippled, the 32nd broke contact in the night and slipped away. But the ARVN force was severely shaken, too. It coiled in place. That night Larson ordered a complete brigade of the 1st Cavalry to Pleiku. Early next morning helicopters placed artillery batteries in position to support the relief column. A day later ARVN armor broke the week-long siege of Plei Me.

By 26 October, with their opening move checked, front headquarters and both NVA regiments were attempting to slip away westward. Sensing big game, General Westmoreland decided to initiate the second phase of his overall strategy: throw the enemy off balance by launching spoiling attacks. Westmoreland's gutsy decision would put Americans and North Vietnamese for the first time in open combat on a more or less equal basis. American marines had already engaged enemy forces, inflicting a major defeat on a Viet Cong regiment in August near Chu Lai, but the enemy there had been trapped on a sand spit with the ocean to their backs; superior American strength and firepower simply chewed them up. In the Central Highlands, on the other hand, the North Vietnamese retained their freedom of movement, and were actually stronger numerically because so many ARVN and U.S. troops were tied down securing bases and towns. Moreover, they were right next to their Cambodian sanctuaries. As the NVA division and the 1st Cavalry squared off against one another, U.S. staff officers in Saigon, aware of the high stakes and the even odds, held their breath.

"Find and destroy the North Vietnamese forces," was the 1st Cavalry's job. General Kinnard described it as a mission of "unlimited offense." He had a tactical area of operations covering over nine hundred square miles of jungle-shrouded mountains, a chunk of terrain roughly the size of Rhode Island. Only two roads touched the area and they served as his northern and eastern boundaries. In that foreboding land, mountains tower as much as five hundred meters above stream-laced valleys. Elephant grass, helmet-high, grows profusely in the few areas not covered by jungle or rain forest. It had long been insurgent country—and for very good reasons. General Kinnard directed his 1st Brigade to start beating the bush for the elusive enemy.

Extensive communications and helicopter mobility permitted a single brigade to sweep so large a sector. With the division's reconnaissance squadron screening the zone's borders to detect any enemy movement in or out, infantry battalions established far-flung patrol bases in methodical patterns throughout the wild area. Helicopters moved artillery batteries in careful coordination with the leapfrogging infantry islands so that every unit always had fire support. The brigade retained no central reserve; when a battle started, every unit not in contact automatically became a reserve to be flown to the sound of the guns.

For four days the whirling search produced no results. Then, on 1 November, an aerial patrol from the reconnaissance squadron spotted movement along the Tae River. The flight commander quickly landed a rifle platoon on a sandy strip for a closer look. The riflemen almost immediately ran into token resistance from a surprised guard force lounging around a complex of buildings hidden back from the river under the thick forest canopy. After a brief firefight the defenders disappeared into the jungle leaving the U.S. platoon leader to discover that he had captured intact a field hospital. Realizing the importance of the find, the squadron commander reinforced with two more platoons. That move was in the nick of time, for a reinforced enemy company counterattacked the three platoons not long after they dug in. By the closest of margins the riflemen held, but they were in dire need of help. As rapidly as helicopters could ferry them in, platoons operating within an arc of twenty-four kilometers from the beleaguered troopers joined their comrades on the Tae River. Then whole companies flew in. Eventually the piecemeal build-up made the American bastion by the hospital too strong for the North Vietnamese. They broke contact and faded into the jungle.

In their first full clash with NVA regulars, the cavalrymen had done well enough, but a prize from that encounter would lead to much tougher fighting. Searchers found on a dead North Vietnamese officer a map showing unit locations and the routes designated for use by both enemy regiments. Based on that intelligence bonanza, General Kinnard redirected his search pattern to intercept the retreating foe.

Air cavalry units promptly began running into elements of the enemy. Frustrated in his attempt to destroy Plei Me, harassed continually by air, pursued by omnipresent air cavalrymen, the front commander, General Man, was attempting to consolidate and reorganize his forces for another effort. His men were struggling to gain shelter under the shadows of the Chu Pong massif. A series of bitter encounters occurred between 3 and 6 November, generally taking the form of NVA attacks against American positions astride avenues of retreat. In all cases NVA units were bloodily repulsed, broke contact, and continued westward by a different route. The 33rd Regiment absorbed the brunt of the action. Upon arriving at its base near the Chu Pong, the weary regiment had only seven hundred effective soldiers of an original twenty-two hundred. Several hundred had been killed. At that point Kinnard rotated his forces, putting in the fresh 3rd Brigade.

After ten days in the crucible of combat, the airmobile division had demonstrated its inherent superiority over the field front in terms of firepower and mobility. Portents of a dangerous weakness had cropped up as well, but in the flush of success Americans discounted it. Once on the ground and out of their helicopters, U.S. units were for all intents and purposes immobilized. NVA units maneuvered, attacked, broke contact, withdrew, sidestepped, and continued their march; Americans dug in, defended, and watched the enemy fade away to fight again. If the enemy chose to fight, a battle ensued and the Americans, with far greater firepower from air and artillery, were almost sure to inflict disproportionately severe casualties; if the enemy chose not to close, the cavalrymen seemed unable to force a fight. In other words, Americans had almost as little foot mobility as their foe had helicopter mobility.

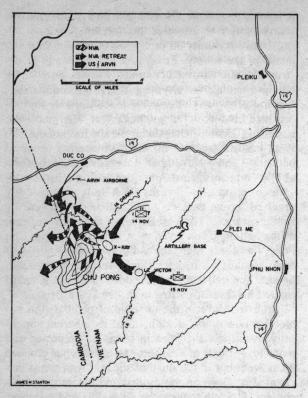

Battle of the Ia Drang

It was not that the units of the 1st Cavalry *could* not match their field front opponents on the ground—they *would* not. Obviously, plunging into the jungle in pursuit of the enemy was to chance higher casualties, an altogether unacceptable risk. It also meant marching away from the womb of the landing zone. All support fed into that cleared area through the division's umbilical cord, the ubiquitous helicopter. Commanders on the ground were neither physically nor mentally prepared to cut loose on their own; they could not imagine fighting any distance away from the security and convenience of the chopper pad. This was the beginning of what would later grow into a fixation on firebases, or, in General Westmoreland's phrase, a "firebase psychosis."

Watching while Kinnard switched the 1st and 3rd Brigades, front headquarters interpreted the change-over as a pullout. The communist commander at once decided to regain the initiative by renewing his attack on Plei Me. Assault elements would be from the newly arrived 66th Regiment—two thousand men strong— while the bloodied 32nd and 33rd would play supporting roles. This time there was to be a battalion of 120-mm mortars to batter the garrison numb before the attack. Also an anti-aircraft battalion was on hand to turn back the locust-like plague of helicopters. Field front orders set 16 November as the target date.

While the North Vietnamese readied themselves for the attack, the 1st Cavalry's 3rd Brigade searched unsuccessfully in the eastern sector of the division area. Satisfied at last that all enemy elements had slipped out of the area, the 3rd Brigade turned westward towards the Chu Pong.

That shift frustrated NVA plans for Plei Me, but it opened the tantalizing possibility of trapping and destroying one of the scattered American battalions. Like a spider watching patiently for a fly to light on his web, General Chu Huy Man kept his forces crouched in the crevices of the Chu Pong, waiting motionlessly. Amazingly, a perfect opportunity presented itself right under his nose in midmorning of 14 November when helicopters began landing an infantry battalion in a small clearing near the Ia Drang. Spoiling for a fight, the 66th Regiment and the weaker but by now rested 33rd rushed to get at the Americans.

Lieutenant Colonel Harold G. Moore, commanding officer of the 1st Infantry Battalion, 7th Cavalry, was among the lead elements in this battalion to touch down. A twenty-year veteran, having entered the army from West Point in 1945, Moore was a rugged professional

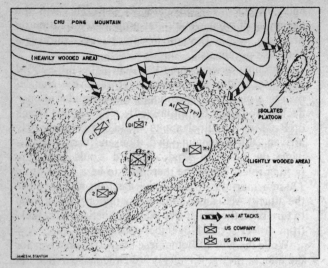

Landing Zone X-Ray

soldier who worried that the North Vietnamese might get away into Cambodia before his green battalion, which had not yet met any serious opposition, could get a taste of them. He needn't have been concerned; commanders of the two NVA regiments similarly hoped the Americans would sit still long enough for their troops to fall on them. Moore was the first man out of the choppers. When he hit the ground, running and firing his rifle into the tree line, he was most worried about getting all of his unit shuttled into the area as rapidly as possible. With singular lack of poetic foresight, he dubbed the 100 by 200 meter landing zone simply "X-Ray." Inspecting the tiny clearing for fighting positions as relays of helicopters ferried his companies in, he glanced with distaste at a number of huge anthills crawling with red ants; soldiers, he knew, hated to dig foxholes near the ferocious insects. Peering into the quiet, sparse tree lines around him, Moore had no idea that he was triggering the biggest battle yet, but he had a clear and eery sensation that a real fight was on the way. By midday most of the battalion had arrived. By then, also, the North Vietnamese had worked their way forward almost into assaulting positions.

While checking the landing zone, one of the squads flushed a North Vietnamese straggler. He was unarmed, dressed in a dirty khaki uniform, and carried an empty canteen. Moore, who had brought an interpreter along with him, quickly questioned the woebegone captive. He stated that he had eaten only bananas for five days, and that there were three battalions on the nearby mountain who wanted very much to kill Americans but had been unable to find them.

Based on the information gleaned from the prisoner, Moore sent "B" Company to occupy a finger of high ground a short distance beyond the landing zone. That precautionary move may have been what saved his battalion. At 1245, "B" Company ran head-on into NVA soldiers, surprising both sides and starting the battle slightly before the attackers were ready. A roaring firefight gradually built up. In a short time, the commander of "B" Company reported that he was under heavy attack by at least two enemy companies. Moore realized that his battalion's baptism of fire would be, in his words, "a fight to the finish."

On hearing the infantry exchanging fire, NVA gunners brought a barrage of rocket and mortar fire crashing down on the landing zone. Hovering helicopters frantically veered up and away to escape the rain of high explosive rounds. Startled soldiers dove to the ground; the anthills, absorbing some of the whistling shrapnel, suddenly looked friendly.

In the initial melee, "B" Company and the North Vietnamese became confusingly mixed. To restore order, the company commander withdrew his men to a defensible position nearer the rest of the battalion, but one platoon was unable to fight its way back. Counting only twenty-six men and himself, the platoon leader grimly gave the order to dig in where they were. Meanwhile, Moore directed "A" Company to move up along-side "B." That company also struck approaching NVA units. About that time "C" Company fought off an assault on the west side of "X-Ray." The entire battalion was engaged.

The 1st Battalion, 7th Cavalry, had entered the day's fighting with only 68 percent of its strength—20 officers and 411 men of an authorized 23 and 610. Sickness, rear area guards, and administrative requirements had robbed Moore of a third of his manpower before the battle ever began. Understrength, the battalion was quickly overextended. While bringing in air strikes and supporting artillery fires, Moore urgently requested reinforcements. Despite the heavy fire on the landing zone, the 3rd Brigade commander sent in a company from another battalion. It landed safely and became Moore's reserve.

With that reinforcement, and with all available supporting fires pounding in close to his position, Moore was able to hold on. Forced to attack prematurely, the North Vietnamese struck "X-Ray" piecemeal, providing the American commander the opportunity to shift his forces in order to repel each assault in turn. The struggle was furious and the outcome often in doubt, although Moore and his men were too busy to worry about their odds. Luck rode with the cavalry that afternoon; at one point, for instance, Captain Ramon A. Nadal, wanting a smoke screen, mistakenly brought white phosphorous artillery rounds right onto his own "A" Company positions, repulsing the attackers and miraculously not hurting a single American. The fortuitous error saved much of the company. Luck, shrewdness, courage, and most of all, overwhelming firepower combined to beat off all assaults.

At dusk action slackened around "X-Ray," but the enemy continued through the night trying to overrun "B" Company's isolated platoon. Only seven members of the gallant little group survived the night intact—eight died at their posts and twelve were wounded—

but they refused to buckle. Dawn's light revealed two score enemy bodies sprawled around their tight position; perhaps that many more had been dragged away by retreating NVA troops.

Having reorganized during darkness, elements of both NVA regiments launched an all-out, coordinated attack at first light against Moore's perimeter. Swarming out of the jungle they surged screaming into "X-Ray." The struggle quickly reached the hand-to-hand stage; victory balanced on bayonets and grenades and guts. It came down to a question of which side would crack first. Fighting with a valor born of discipline and desperation, the Americans held, sending the North Vietnamese streaming back with awesome losses. Throughout, fire support was massive. Artillery rounds rained in by the thousands, tactical air strikes came by the score, and starting that afternoon, B-52 bombers began to work over the Chu Pong redoubt. By noon more U.S. reinforcements had arrived, some by air, some overland through the jungle. Lieutenant Colonel Moore immediately mounted a counterattack to recover the survivors of his cut-off platoon. That ended the fighting for the day.

During the second long night in "X-Ray," cavalrymen fended off several weak, piecemeal attacks. When daylight on the 16th showed Americans still in possession of the landing zone, the chagrined North Vietnamese withdrew. They had had enough.

The back of the front had been broken. The NVA regiments left the battlefield littered with some six hundred corpses—and may have carried away hundreds of others. Perhaps half of the 66th Regiment's two thousand men never fought again, being killed or permanently disabled in their very first battle. Seventy-nine Americans had been killed.

Admitting complete failure, General Man ordered the remnants of his three regiments to retreat into Cambodia. There were one or two more bitter clashes with air cavalrymen, costly to both sides, but the NVA forces succeeded in withdrawing. However, they were not to escape without one last, punishing blow.

While the fighting had raged around "X-Ray," the South Vietnamese high command had airlifted five battalions of paratroopers from Saigon to Duc Co. A short hop by helicopter and they were strung out in a line across the Ia Drang valley, tight against the Cambodian border. Unsuspecting NVA units walked right into the trap. American artillery and charging ARVN paratroopers decimated them. Shattered, beaten bloodily at every turn, the enemy division—or what was left of it—finally straggled across the border to safety. The Battle of the Ia Drang was history.

It had been a test of mobility and firepower on one side versus manpower and choice of terrain on the other. The tactics employed by the North Vietnamese had been good enough to beat the French, would have been sufficient to defeat South Vietnamese forces, but had failed miserably in the face of technological and tactical advances. Simply put, Americans unfailingly got there first with the most. For example, artillery batteries had displaced by air a total of sixty-seven times, and had still managed to fire 33,108 rounds of 105mm alone! Airplanes had orbited overhead throughout and reserves had never failed to arrive when needed, even at night. The supreme example of both strategic and tactical mobility was the movement in a single day of six battalions from Saigon to blocking positions in a trackless jungle two hundred miles away. The more mobile force will be superior—a story as old as warfare itself.

Victory in Vietnam was hard to measure. There were no rubble-crested ridges on which to plant a flag, no great cities to liberate, no surrendered armies. As the troopers of the 1st Cavalry Division choppered out of the Ia Drang valley heading for other battles, they left behind no occupying force. Their nearly three hundred dead had already been evacuated. Except for a number of felled trees the jungle appeared untouched.

After a few rains even the scars would disappear. And surely the enemy would come back. But the outcome of the fighting along the Ia Drang and under the Chu Pong was a victory in every sense of the word. On the strategic scale, a brilliant spoiling attack had completely derailed Hanoi's hopes of earning a decisive victory before full American might could be deployed to South Vietnam. Moreover, in a head-on clash between an American and a North Vietnamese division, on the enemy's chosen ground, the NVA unit had been sent reeling in retreat. For the moment, at least, an adverse tide had been reversed. Victory along the River Drang had turned the NVA from hunter to hunted.

Though *Ia* means river in the Montagnard dialect, it has an altogether different meaning in the Vietnamese language itself. It is, ironically, a splendidly appropriate, earthy expletive to sum up the North Vietnamese reaction to the disaster which befell them in the Ia Drang valley.

Time Magazine did not have to search far to find the obvious 1965 recipient for its prestigious "Man of the Year" award. General William Childs Westmoreland was the popular choice. Successful completion of the vast build-up in the face of all odds amounted to a logistical miracle, reason enough to consider the general for the honor. But on top of that, his daring and brilliant repulse of North Vietnam's invasion cinched his selection. It was Westmoreland's finest hour.

PART III

THE SEARCH FOR A STRATEGY

1966–1967

CHAPTER 13

"An Escalating Military Stalemate"

Winning is not the same as not losing. By the end of 1965, Allied forces had stopped losing in Vietnam, but they were only beginning to comprehend what was required to win.

Just days after the Battle of the Ia Drang, Secretary of Defense McNamara flew hastily to Saigon. A new call from General Westmoreland for greatly increased reinforcements had raised dark questions in the Pentagon. Back in July of 1965, MACV staff officers had estimated that some twenty-eight additional U.S. battalions, about 112,000 men in all, would be needed for Phase II of Westmoreland's plan. Now, however, as he was about to enter that second phase, the general was saying he needed more fighting units than predicted. Many more. Unanticipated increases in infiltration from the North and the enemy's willingness to stand and fight large-scale engagements were twin reasons for his revision.

After hurried consultations in Saigon, McNamara returned to Washington in uneasy agreement with his field commander. More troops were indeed necessary. The contemplated addition of twenty-eight U.S. battalions, the secretary wrote in a memorandum to Pres-

135

ident Johnson, would permit the Allies "only to hold our present geographical position." In a word, stalemate. There were really only two options, he told the president: to seek a compromise solution or "to stick with our stated objectives and win the war, and provide what it takes in men and materiel." What it would take, he continued, would be heavier bombing of the North, a total of four hundred thousand men by the end of 1966, an understanding that another increment of two hundred thousand troops or more might be needed in 1967, and a willingness to accept up to one thousand combat deaths a month. Even then, the secretary warned, success could not be guaranteed. Noting intelligence estimates of Hanoi's resolve to continue a vigorous prosecution of the war and to match any U.S. augmentation of forces, even to the point of accepting Red Chinese volunteers, a subdued McNamara told the commander-in-chief, "... the odds are about even that, even with the recommended deployments, we will be faced in early 1967 with a military standoff at a much higher level, with pacification still stalled, and with any prospect of military success marred by the chances of an active Chinese intervention."

That gloomy prediction shook the confidence of several previously complacent members of the administration. Assistant Secretary of Defense John T. McNaughton captured the mood of many when he wrote in January 1966, "We are in an escalating military stalemate."

The frightening vision of years of fighting and tens of thousands slain, with nothing to show for it all, sobered Washington's strategists. Rather late in the game Department of Defense wordsmiths began casting around for a definition of victory, for the meaning of "win." In response to a query from Secretary McNamara, a Pentagon study group, comprised of both officers and civilians, had written in mid-1965, "Within the bounds of reasonable assumptions there appears to be no reason we cannot win if such is our will—and if that will is manifested in strategy and tactical operations." The working definition used by the study group said victory "means that we succeed in demonstrating to the VC that they cannot win." McNamara himself tried to wriggle off the hook in February 1966, saying he preferred to avoid "color words" like "victory" or "win." He suggested using the euphemism, "favorable settlement." Another highly placed Defense Department official went on record about the same time as believing that the U.S. objective should be simply "to avoid humiliation," that victory could be attained by somehow camouflaging an obvious defeat, even if South Vietnam should fall. With that kind of thinking at the top, it is not surprising that a debate raged for the duration of the war over just what would constitute a win.

Douglas MacArthur's famous dictum—"There is no substitute for victory!"—had served the United States well over the years, but it had been discredited ever since the Korean War. The trouble was, although America's intellectual community had almost in a body damned MacArthur's statement, no one had yet discovered what the substitute was.

Soldiers, who are the ones ultimately charged with winning wars, need and want firm guidance from their political leaders. Speaking in general terms, but with his remarks aimed specifically at Vietnam, Army Chief of Staff Harold K. Johnson told a college audience, "We accept the fact that there are degrees of victory and that each degree must be defined in terms of political, economic, and military objectives, as well as the aggregate price that must be paid to achieve them." That is, decide what you want and how much you are willing to pay to get it—and you have defined victory. The mission in Vietnam, commanders were told, was to convince Hanoi to stop its aggression. Not make—convince. The difference in the two words is all-important. Regarding the acceptable price, instructions were notably absent. Never during the critical years of the build-up did the president say what he was willing to spend in terms of time or money or lives. In fact, speaking on 9 February 1966 to key Vietnamese and American officials at a conference in Honolulu, President Johnson candidly admitted his deep reluctance to come to grips with the vexing problem of establishing troop strength: "I want to put it off as long as I can, having to make these crucial decisions." About as close as anyone came to proffering guidance in late 1965 or early 1966 was Secretary McNamara when he recommended providing everything "it takes in men and materiel." Put another way, the American commitment to the Vietnam War was open-ended.

Over four years earlier, on 1 November 1961, General Maxwell Taylor had warned President Kennedy of the likelihood of escalating manpower requirements—and in a parenthetical afterthought had provided the solution. "If the first contingent is not enough to accomplish the necessary results, it will be difficult to resist the pressure to reinforce. If the ultimate result sought is the closing of the frontiers and the clean-up of the insurgents within SVN, there is no limit to our possible commitment (unless we attack the source in Hanoi)." Prophetic words, those. They could have been re-read with profit on 1 November 1965. Or 1966. Or 1967.

But the Johnson administration had already barricaded the one sure route to victory—to take the strategic offensive against the source of the war. Memories of Mao Tse-tung's reaction when North Korea was overrun by United Nations troops in 1950 haunted the White House. America's fear of war with Red China protected North Vietnam from invasion more surely than any instrument of war Hanoi could have fielded. For precisely the same reason, the air campaign against the North was constrained from striking for the jugular. Thus North Vietnam became a sanctuary, safe from all attack except the irritating but endurable aerial campaign. Hindsight might hint that the United States unnecessarily limited itself, but since China never did enter the war, there is little to be gained by second-guessing Washington's cautious position. Suffice it to say that it was a tough decision, taken with full knowledge that it greatly complicated the management of the war in South Vietnam.

Less defensible, however, was the prohibition of fighting beyond South Vietnam's borders with Laos and Cambodia. The Johnson administration's avowed purpose of limiting the ground war to South Vietnam alone was patently irrelevant. The North Vietnamese themselves had already involved all of Indochina. They had established base camps, artillery positions, supply depots, major control headquarters, training complexes, and hospitals just behind the borders. Enemy forces staged in safe areas, struck swiftly into South Vietnam, and retreated as quickly back to secure havens. In full view of the Allies, they contemptuously stockpiled supplies to support guerrilla and regular forces operating within South Vietnam. American military leaders were not the only ones who wondered why their hands were tied. General Tran Van Don, a senior South Vietnamese officer, later wrote that "the pouring of more and more men into the country without some clearly defined plan for military victory was a useless endeavor." He added, "We Vietnamese had trouble understanding why this vast and highly competent force did not come in and really get to the business of winning the war. It seemed to serve as more of an instrument of intimidation and reinforcement of policy than as a genuine war machine." Ex-President Eisenhower could not understand Lyndon Johnson's reluctance to hit the enemy bases. "Tell 'em they have no sanctuaries!" he counselled Johnson. But the old soldier's advice, along with that of the Joint Chiefs of Staff, was not heeded. The bases remained "off-limits." Granting the enemy that unrestricted use of sanctuary lands on South Vietnam's flank was at least naive, at worst an egregious strategic blunder.

Even a surface perusal of military history would have informed U.S. strategists of the vital necessity for closing the communist sanctuaries. British counter-insurgency expert, Sir Robert Thompson, has noted, "In all the insurgencies of the past twenty-five years, since the Second World War, none has been sustained, let alone successful, without substantial outside support." Writing some five years earlier, Bernard Fall said, "In brutal fact, the success or failure of *all* rebellions since World War II depended entirely on whether the active sanctuary was willing and able to perform its expected role." Apparently, policy makers along the Potomac thought they could flaunt that historical imperative. They couldn't, but four more years were to pass before they would face up to it.

General Westmoreland, on whose shoulders fell the task of actually conducting the fighting inside South Vietnam, thus had fairly explicit directives on what he was not to do, imprecise instructions on what he was expected to accomplish, and very vague information on what he would have on hand to do it with. His limitations and strictures were carefully delineated, his missions and resources were left more or less open for interpretation.

In groping for an operational strategy, Westmoreland had to consider two major factors in addition to the shackles imposed by Washington's policy restraints: the peculiar nature of the war, and the intentions of the enemy. Both, of course, would affect significantly how he could conduct his fight.

The conflict itself had evolved into two parallel wars. First was the insurgency, a continuation of the long-standing contest between Saigon and the Viet Cong for domination of the countryside. Superimposed on the older war was the more recent and more conventional struggle between the North Vietnamese army and Allied forces. Giap described the dual situation as "many-sided war." Westmoreland said it was "a war of no frontlines but many sidelines."

Waging revolutionary and regular warfare simultaneously complicated matters for both generals. For instance, assembling an overwhelming force to defeat NVA regulars caused serious economic disruption in South Vietnam, seriously hindering efforts to build up the country. It was paradoxically possible that the minimum strength needed to secure the country would be more than enough to sink it. Similarly, the drastic demands of supplying regular Northern units with men and food and shelter detracted mightily from local Viet Cong efforts and all too often discredited that part of Hanoi's propaganda striving to portray the NVA as liberators. Major battles raging about the very ears of the populace set back Saigon's pacification programs and Hanoi's insurgent exertions alike. The memorable statement alleged to have been made by an American officer—"We had to destroy the village in order to save it!"—points out as nothing else can the cruel dilemma so often encountered in waging the dual wars. Soldiers had to build as well as destroy, had to heal as well as kill, to practice peace as well as war. At the Honolulu Conference in February 1966, which was devoted principally to matters of Vietnam's economy, rural development, health and education, production of consumer goods, and refugees, President Johnson chided Westmoreland for naming an operation then in progress "Masher." In keeping with the complex nature of the war, offensive actions had to have inoffensive names.

Intelligence agencies which had opined all along that Hanoi would match America's gradual escalation step by step were proven right. They confirmed that, unless the ground rules were changed, the open-ended commitment meant open-ended escalation—and continued stalemate. As Secretary McNamara summarized the intelligence community's consensus for President Johnson:

> Our intelligence estimate is that the present Communist policy is to continue to prosecute the war vigorously

in the South. They continue to believe that the war will be a long one, that time is their ally, and that their own staying power is superior to ours. They recognize that the U.S. reinforcements of 1965 signify a determination to avoid defeat, and that more U.S. troops can be expected. Even though the Communists will continue to suffer heavily from GVN and U.S. ground and air action, we expect them, learning of any U.S. intentions to augment its forces, to boost their own commitment and to test U.S. capabilities and will to persevere at higher levels of conflict and casualties.

In a way it was the World War I "race to the sea" all over again. That race had ended with a stalemate on the western front which was broken only after four years of bloody attrition warfare.

North Vietnamese General Nguyen Chi Thanh, field commander in the South, had well over two hundred thousand men at the start of 1966—and twelve new battalions were pouring out the end of the Ho Chi Minh Trail monthly. American predictions were that, after losses and even in the face of the air interdiction program, enemy strength would climb in the coming year by eighty thousand men, or about forty battalion equivalents. That was a remarkably accurate forecast; even though the infiltration rate was as usual higher than expected, mounting casualties cancelled the unanticipated increase. All things considered, General Westmoreland entered 1966 with an excellent grasp of enemy intentions and capabilities. He was surprised neither at their intransigence nor their decision to continue pressing the offensive.

That is not to suggest that leaders in Hanoi did not devote considerable thought to selecting their course of action. Their galling repulse in 1965 had indicated that something was awry with all previous calculations, that superior American technologically-derived firepower and mobility had cast a new component into the equation of war. Essentially, Giap recognized that victory via a decisive military campaign was very unlikely. But there remained at least three ways the North could win yet: failure of American or South Vietnamese resolve; an Allied inability to adopt a correct counter-strategy; or a miscarriage of Saigon's attempts to build a strong nation in the South. In the event either of the first two occurred, the NVA could overrun South Vietnam; in the third instance the insurgents would emerge victorious after all. Importantly, victory could come by any one of the three steps.

Observing the overall situation, General Giap found ample room for optimism. In America opposition to the war grew daily more vocal and violent; in Saigon war weariness was evident and the political situation potentially explosive; on the battlefield, Allied forces forfeited much of their strength by assuming the strategic defensive and by surprisingly permitting snug sanctuaries to exist right under their noses; in the countryside, the history of pacification was sorry, and current efforts weren't promising. Of course, the rule book of revolutionary warfare still had a plain answer: in the face of superior force fade back to a lower level of intensity and put time to work again. But Hanoi had gone against doctrine before, and having once violated dogma it is always easier to breach it a second time. Besides, it requires a great deal of emotional and intellectual fortitude to back away simply for the sake of doctrine when final victory beckons tantalizingly just out of reach—and when the price to come so close has been so terrible. Part of that price had been to make the insurgency even less popular with the people than it was before. Brutal conscription and equally brutal taxation, both predicated on gaining a total victory in 1965, had embittered the peasantry. A contraction of the war effort at this time, then, in addition to being a rankling admission of temporary failure, might also be dangerous. Theory called for contraction, instinct for continuation. When a similar situation had occurred while they were fighting the French, Giap and Ho had unhesitatingly eased off—and had won in the end. But that had been almost two decades ago.

Neither was any longer a young man; they could not afford to be so patient in 1966. They did not have another decade to wait. The politburo agreed—press on!

Accordingly, the tempo of the fighting picked up in early 1966, both in the military and the political arenas. North Vietnamese units opened a new front by coming straight across the Demilitarized Zone separating the two Vietnams, and they increased the armed pressure everywhere else at the same time. Internationally they used every ploy at their disposal to fan the flames of dissent, especially those inside the United States. Two years earlier the leaders in Hanoi had with typical candor declared, "Along with the intensification of our armed and political struggles in South Vietnam we must step up our diplomatic struggles for the purpose of isolating warmongers, gaining the sympathy of anti-war groups in the United States and taking full advantage of the dissensions among the imperialists to gain the sympathy and support of various countries which follow a peaceful and neutral policy." Now in 1966 those words had more meaning than ever.

With forces numbering around two hundred thousand troops—exclusive of ARVN units—and promises of that many more within the year, General Westmoreland entered in earnest the second phase of his three-phase plan. In his own words: "In the second phase, U.S. and Allied forces would mount major offensive actions to seize the initiative in order to destroy both the guerrilla and organized enemy forces, thus improving the security of the population. This phase would be concluded when the enemy had been worn down, thrown on the defensive, and driven well back from the major populated areas." Ringing in his ears as he embarked on what clearly would be a long, hard struggle, must have been the gloomy words of the secretary of defense, ". . . the odds are about even that . . . we will be faced in early 1967 with a military standoff at a much higher level."

At that time, early in 1966, there were four components to America's grand strategy in Vietnam: the air campaign against North Vietnam; a nation-building effort within South Vietnam; a diplomatic offensive to put pressure on Hanoi to cease its aggression; and Westmoreland's ground battle in the South. It had already been amply demonstrated that the hamstrung air campaign could not be decisive. Nation-building could only succeed when security could be assured. The diplomatic "peace offensive" was mounted mainly to provide the North a face-saving way out and to mute international criticism, not with any real hope of ending the war before the invaders were physically beaten back. Therefore, success or failure depended ultimately on the outcome of the fighting in South Vietnam.

In their search for the meaning of victory, theoreticians had peremptorily cast aside "military victory" as an anachronism. It became popular sport to deride anyone who spoke of winning militarily in Vietnam. Obviously, achieving final victory in a revolutionary war entailed eliminating those factors feeding the insurgency. But, just as obviously, they could never be eliminated unless a shield of security could first be fashioned for the people, unless the North Vietnamese invaders could be defeated and ejected. In short, nothing at all could be won unless the military phase of the struggle ended successfully. So General Westmoreland, the field commander, had of absolute necessity to emerge triumphant in the military encounter in South Vietnam. In that sense a military victory was indeed necessary.

Unfortunately, political limitations obliged the American commander to fight only inside South Vietnam, while his enemy could move in and out of the country at will. The location, timing, size and duration of each battle was to be the choice of the invader. Westmoreland had to wait for his foe to move. So long as the sanctuaries existed, Allied forces remained on the strategic defensive. Unless one's opponent is rather foolish, about the best that can be expected from a defensive strategy is a stalemate. "But in a People's Revolutionary War," Sir Robert Thompson later states, "if you are not winning you are losing, because the enemy can always sit out a stalemate without making concessions. It was, therefore, a no win strategy."

That was not quite so. There was a way to win.

CHAPTER 14

"A Protracted War of Attrition"

Denied the capability of chopping at the roots of aggression, General Westmoreland was compelled to attempt killing the tree by plucking leaves faster than new ones could sprout. With Allied ground forces restricted to the borders of South Vietnam, the only feasible strategy was to try to kill North Vietnamese and Viet Cong soldiers faster than they could be replaced. In Westmoreland's own words, written in August 1966, the conflict in South Vietnam had evolved into "a protracted war of attrition."

The general's rationale for conducting attrition warfare was simple and straightforward. Forced by political factors—those unavoidable back seat drivers in any limited war—to forfeit the strategic initiative to the enemy, his forces could in no way reach out to choke off the invasion at its source or even to smite it in its vital and vulnerable sanctuaries. They could only wait like a crouching, muscle-bound boxer for the opponent to move into range for a punch. If that opponent could be sent reeling back each time with a progressively more battered face, at some point he would surely lose his desire to continue the mauling. It was a purely defensive concept depending entirely on the other guy's constant willingness to press the offensive. The two indispensable ingredients for such a scheme to succeed were an absolutely impregnable position of strength to deny the attacker any victories whatsoever and the tactical power to thrash him roundly each time he sallied forth. The Allies possessed both of the required tactical capabilities—and no strategic alternatives. Therefore, the only answer was attrition.

Moreover, the air and naval campaign against the North was also one of attrition. Ostensibly controlled from Honolulu, but monitored so closely in the Pentagon and the White House that Washington was obviously the actual directing headquarters, the campaign was designed to reduce the flow of men and material southward and to raise the threshold of pain sufficiently to induce Hanoi to back away. Since many key targets in the North were "off-limits," fliers were not allowed to destroy reinforcements faster than they could be accumulated and dispatched to South Vietnam. Hence, in a very real sense, the bombing of the North, like the ground fighting in the South, was a campaign of attrition, a jabbing against supply lines and nerve ends rather than a knock-out blow at sources and command centers.

One should carefully note that while American field commanders openly admitted that they were waging a war of attrition, they winced at calling it a strategy of attrition. Attrition is not a strategy. It is, in fact, irrefutable proof of the *absence* of any strategy. A commander who resorts to attrition admits his failure to conceive of an alternative. He rejects warfare as an art and accepts it on the most non-professional terms imaginable. He uses blood in lieu of brains. To be sure, political considerations left military commanders no choice other than attrition warfare, but that does not alter the hard truth that the United States was strategically bankrupt in Vietnam in 1966.

As the Germans learned to their horror at Verdun in World War I, attrition is a two-edged sword. Manpower costs to both sides are great. What is more, it never achieves results swiftly. Planners who opt to wage war by that macabre means must have the courage to face squarely one unpleasant question: are they willing to accept high casualties to their side over a prolonged period of time in return for imposing heavy losses on the enemy? Placing that sanguinary question directly into the context of the Vietnam War, would the United States be willing to trade "body counts" with North Vietnam for years or even decades? It is not at all clear whether policy makers in Washington honestly asked themselves that question, and they surely never answered it, for America was not in the least prepared to tolerate a high toll of lives. And certainly not for years.

Nevertheless, lacking freedom of maneuver, Westmoreland had no choice but to make the best of an unenviable situation. There was nothing he could do to his foe outside South Vietnam, but he could strive to seize the tactical initiative inside the country. And that is what he did. (Of course, he could have resigned in protest at the shackles placed on him, but generals of the 1960s had watched some of their predecessors take that route in the 1950s to no avail. Moreover, President Johnson had pointedly warned Westmoreland "not to pull a MacArthur on me." The general did as he was told, and kept his doubts in official channels. In his memoirs he said he had not resigned because he believed the war could have been won despite all the political limitations.)

Starting off the year, MACV had two primary military missions—keep the enemy off-balance and away from the population centers, and complete the massive build-up begun in 1965. Concluding that the most critical areas were the heavily populated zones around Saigon and in the coastal lowlands from Nha Trang to Hue, Westmoreland funneled reinforcements directly into those localities. Two U.S. divisions and a newly constituted ARVN division formed a shield north and west of Saigon, while a second Korean division and two more American divisions—one marine and one infantry—landed along the coastal strip. As soon as the various elements debarked they began aggressively seeking battle, operating under broad orders telling them "to undertake operations which will find, fix, and destroy" enemy units.

During the year over 200,000 more Americans arrived, raising the total U.S. strength to nearly 400,000 men. At the peak, reached a couple of years later, the number of American servicemen in Vietnam would be well over half a million. Combat troops from other nations continued to flow in as well, totalling some 60,000 men by 1967, a number easily surpassing the 39,000 soldiers sent by the United Nations to fight in the Korean War. (On a monument in downtown Saigon were carved the simple words, "List of Nations having provided aid to the Republic of Vietnam." There, in alphabetical order from Argentina to Venezuela, were the names of forty-five countries which sent men, money, or supplies to help South Vietnam defend itself.) For the most part, the build-up was completed in 1966, although new units continued to arrive until early 1969. Westmoreland reported: "By the end of 1966 sufficient forces had been deployed, together with their logistic support, so that the total Allied military establishment was in a position for the first time to go over to the offensive on a broad and sustained basis in 1967."

Throughout 1966 the American commander bent his every effort to disrupt Giap's plans, to make enemy base areas inside South Vietnam untenable, to push the invaders away from populated areas back into the sparsely settled border regions. Terrain itself, in the kind of war in which Americans found themselves, had little intrinsic value. People were the key. The population had to be protected, which meant the fight should be waged in remote areas, but the purpose remained to kill enemy soldiers, not to hold or take any piece of ground. Thus, terrain was important only if it could be turned into a killing ground.

Relying mainly on massive operations conducted by brigade and division and multi-division sized forces, the Allies penetrated previously untouched redoubts and criss-crossed the countryside, seeking constantly to corner and destroy the elusive foe. Backed by an ever growing array of firepower, including B-52 bombers flying in formations too high to be heard and able to place awesome amounts of high explosives with shocking suddenness right into enemy laps, Allied forces inflicted terrible losses on the stubborn communist troops—and also watched their own death lists lengthen.

From the concept of attrition sprang one of the war's more ghoulish terms—"body count." Having decided to engage in a killing contest, an army thereafter scores its points in terms of cadavers. Thus, a company commander might be careful to the point of timidity about endangering the lives of his own troops in battle, but at the same time being illogically prone to risk taking casualties while scouring the bushes for one more dead enemy to raise his corpse count for that engagement. Other standards used to measure progress in past wars— ground taken, miles advanced, cities liberated—were manifestly irrelevant in a war of attrition. "Body count" became a morbid fixture of military jargon. The news media tabulated the number of Americans killed each week and compared it with South Vietnamese losses to see if they were bleeding equally. Then the combined figures were contrasted with reported Viet Cong and NVA deaths to ascertain the weekly kill ratio. Since the Allies had no strategic plan on which to anchor their perspective, it is hardly surprising that in all too many instances the body count, the indicator, came to be considered the actual goal of military operations. That transmutation gave rise to considerable misunderstanding among soldiers and civilians alike, a lack of comprehension on the military side which made it difficult to discern the difference between legitimate attrition and indiscriminate killing. Virtually by definition, a dead person was an enemy, one more tally to boost that day's body count. This attitude led to abuses, most notoriously the massacre at My Lai in 1968. It was a sad and perhaps inevitable legacy of the protracted war of attrition.

During 1966 there were eighteen major operations each netting over five hundred supposedly verified—counted and re-counted—enemy dead. The most successful was "Masher" which accounted for nearly twenty-four hundred bodies in forty-two days; the least effective, in terms of attrition, was "Macon" with just over five hundred corpses tallied after 116 days. Of course, there were scores of other actions which did not result in five hundred or more deaths, but which took a heavy cumulative toll nonetheless.

It would be incorrect to depict North Vietnamese and Viet Cong troops as continuing to hurl themselves blindly at Allied positions in mindless human wave attacks. Hanoi's commanders were not stupid. They realized their inability to win decisive battles in large-unit engagements. But, capable of nimbly evading most of the massive Allied blows, and invariably able to disengage from contact to slip away into havens in Cambodia or Laos, they retained sufficient flexibility to hit when and where circumstances offered good chances of success. So, by constantly coming back for more, General Giap's divisions kept heavy pressure on South Vietnam, albeit in repetitive surges at various points around the country rather than in a single onslaught against any given area. Guerrilla warfare, of course, continued unabated across the land. Thus, combat, large and small, was constant throughout the year, and the communist drumfire of probe and pressure kept the killing high.

Not every North Vietnamese strategist agreed with Hanoi's decision to continue pressing the unequal battle. General Nguyen Chi Thanh, NVA field commander in the South, was one who argued bitterly against it.

In the summer of 1966, having seen firsthand the futility of continued confrontation with American firepower and after watching his men fall by the thousands with no commensurate gain, the NVA leader protested so vehemently that the matter verged on public debate in the North. Allied long-range weapons, airpower, and mobility were plainly too much for the communists to overcome. Despite Hanoi's rhetoric, the general said wryly, willpower alone could not overcome firepower. But Thanh and his supporters did not prevail in the heated exchange. Hanoi resisted altering its strategy. Ho Chi Minh stoically shrugged off the spiraling death rate (perhaps fifty thousand in 1966) and responded by increasing his infiltration rate (about sixty thousand the same year). Providing an ironic footnote to the debate, General Thanh himself was fated to become a victim of a B-52 strike in 1967.

With Viet Cong recruitment and North Vietnamese infiltration, communist strength actually rose during those bloody twelve months to a total of nearly three hundred thousand soldiers. At the same time, counting six hundred and twenty-five thousand South Vietnamese, well over a million men bore arms for the Allies by the end of 1966. There was no shortage of attrition fodder on either side as 1967 began.

CHAPTER 15

More Rolling Thunder

The most powerful god of ancient Etruria was called Tinia. Tinia had three thunderbolts to cast while all the lesser deities had but one. The first he could hurl at his pleasure, the second only upon approval of the others, the third terrible bolt not until all his companions in concert demanded it. As a result, despite his vast potential strength, Tinia was unable to accomplish more than the ordinary gods for they saw to it that his extra two thunderbolts, his margin of superiority, remained idle. Etruria fell to Rome, whose celestial warriors were not so limited.

The bombing of North Vietnam lasted from its beginning in the spring of 1965 to the eve of the American presidential election of 1968—a total of three and a half years, the longest sustained strategic bombardment in the history of warfare. Throughout that entire period it remained a separate and distinct operation from the war in South Vietnam, directed from a different headquarters and subject to different policy considerations. Yet it obviously was a part of the Vietnam War, always related to and affected by events in the South. It was one component of America's three-sided approach to the war, supplementing nation-building and the ground

154

battle in the South. More, it was a hulking factor in policy discussions and strategy sessions in both Hanoi and Washington, an unavoidable backdrop to everything that occurred below the 17th Parallel. And, perhaps more than anything else in the war, the long aerial campaign engendered domestic controversy and typified military ineffectiveness.

When President Johnson ordered a pause in the bombing in May 1965, he hoped for but did not expect a favorable reaction from Hanoi. As a matter of fact, he secretly informed Ambassador Taylor that "the days of Buddha's birthday seem to me to provide an excellent opportunity for a pause in air attacks . . . which I could use to good effect with world opinion." Buddha's birthday might have been a valid excuse for the timing of the pause, and world opinion a good reason, but military factors of any sort certainly were not considered, for the pause coincided precisely with one of the darkest moments of the war, when Saigon had its back to the wall and Westmoreland was urgently pleading for American combat troops to save South Vietnam. Militarily, more strength not less was needed. Politically, however, before making a major escalation of the war, the White House deemed it prudent to demonstrate a willingness to de-escalate so that North Vietnam could be shown as the belligerent insisting on continuing the conflict. That first pause set the pattern. Rolling Thunder, though ostensibly a military operation, was and remained essentially a political tool. That fact accounts for many of the campaign's apparent failings and helps explain the bitter controversy over its conduct and eventual demise.

Noting that the powder puff approach taken from March to May had failed to impress the hardheaded men in Hanoi, Admiral U.S.G. Sharp, who directed air and naval actions from his headquarters in Hawaii, requested authority to reshape Rolling Thunder. He wanted to design raids in consonance with the capabilities of his attack aircraft and in consideration of enemy vulnerabilities, not according to some loosely reasoned design of how the opponent ought to react. The implied threat of devastation had not convinced Ho Chi Minh to reconsider; the actual fact of destruction, Admiral Sharp believed, would force him to do so. Taking advantage of what he called "the ubiquity of our air power," the admiral proposed to wage "an around-the-clock program of immobilization, attrition, and harassment of North Vietnamese military targets." But Washington did not agree. The bombing resumed on 18 May with most of the previous restrictions remaining in effect.

The principle of continually and steadily increasing the pressure against the North was the foundation of Secretary McNamara's policy of graduated response. The purpose behind his scheme was to "drive home to the North Vietnamese leaders that our staying power was superior to their own." The purpose was never accomplished because, for one reason, the principle was never followed. It is widely understood that a poor plan well executed usually attains better results than an excellent plan poorly executed. Graduated response had been widely condemned as a faulty policy, and probably it was. But, even worse, it was not redeemed by bold and proper implementation.

Air strikes continued unbroken from their resumption in May into the desperate days of the build-up and through the Ia Drang fighting until a second pause beginning just before Christmas 1965. Taking stock of results at that time, all hands, military and civilian, professional and amateur, agreed for once: the objectives of the bombing campaign had not been achieved. Far from being awed into submission, Hanoi was if anything more determined than ever not to cave in. Indeed, the infiltration of men into South Vietnam had actually increased, causing American officials to call for even more U.S. troops. Moreover, patriotic spirit in the North had been unified and strengthened by American attacks against the homeland—neither a new nor a surprising reaction from a national population threatened by foreign arms.

Throughout, Admiral Sharp and the Joint Chiefs of Staff had argued stoutly if unsuccessfully for a more forceful and realistic aerial strategy. They also constantly fought restraints which precluded even the basic, minimum implementation of the administration's enunciated policy. In this, too, they were unsuccessful. Instead of a gradually increasing pressure, Rolling Thunder's momentum actually lessened. Admiral Sharp, admitting unhappily that armed reconnaissance missions and strikes against fixed targets had gradually declined, explained it this way:

> The overall decrease in pressure was caused in part because the authorized armed reconnaissance area had fewer significant targets than before. Further, the reduced number of fixed targets for each succeeding Rolling Thunder period had lessened the pressure on North Vietnam. Finally, the most important targets were in the northeast and in the large sanctuaries around Hanoi and Hai Phong, where air operations were not authorized.

To military men the politically imposed restraints simply didn't make sense. For instance, normally the only military facilities fliers were permitted to strike were troop barracks; Sharp wanted to go after ammunition dumps and storage depots as well, and he wanted to destroy them anywhere they could be found, not in the southern part of North Vietnam alone. "In the eyes of a military commander," he wrote, "the objectives of the Rolling Thunder campaign had not been achieved—and to achieve them required adherence to the basic concept and principle of applying a continual and steadily increasing level of pressure."

On 26 November the admiral strongly recommended destruction of war supporting targets all across the North, disruption of major port facilities, and interdiction of road, rail, and water routes from China. Virtually every military official agreed with him. Thus, when some advisors in Washington recommended a bombing pause instead, two distinct camps emerged. Secretary McNamara and most key civilians in the Pentagon were for the halt, while Ambassador Lodge (back in Saigon for a second tour after replacing General Taylor) and Secretary of State Dean Rusk joined the military experts in arguing against it. Once again, in spite of Rusk's stand, political considerations overrode military imperatives. The bombing was lifted from Christmas 1965 to 31 January 1966.

As before, and as they would do in every future break in the bombing, the North Vietnamese displayed not the slightest interest in stopping the war. Instead, they took maximum advantage of the opportunity to rush supplies and men southward in broad daylight without fear of attack. In South Vietnam, Allied forces dug in to meet this added increment of communist weight. Pilots braced to face the improved and enlarged air defense system they knew would be waiting for them.

During the six-week pause, various agencies conducted a survey of Rolling Thunder operations. Since the aerial strategy's inauguration a year earlier, the nature of the war had changed dramatically, indicating a definite need to review the objectives and techniques of the campaign. Besides, the underlying assumption that North Vietnam would retire rather than accept continued pounding had proven to be false.

The original objective of the bombing was threefold: to slow the flow of men and material into South Vietnam; to boost South Vietnamese morale; and to convince Hanoi that aggression in the South was not worth the price to the North. The first two had been attained, although it would have been possible to do a more effective job in reducing the infiltration rate. In the attempt to reverse Hanoi's will to persevere, the strategy had not only failed, it had been counterproductive. It had solidified North Vietnam's national tenacity and, by its self-evident streak of restraint, had beamed a signal which Northern leaders interpreted as a basic unwillingness to escalate—a lack of resolve. This was an apparent American weakness supporting Hanoi's strong conviction that public patience in the United States would ebb before long, that Washington could not hold out long enough to achieve victory. It was evident to Pentagon staff officers, therefore, that some changes were overdue if Rolling Thunder were to attain its third, and primary, objective.

Unfortunately, this was the same time when the same planners were probing for a workable but safe concept for the fighting in South Vietnam. And, just as they could discover no cheap way to win inside the South, they could come up with no easy way to gain the objectives of Rolling Thunder. Apparently, Washington's policy-making apparatus had difficulty relating operations to objectives, a most grievous failing for a major power in the modern world, a failing, in fact, fraught with the breath of Armageddon. On the ground, Westmoreland was denied authority to strike enemy sanctuaries; in the air, Sharp met the same stiff policy restrictions. Hostile bases beyond the borders of South Vietnam remained inviolable to ground attack, and most of them were similarly protected from air action. As ground planners turned for lack of alternatives to attrition warfare, so too did air planners. Even in emasculated form, though, the bombing had a role. All of President Johnson's principal advisors, including McNamara, recommended resuming it in one degree or another. The president concurred, but, still afraid of antagonizing China or Russia, he flatly rejected military advice to conduct a crushing campaign designed to force Ho to withdraw his support of the Southern insurgency. Restrictions remained. The most Rolling Thunder could do, then, was more of the same.

When 1966 ended, all Admiral Sharp could claim of the year's actions was merely an unhappy echo of his remarks after 1965: "The application of steadily increasing pressure was denied us in 1966 through operational restrictions and as a result the tasks were not accomplished."

One example, the memorable POL campaign, will suffice to describe why fliers generally were unable to achieve established goals in 1966 even though they flew thousands upon tens of thousands of sorties.

In military shorthand, POL stands for petroleum products—fuel, oil and lubricants. Without POL a modern country quickly grinds to a virtual halt. Transportation ceases, fuel and power levels dip dangerously, factories close. Not an industrial nation, North Vietnam nevertheless depended heavily on POL to continue waging its war in South Vietnam. Especially critical was the fact that all petroleum and oil had to be imported, most of it from Russia. POL facilities were natural targets for strategic bombing. In 1965 the military had asked for authority to wipe out Hanoi's entire POL capacity. It could have been done then either by closing Haiphong harbor or by destroying the few major storage centers, which were at that time extremely vulnerable. The White House denied permission.

When the bombing first began, Hanoi immediately recognized the vulnerability and the importance of its POL system. With an alacrity born of anxiety, the Northerners began dispersing and protecting their tank farms. Buried or bunkered storage tanks soon dotted the countryside by the hundreds, while stacks of 50-gallon barrels served to spread POL stores over an even larger area. Taking advantage of the well publicized American aversion to bombing population centers, supply officers placed many of the tanks in or adjacent to villages along key highways. By declining to hit POL targets in 1965, the United States had lost the opportunity to deal a damaging blow when it could have been done with relatively little expense or effort.

Still, POL remained a vital resource quite worth attacking. Field commanders and the Joint Chiefs of Staff continued to plead for permission to bomb the major storage areas. Admiral Sharp probably spoke for most of them when he predicted that destroying Hanoi's POL system would cause Ho Chi Minh either to enter into negotiations or to phase back the war in South Vietnam. The intelligence community, on the other hand, though acknowledging the importance of the North's POL, doubted that even such a severe blow would knock the determination out of "Uncle" Ho. Secretary McNamara, after considerable soul-searching, sided with the Joint Chiefs. Still, President Johnson was unconvinced. He asked others. Walt W. Rostow prepared a memorandum which apparently persuaded the vacillating commander in chief. Rostow thought "the military effects of a systematic and sustained bombing of POL in North Vietnam may be more prompt and direct than conventional intelligence analysis would suggest." Then he carefully reiterated the words "systematic and sustained." For decisive results, he warned, one "must cut clean through the POL system—and hold the cut . . ." A one-time attack would not do the job.

Johnson gave the go-ahead, but his uncertainty and fear remained. The implementing order was choked with overly explicit and wholly unnecessary instructions on such details as composition of crews, flight patterns, defensive measures, etc. The crews who dropped the atomic bombs on Japan in 1945 received more careful coaching, maybe, but then they had not been making similar attacks with similar weapons for over a year.

The first POL attacks, carried out in mid-1966, a year after they were initially recommended, were quite successful in destroying the large tank farms, including those near Hanoi and Haiphong. A year earlier those attacks would have for all intents and purposes sent the bulk of North Vietnam's gasoline up in flames. But not in the summer of 1966; most of the fuel was stored elsewhere. For the next few months bombers ranged wide over the countryside searching out the POL sites, but because of their dispersed locations near restricted targets many could not be hit even when found. In Haiphong, bombers had destroyed all but a marginal storage capacity, but the port itself remained open. Soviet tankers continued to arrive and to discharge POL modules which could be placed with impunity right onto waiting trucks and be driven away. The POL system had been sorely damaged; it had not been destroyed. The bombing had been too late and too little. To pilots it was a familiar tale.

By and large the story of 1967 was a repeat of 1965 and 1966. Bad weather in the winter months, political restraints during good weather, North Vietnamese resilience and resourcefulness year round. Admiral Sharp's annual overview was a monotonous paraphrase of earlier summaries: "It is of vital importance ... to bear in mind that the objective of applying continuing and steadily increasing pressure over an extended period of time was not attained."

There was, however, one significant difference in 1967. Never before had airmen been allowed to implement the policy of gradualism as it had been envisioned. Then, two years after its inception, in the spring of 1967, President Johnson finally granted the means necessary to achieve his long-standing goal. He gave authority to hit previously proscribed areas. Targets in the northeastern part of North Vietnam and selected sites in the Hanoi-Haiphong area suddenly showed up on mission briefing charts. And, except for Haiphong and two other deep-water ports, river mouths were to be mined. Rolling Thunder grew fangs. Eagerly responding to the release from so many restraints, air crews brought the air war to a rising crescendo of pressure in June, July, and August. Their sustained activity began to make inroads on enemy morale and to inflict real damage on Hanoi's war-making resources. Admiral Sharp was delighted with the results and trends. But, inexplicably, Washington eased off, letting the pace of the campaign go slack and then ebb. Sharp could not keep a tinge of bitterness from his words as he reported, "The pressure period was foreshortened, even as the enemy began to hurt."

What had happened was not so much any new decisions on the air campaign itself as it was a reflection of growing unrest with the course of the war inside South Vietnam. In the spring of 1967 General Westmoreland had asked for some two hundred thousand additional troops, and the Joint Chiefs had renewed their demands on the president to mobilize reserves. Both requests struck a politically sensitive nerve in the White House and caused yet another introspective evaluation within the administration of the whole Vietnam question. At about that time, also, Secretary McNamara began to urge that the open-ended aspect of the war be closed, that the United States should set a ceiling on its commitment and prepare for the long haul. He was manifestly disappointed with the unpopular conflict which many were calling "McNamara's War."

President Johnson, whom history may well remember as our most reluctant and indecisive wartime commander in chief, found himself torn two ways. On one side, his military advisors told him victory was near if he would just summon the courage to close for the kill; on the other, trusted advisors were passionately urging him to hold the line against escalation. General Wheeler said to cut back on the bombing of North Vietnam would be tantamount to an "aerial Dien Bien Phu," while McNamara thought heavier bombing "would not be stomached either by our own people or by world opinion; and it would involve a serious risk of drawing us into open war with China." At the same time, a rising swell of sentiment among public and press cried for an end to the bombing. The air war was a prime source of debate and dissent and became daily a more potent political liability to President Johnson's Democratic party. Opponents could point with unanswerable logic to the great costs and small gains; proponents could not counter with provable claims of success. Furthermore, the summer of 1967 was "the long hot summer" in America. Riots, demonstrations, and violence were its hallmark. There were many contributing reasons for the internal upheaval, but the war, and especially the air war, was high among them. One result of the national malaise was that Rolling Thunder, at its single bright moment of promise, lapsed back to an ineffectual aerial campaign of attrition.

For all the bitter policy arguments and for all the evident shortcomings, the air war itself was an intensely active and determined affair. The overall failure of the air war was not the result of any lack of professionalism or dedication on the part of air crews or staffs, although McNamara at one point had confided to the president his fear that limitations on the bombing would "cause serious psychological problems among the men who are risking their lives to help achieve our political objectives." Nor did the campaign suffer from a lack of material support. A glimpse of the statistics, friendly and enemy, indicates how profusely Rolling Thunder was pursued.

To begin with, the extraordinary communist reaction was itself a direct measure of the tremendous weight of the American air effort. At the start of the bombing in 1965, Hanoi had no jets, very limited airfields, no missiles, fewer than twenty radar sets, and just a handful of obsolete anti-aircraft guns. By 1967, fliers had to penetrate defenses far more formidable than those encountered over Germany in 1944. Russian made surface-to-air missiles (SAM) claimed their first victim, an F-4C jet, on 24 July 1965. At year's end there were around sixty SAM sites in the North. Jet fighters of the MIG-15 and MIG-17 type arrived that year also, and shot down two F-105 bombers on 4 April. Radar sets of all kinds proliferated, as did anti-aircraft artillery and automatic weapons. By the end of 1966, SAM sites had grown to about one hundred fifty; some seventy MIGs challenged U.S. aircraft; maybe five thousand anti-aircraft guns were in operation, and over one hundred radar stations provided early warning, tracking, and intercept capabilities. The next year witnessed similar growth. Photographic interpreters identified another one hundred SAM sites, for instance. Rates of engagement also soared. SAM firings are a good indicator: in 1965 pilots observed just a few score SAM launchings; gunners fired a thousand missiles in 1966; the figure rose to thirty-five hundred in 1967. American losses of planes and pilots climbed in direct proportion to the burgeoning defenses.

Against those defenses Admiral Sharp threw wave upon wave of the most advanced aircraft in our inventory, supported effectively by sophisticated counterelectronic measures. Sorties over North Vietnam numbered more than ten thousand a month in 1966, reaching beyond thirteen thousand monthly in 1967. A sortie is one flight by one warplane. Altogether, some two thousand fixed targets were bombed, most more than once, and many thousands of moving targets—trucks, trains, ferries, ships—fell prey to attack aircraft. The tonnage of bombs expended surpassed that dropped during World War II and doubled the amount used in the Korean War. Through the end of 1967, well over a million tons of high explosive had fallen on North Vietnam. On any given day, American bombers could—and often did—deliver more ordnance than the French could in all the months of the siege of Dien Bien Phu. The extravagant array of trained men and sophisticated weaponry which America committed against North Vietnam constituted one of the most munificent armadas ever sent to war. Sadly, that lavish expenditure could not rescue a strategy which was itself bankrupt. The strategy stopped short, so the expenditure was futile.

Rolling Thunder failed to accomplish the primary mission assigned to it by failing to convince the leaders in Hanoi to cease their aggression against the South. In retrospect, that was neither a remarkable nor an unpredictable result. For, as historian Theodore Ropp wrote early in 1965, "What is 'unbearable' in terms of Western values may seem normal to the peoples of emerging nations." The bombing campaign, as it was applied, was bearable to North Vietnam. Nonetheless, it did provide crucial assistance to the war effort in South Vietnam. Knowing that their cousins in the North were not escaping unscathed for all the devastation they were causing in the South gave the South Vietnamese extra motivation to sustain the long resistance. And, despite their outward show of unity and determination, the widespread damage to their painstakingly developed industry and commerce simply had to make communist leaders ponder the wisdom of continuing. Nor could the disruption of daily life be ignored—over half a million men had been diverted from farming and other pursuits to repair bomb damage, while other thousands manned the intricate air defense system. Finally, had it not been for Rolling Thunder, one can only guess at how many more men and guns General Westmoreland would have had to counter in the South. "Perhaps the most important measure of the effects of the bombing," Admiral Sharp said, "would be the consideration of the situation if there had been no bombing at all."

For all intents and purposes 1967 saw the end of Rolling Thunder. That winter brought prohibitively bad flying weather, President Johnson sharply curtailed the campaign in March 1968, and he killed it completely during the final days of the presidential race in a last ditch effort to swing votes to Vice President Hubert Humphrey. Begun, and for the most part conducted, principally for political reasons and in hopes of political gain, the first aerial bombardment of North Vietnam ended on the same note.

In the long history of warfare, airpower is a very new factor. Only in the last half century has it joined land and sea elements to add a third dimension to strategic thought. As might be expected, its incorporation into the overall equation of combat has been accomplished with only partial success. The primary reason for its incomplete utilization is that the amazing technological advances of aerial weapons systems have far outstripped the development of a comprehensive theory for their employment. In his book, *Commander of the Air*, published in 1921, Giulio Douhet, the Italian infantry officer who became the world's first recognized airpower theoretician, wrote, "The disintegration of nations [which] in the last war was brought about by [attrition] will be accomplished directly by ... aerial forces." Airplanes have fueled the imaginations of men ever since. In every decade since Douhet wrote, prophets have proclaimed the omnipotence of strategic airpower. However, in every test the theory has failed. Hitler had his high hopes dashed in the 1940 Battle of Britain, Americans learned after World War II that Germany and Japan had actually increased production while being pounded incessantly by Allied long-range bombers, and General MacArthur discovered that even total air superiority could not prevent Chinese armies from entering and fighting in the Korean peninsula. Now historians will have for their studies yet another example of a strategic air campaign which miscarried—Rolling Thunder. Speaking at West Point in 1967, General Westmoreland told the cadets, "Airpower alone didn't do the job. It never has, but we give it a chance in every war." He might more accurately have said our *theory of employment of airpower* didn't do the job.

If the officers who were charged with conducting Rolling Thunder had ever heard of Etruscan gods, they must have sympathized mightily with the numbing sense of frustration Tinia had suffered.

CHAPTER 16

The Iron Triangle

The ground war of attrition in South Vietnam paralleled the ineffectual air war against the North in time and, to a degree, in style. Both seemed to observers to be somewhat ponderous, clumsy, and inefficient applications of power. There was an inescapable sense of elephants stamping on ants, of a tremendous expenditure of energy when far less would have sufficed, of wielding a bludgeon when a scalpel was required. In truth, such impressions were not totally inaccurate. Neither Sharp's limited air war nor Westmoreland's ground campaign of attrition will ever be viewed as skillful examples of the practice of the military art. And for much the same underlying reason: policy restraints hindered—if not absolutely precluded—the proper utilization of available forces.

After he had so brilliantly stopped the North Vietnamese invasion in late 1965, Westmoreland mounted a counter-offensive aimed at gaining the initiative and destroying hostile forces inside South Vietnam. Denied authority to strike decisively at enemy bases and concentrations in Cambodia, Laos, and North Vietnam, the American commander could only wage a strategically defensive campaign behind friendly borders. To win such a contest he had to protect South Vietnam's population and to make aggression so terribly costly that General Giap would call his divisions home. To accomplish that twofold task, Westmoreland gave ARVN forces the primary mission of protecting and pacifying population centers while U.S. and other Allied combat units actively sought to engage communist divisions in the unsettled stretches near the western borders and in the numerous insurgent sanctuaries throughout South Vietnam. Whatever he did, moreover, had to be done in such a manner as to minimize friendly casualties, for, in attrition warfare, that is the name of the game. Thus, American field commanders found themselves attacking fortified base areas in generally isolated sections of Vietnam using massive search-and-destroy tactics—and worrying all the while about the statistical results of body-counting.

Search-and-destroy was one of several operational terms coined long before American combat units entered Southeast Asia. Actions of this type were designed to locate and neutralize hostile forces and bases and supply caches. By definition it was an attack conducted away from populated areas and in localities where the enemy was strong. It entailed violent assault by infantry and armor, in conjunction with the use of heavy supporting fires, to destroy an armed opponent who could probably be expected to defend himself in a conventional way. So, to minimize friendly casualties, only very large units could execute the operations. Later in the war, when the term became synonymous in the public mind with aimless thrashing about in the jungle and purposeless destruction of property, General Westmoreland dropped it and substituted more normal names. But, whether called offensive sweep, reconnaissance in force, spoiling attack, or search-and-destroy, the principle was the same—a large-scale, tactical offensive seeking an opponent to fight, a base to destroy, or both.

South Vietnam had no shortage of hostile bastions—

eighty or so major strongholds and hundreds of minor ones laced the land. Used for resupply, rest, training, hospitals, staging, or simply for refuge, that extensive network of bases had sustained the insurgency for years. Carefully sited in hard-to-reach areas—jungles, mountains, swamps—and shrewdly provided with redundant escape routes, always defended in depth and often with tenacity, extensively booby-trapped and mined, those asylums were by no means simple or safe even to enter. They were exceedingly tough to destroy. The story of Allied efforts to destroy one such base—and not one of the largest, at that—will demonstrate the magnitude of Westmoreland's task and will help explain why his search-and-destroy tactics seemed in the end to have required so much to do so little.

The Iron Triangle was a formidable arrow tip pointing straight at Saigon and located not twenty miles north of the city. Situated strategically between two superbases—war zones C and D—the communist citadel was both a secure stopping place for units in transit between the two larger fortresses and a staging point for major assaults against government installations near the capital. Bounded on two sides by rivers, on the third by jungle, and elevated well above the water level, the redoubt included forty square miles of close-packed second growth jungle, a natural barrier of tangled vine and briar. Any movement was at machete pace. The strength of the position lay in its all but impenetrable top and its amazingly complex underground network of tunnels and chambers. Begun as a refuge when the Japanese had occupied Indochina in World War II, improved by the Viet Minh in their struggle to oust the French, consolidated by the Viet Cong as they fought first President Diem and then the Americans, it was a fortification in every sense of the word. Millions of manhours of labor had gone into developing the subterranean labyrinth. Thousands of men could live there, could move unseen for miles to counterattack or escape, and could fight from under the earth as well. It was a human anthill. Hospitals, printing plants, classrooms, storage areas, offices, and, of course, traps and fighting tunnels saturated the area. For more than twenty years it had protected insurgents against all comers. It was most aptly named.

No one seems to remember or to have recorded just when the first effort was mounted to rid the tract of its denizens. It must have been some time prior to 1962, however, for by then the Iron Triangle had its foreboding name and a fierce reputation to match. Large ARVN forces made occasional forays against it, but with only sniper and booby-trap casualties to show for their pains. The redoubt could simply swallow a regiment. In November of 1964, in fact, an entire ARVN regiment, reinforced by an armored squadron, several battalions of artillery, and a heavy concentration of aircraft, spent ten days beating around in there with absolutely no results—unless one counts several swaths cut through the dense vegetation and the destruction of a few dozen tunnel entrances as worthwhile accomplishments for so large a force over so long a time.

Shortly after that futile incursion, General Westmoreland invited an American captain who had been on the operation to have dinner with him and his family in Saigon. During the course of the evening, the young officer described the difficulties involved in attempting to root an entrenched foe out of the area. The best solution, he thought, would be to burn the place to the ground. Interested, Westmoreland asked his guest to elaborate over coffee after Mrs. Westmoreland and the children had gone to bed. From the midnight session between the general and the captain sprang the next attempt to neutralize the Iron Triangle.

At the beginning of the dry season, aircraft saturated the dense jungle with chemical defoliants, killing the luxuriant plant covering. After a couple of months under the broiling sun, the Iron Triangle became a vast, tinder-dry fire trap. Leaflets and loudspeakers then warned noncombatants to get out fast. Cargo aircraft flew low over the baked forest, priming it with barrels of oil and gasoline, and attack planes swept in to ignite it with napalm and incendiary bombs. Raging flames roared high into the sky. Success seemed certain. Then an incredible phenomenon occurred. The intense heat triggered an atmospheric confluence in the wet, tropical air, loosing a gigantic cloudburst. As *Time* Magazine described the astounding event, "a drenching downpour...doused the forest fire and left [the] Viet Cong safe and unsinged in their caves." Monsoon rains soon revived the jungle cover. All effort had been for naught.

Late in 1965 the American 173rd Airborne Brigade, reinforced with Australians and New Zealanders, undertook to accomplish what all others had failed to do. Placing a battalion in a blocking position west of the Iron Triangle, the Brigade commander, Brigadier General Ellis W. Williamson, poked the remainder of the 173rd into the jungle fortress from the east. We have the Iron Triangle "like a nut in a nutcracker," Williamson crowed. "Now we have to see whether the Viet Cong will stand and fight."

The Brigade remained there three days. Airborne troopers captured documents, uncovered stacks of supplies, destroyed assorted structures, captured sixty-seven Viet Cong suspects, and reported killing forty-four enemy soldiers. Williamson happily wrote in a magazine article: "...we turned our attention to the southwest and tore apart the great unknown, the Iron Triangle...The Iron Triangle was destroyed...The Iron Triangle was thoroughly searched and investigated, and all enemy troops and installations were destroyed..."

The general could not have been more wrong. He had entered the Iron Triangle, had stayed three days, had caused the inhabitants a certain amount of inconvenience, and had inflicted a modicum of damage. But he had by no stretch of the imagination "torn apart" the Iron Triangle. Dented perhaps; destroyed not at all. Captain Henry B. Tucker, one of Williamson's company commanders, was more observant: "We burned the buildings, but we could not do anything to the fortifications; they were just dug too damn deep." The proof that General Williamson was wrong lies in the massive operation which had to be conducted a year later over the same ground.

Not that the general was the only senior officer to fail to discern the real nature of the problem; at that early stage of the conflict most American military men were just beginning to learn how different this war was, how drastically the measures for recording success or failure had changed. Reducing a fortified base area was deceptively easy in concept, difficult in the extreme in execution. To completely deny insurgents the use of a fastness like the Iron Triangle, counter-insurgency forces must either occupy it or render it totally unlivable by such means as nuclear seeding or chemical poisoning, or by physically changing the geography through flooding or filling. That is why so many search-and-destroy operations appeared to be unremunerative despite commanders' claims of success. Which is at least partly why the American public came to view them as pointless flailings in the jungle.

When it became obvious that the 173rd had failed, that the Iron Triangle functioned still as a major communist preserve, Westmoreland determined to mount a final assault so powerful that it could not fail to eliminate the dreaded fortress once and for all. Two entire infantry divisions, the 1st and 25th, the 173rd Airborne Brigade, and the 11th Armored Cavalry Regiment were the principal ground units involved. Fleets of helicopters and a superabundance of firepower supported the attacking elements. Dubbed "Cedar Falls," the operation got underway with B-52 strikes on 4 January 1967.

On 8 January, in a smoothly coordinated maneuver, ground units moved swiftly into pre-arranged positions to seal in any remaining enemy forces. Sixty helicopters dropped an entire infantry battalion (the 1st Battalion, 26th Infantry, commanded by Lieutenant Colonel Alexander M. Haig) smack on the village of Ben Suc, a known Viet Cong nest. That swift blow caught several Viet Cong soldiers before they could scurry away. Meanwhile, spearheaded by mechanized and armored battalions, the 25th Division, commanded by Major General Fred Weyand, occupied blocking positions along the Saigon River west of the Iron Triangle, effectively precluding any escape in that direction. Next day, Major General William DePuy's 1st Infantry Division, with the 173rd attached, executed an airmobile assault with six battalions to block exits along the northern flank. Reconnaissance units, including air cavalry, screened to the south and east. Artillery batteries rolled into firing positions already surveyed. Before dusk of the second day an entire American corps surrounded the Iron Triangle.

As DePuy's airmobile elements were being inserted, armored columns from the 11th Armored Cavalry Regiment thrust westward from Ben Cat, crossing the Tinh River and crashing into the jungle. In a single lunge the leading squadron slashed five miles to reach the Saigon River, halving the Iron Triangle. Armored troopers, plowing directly through the tangled thickets in their tracked vehicles, then swept north to link up with the air-landed elements holding there. Next, the cavalrymen turned southward and battered their way to the far point of the triangle. The fabled Iron Triangle was theirs.

But the enemy was gone. Most of the defenders had scattered and fled. Notwithstanding the vastly superior American mobility—derived from armored vehicles and helicopters—the decision to fight or not had remained with the Viet Cong commander. And he had opted to avoid battle. A battle of annihilation against a foe who retains that option is unlikely, maybe impossible—unless he happens to be a Varro, the dupe at Cannae, history's classic battle of annihilation.

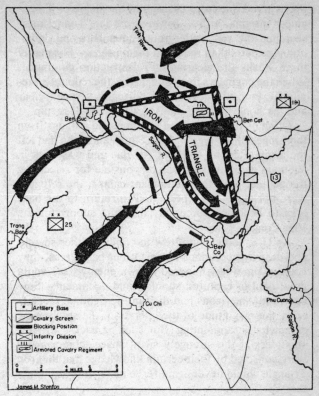

Operation "Cedar Falls"

The enemy might have fled, but the bastion itself was in American hands. Part of the operation's purpose was to destroy it, to inflict so much damage that insurgents could never again return. Even before the shooting stopped, army engineers were at work altering the face of the Iron Triangle. They blasted clearings for helicopter resupply and evacuation, improved existing trails, cut new roads to handle the movement of supplies and fighting units, and bulldozed great lanes crisscrossing the whole expanse of smoking land. Leaving their brand in the proper "Old West" style,

175

they carved one huge clearing in the shape of the engineer insignia, a three-towered castle. "Tunnel rats" searched the vast underground chambers and demolitions experts then rendered them useless. For nearly three weeks the clearing and destruction continued. When the engineers finally departed, the redoubt's previously tangled surface was virtually scraped clear and the honeycombed interior was a hopeless ruin.

Officials removed some six thousand persons from the fringes of the region. John Paul Vann, who had left the army after the battle of Ap Bac and was back in Vietnam as a civilian, was responsible for relocating the people. Sent to resettlement camps, the refugees were not again to be permitted to return to the base area to become sources of labor and supply for the Viet Cong.

As U.S. forces withdrew to conduct other search-and-destroy operations against other base areas, they could claim a few hundred known enemy dead and a great haul in captured supplies and documents. Seventy-two Americans had died in the fighting. Considering the magnitude of the operation, the spoils were somewhat disappointing. But, looking back over their shoulders at the strangely silent space, commanders were consoled by their certain knowledge that the Iron Triangle would never again serve insurgents as a sanctuary.

They were wrong.

CHAPTER 17

The Phalanx of Fire

Tactics are affected markedly by considerations of policy and strategy. Saddled with a policy of graduated response, which assured a long war, and a non-strategy of attrition, which made the kill ratio the primary measure of success, American generals not surprisingly tailored their tactics accordingly.

There were some differences, of course, from unit to unit and between one geographical area and another. Tactics employed in the Delta, for instance, where the watery terrain is more water than terrain, were obviously unsuited for use in the towering mountains farther north. But, throughout, there were two common elements: the all-pervasive impact of technology and the virtually complete reliance on fire tactics to the all but absolute exclusion of shock tactics. Technology made fire tactics possible while politics precluded the use of shock tactics.

It was not always so. When the internal war had flared up in the late 1950s, demonstrating beyond all doubt that aggression was to be cloaked in the sheep's skin of internal war, the U.S. military establishment found itself unprepared for the challenge. Doctrine, thinking, equipment, organization, and training had all been oriented on large-scale, atomic warfare, with Europe seen as the likely battleground. Insurgency was a germ almost foreign to our soldiers, while fighting on the land mass of Asia was officially unmentionable. Obliged to adjust abruptly to the style and pace of a conflict at the far end of the spectrum from the one for which they had prepared themselves, many military men overreacted. For years thereafter there persisted a strong feeling that modern weapons, equipment, and firepower were next to useless—maybe even counter-productive—in an insurgency environment. To beat a revolutionary, the reasoning in vogue went, one must engage him on his own ground on his own terms with his own weapons. In short, fight guerrillas with guerrillas. That early, simplistic conclusion demonstrated as perhaps nothing else could that U.S. policy makers had not grasped the essence of insurgency. And it led to not a few bizarre applications of force, the best known example being the unusual role handed to special forces teams.

Gradually, however, the pendulum returned to center—and, as is normal in such swings, may have gone too far in the other direction. The change, though, was for the better. Someone had remembered in time an anonymous admonition: "Let him who would enter battle armed only with the weapons of his enemy ponder carefully the difficulty of stinging a bee." Military leaders, after their generally unsuccessful flirtation with guerrilla versus guerrilla techniques, recognized that trying to fight on the insurgents' terms—attempting to sting a bee—was to sacrifice what was probably the greatest asset in America's arsenal, technology. If the United States was unable to match Asian opponents in manpower, the Asians could by no stretch of the imagination compete with American technology. Soon, then, MACV was asking for armored personnel carriers and tanks to provide mobility and shock action; for fighter-bombers and artillery to increase fire support; for B-52 bombers to pummel Viet Cong bases;

for armored boats to invade river redoubts; for infra-red and radar to find the foe in the night; for helicopters to shuttle entire divisions; for aircraft carriers and landing ships; for improved small arms; for computers to keep tabs on enemy activities. And the list is but begun. Fertilizers and hybrid plants and modern medicines and, yes, even television were technological weapons used in the struggle to build the nation. Bulldozers and road graders went to battle—and also helped reconstruct the devastated country. As the impact of technology came fully to bear in the early 1960s, observers agreed that effective counter-insurgency could not be conducted solely at the level of garrote and punji stake. Techniques had to be many-layered.

Tactical changes wrought by recent technological advances have been described with some justice as more revolutionary than evolutionary. Beyond a doubt, the World War II or Korean War forebear of the Vietnam War G.I. would have been flabbergasted could he have been suddenly transported into the midst of a battle in Vietnam. For instance, consider the work-horse whirlybird, the ubiquitous helicopter which would have been the most obvious and most astounding difference the old soldier would have seen. It was every-where. And did everything. It put soldiers into battle, moved artillery pieces, carried reinforcements and supplies, evacuated casualties, conducted reconnaissance, provided an aerial armchair for commanders, and contributed its own increment of firepower to support the men on the ground. It is every bit as hard to imagine the trooper in Vietnam without a helicopter as the old-time, Indian-fighting cavalryman without a horse.

Not that technological advances produced unmitigated blessings. Consider the helicopter again. It was of minimum value at night, when insurgents were most active. And bad weather, a feature of the climate in Southeast Asia, limited its effectiveness. Now, natural conditions have always affected military operations, but never qu   the degree reached in Vietnam, a

179

result of placing such great reliance on a machine which was so very susceptible to the vagaries of weather. Moreover, MACV's already fat logistical tail grew fatter still by virtue of vastly increased requirements for fuel and parts and mechanics; fleets of helicopters don't fly without immense supporting facilities. In the final analysis, though, the helicopter's most pernicious contribution to the fighting in Vietnam may have been its undermining of the influence and initiative of small unit commanders. By providing a fast, efficient airborne command post, the helicopter all too often turned supervisors into oversupervisors. Since rarely was there more than one clash in any given area at any given time, the company commander on the ground attempting to fight his battle could usually observe orbiting in tiers above him his battalion commander, brigade commander, assistant division commander, division commander, and even his field force commander. With all that advice from the sky, it is easy to imagine how much individual initiative and control the company commander himself could exert on the ground—until nightfall sent the choppers to roost. Nor did Viet Cong or NVA leaders fail to note that the importance of an operation was directly proportional to the number of helicopters stacked above it. An Englishman, sympathetic to U.S. efforts in Vietnam, observed that the helicopter "exaggerated the two greatest weaknesses of the American character—impatience and aggressiveness."

Nonetheless, for better or for worse, American soldiers in Vietnam became firmly wedded to technology. It was the equalizer in a war which seemed in so many other ways to favor the enemy. Eventually, it came to dominate Allied tactical thinking and to dictate the very manner of fighting.

Like the changing opinions of the proper role for modern weaponry—and in large degree because of those changes—tactical concepts of fire and maneuver also underwent a complete flip-flop during the war. Prior to the introduction of American ground combat units in 1965, U.S. Army doctrine called for—and advisors so urged their counterparts—closing with the enemy and destroying him in place, for maintaining close and continuous contact, for pursuit. Advisors railed at South Vietnamese commanders, inwardly at least, when they were hesitant to come to grips in close combat with Viet Cong units. Senior American advisors hammered at subordinate advisors trying to get them to make their units keep contact once it was made. And they despaired of ever witnessing a pursuit. Many a wishful beer was drunk to the refrain, "One good American division would show them how!" Without doubt, officially proclaimed tactical doctrine was to grapple with and destroy the enemy using fire and maneuver.

But that began to change in 1965; by 1967 only a foolhardy or a desperate commander would ever engage hostile elements by any means other than with firepower. Early signs of the drift in that direction could be seen in the Ia Drang campaign during the autumn of 1965 in which practically all combat was in the form of communist attacks on American positions, and North Vietnamese soldiers could walk away at their pleasure from American units in contact with them.

As the months of the war of attrition bled by, the new tactics quickly became standard. Infantry units were all but forbidden to practice their traditional mission of closing with and killing the enemy. Instead, maneuver elements *found* the foe while firepower eliminated him. B-52 usage, for instance, leaped from sixty sorties a month in 1966 to over eight hundred monthly in 1967. When contact was made, American units, preoccupied with avoiding casualties, generally fell back into a defensive perimeter to call for air and artillery. Tactical maneuvers to roll up an open flank or strike an exposed rear were usually attempted only by the enemy. Not that field manuals were changed. Not even that service schools taught the new doctrine. But, in practice in Vietnam, U.S. Army policy was to locate the enemy with infantry and then attack him by fire.

Sidney B. Berry, Jr., one of the war's most successful brigade commanders, authored a pamphlet in mid-1967 describing the new tactics. Endorsed by the chief of staff, it was given wide dissemination in the army. In it he made abundantly clear that the time-honored technique of fire and maneuver had switched over to one of maneuver and fire, as these excerpts show: "...growing quickly into intense fire fights, battles end abruptly with the enemy's withdrawal...During battles, enemy forces move in a relatively wide area around a point of contact, seeking to encircle, reinforce, or withdraw...[The brigade commander] uses his soldiers to find the enemy and supporting firepower to destroy the enemy. He spends firepower as if he is a millionaire and husbands his men's lives as if he is a pauper...during search and destroy operations, commanders should look upon infantry as the principal combat reconnaissance force and supporting fires as the principal destructive force."

Colonel Berry also made frequent references to American units being pinned down. In spite of the massively overwhelming U.S. firepower, one searches in vain through all the literature of the war for an example of enemy units being pinned down!

A division commander, in an article published in September 1967, thus described what he called a victorious fire fight:

> This contact (made by B company) was with a platoon-sized enemy force, but by 1200 hours, the company was engaged with an entrenched enemy who was committing more and more units to the battle. As the fire fight increased in intensity some elements of B Company were pinned down. The enemy, now in battalion strength, began to encircle the company. Company C...wheeled about and made a forced march back to the scene of the fight. It began crossing the river and came under heavy fire. Air and artillery strikes were called in, but neither B nor C

Company was able to muster enough firepower from its own position to maneuver decisively.

As darkness approached, both sides began to disengage; C and B Companies to prepared positions for the night and the NVA, as it turned out, to slip away.

In that short description, meant to be laudatory, we see American units "pinned down" and, while "under heavy fire," unable to "maneuver decisively." The North Vietnamese, on the other hand, commit "more and more units," they "encircle" the Americans, and they "disengage" to "slip away." When one considers that this happened in broad daylight, over the space of a day, that superior American fire support was employed, and that the estimated NVA battalion had at most only a few more men than the two U.S. companies, it somehow doesn't seem quite so "victorious."

Mobility, clearly, is derived from more than physical or technological factors—it is also a state of mind.

In fight after fight, time after time, as a result of American reluctance to maneuver, Viet Cong or NVA leaders decided when to break contact. And they invariably succeeded. Pursuit became a forgotten art; no sizable communist force was ever hounded to its lair and wiped out. In a war of attrition such passive tactics can perhaps be justified by the explanation that many enemy soldiers can be killed at a very low cost to friendly troops. At Loc Ninh, as a case in point, in late 1967, the killed-in-action (KIA) ratio during the first five days of the fighting was several hundred North Vietnamese to eleven Americans. And that is no isolated example. The peculiar political nature of the Vietnam War made those fire tactics expedient, but one should assiduously avoid confusing expediency with doctrine. Sir Robert Thompson, in *No Exit from Vietnam*, wrote incisively, "When lives are at stake it takes a very tough commander, as required in this type of war, who is prepared to risk increased casualties to achieve the right effect rather than hold down casualties (by using massive fire-power) to get a statistical result but the wrong effect. *That the fewer casualties may have been entirely wasted* does not occur to the many." (Italics added.)

The utter dependence on firepower represented a failure of the U.S. system of fighting in Vietnam—a failure, to be sure, which contrarily provided success time and again. Therein, in that paradox, lies a danger for the future: a system which works is seldom scrutinized critically. If the tactics of Vietnam are to predominate in other wars of a similar nature, a far-reaching reorganization of at least some of our combat divisions would seem to be in order. If the mission of infantry is to remain one of finding the enemy, not fighting him, then a structure designed primarily to fight is not the most efficient organization to employ. Something in the pattern of long-range patrols, rangers, or commando units could do the job better and more economically. But a failure to discern and implement needed organizational changes carries far less danger than a failure to recognize the philosophical factors springing from the Vietnam experience. In a future conflict such colossal amounts of firepower might not be available, or the enemy may have equal strength. It has been a long time since the American army has had to cope with a foe on even terms. To enter the next war with the tactics employed in Vietnam could be bloody. Or even disastrous.

Only after leaving Vietnam and becoming army chief of staff, would General Westmoreland recognize the long-range danger. The fighting in Vietnam, he later admitted, produced "a defensive, stereotype, tactical philosophy." He labelled it "firebase psychosis." He would also be obliged to report, "Our company and junior field grade officers and many of our non-commissioned officers, whose sum total of combat experience has been restricted to Vietnam, will require reorientation to overcome such doctrinal narrowness."

The substitution of fire for maneuver, for good or bad, has an analogy in military history. In the days before Rome became supreme, the Greeks had developed a method of fighting built around an organization known as the phalanx. A phalanx was an inflexible formation which could maneuver only with extreme difficulty. The Greek soldiers stood behind a porcupine wall of thickly bristling spears, fully expecting foemen to cooperate by impaling themselves on the protruding pikes. In lockstep and shoulder-to-shoulder, the men of Athens and Sparta marched straight ahead to shatter opposing formations, driving them from the field. The phalanx had shock effect and killing power, but could not maneuver to protect itself or to kill an adversary who refused to stand in front of it. Nonetheless, in its day it was hugely successful.

Then the Romans developed their famous legion, which was designed to take advantage of the weakness of the phalanx. The legion, featuring mobility and flexibility, could maneuver in the heat of battle. In a climactic encounter at Cynoscephalae, the agile legion destroyed the cumbersome phalanx—and ended forever the power of Greece.

History often comes full cycle. In Vietnam the American army replaced the phalanx of spears with a phalanx of fire.

CHAPTER 18

The Search Fails

President Lyndon Baines Johnson, deep furrows of anxiety darkening his already craggy face, leaned forward intently, chin propped on elbows. Across the table General William Childs Westmoreland spoke earnestly of the pressing need for reinforcements in Vietnam. It was not a comfortable topic for either man; both understood only too well the grave domestic and international implications inherent in any further escalation of the fighting. The date was 27 April 1967. The place, the White House. The two had last met six months earlier when Johnson had flown to Cam Ranh Bay to award Westmoreland a Distinguished Service Medal for his outstanding management of the war.

The general had returned to the United States that spring for a brief respite and to report on progress in the war zone. A speaking tour had taken him to West Point, then to New York City, and finally to Washington where he addressed a joint session of Congress. Never once, though, in all his encounters with public or press did he betray the real reason for which he had returned: to convince an irresolute commander in chief to authorize reinforcements. In fact, so well did the general expunge any hint of dissatisfaction from his public words that a key White House aide sent Johnson a memorandum warmly approving of his self-restrained conduct. He had been "a model of discipline in his public pronouncements," the aide said. But, privately, Westmoreland did not mince words. He told the chief executive in blunt, soldierly fashion the bad news he had withheld from the nation—without a major increase in American strength, the war might very well drag on for another five years or more!

"In the final analysis," the general pointedly reminded the president, "we are fighting a war of attrition in Southeast Asia." Defeat is not a real worry, he confidently asserted, but achieving victory will take both time and men; at the presently authorized total of 470,000 troops, at least five years. An increase of 100,000 soldiers would cut that to maybe three years, while adding still another 100,000 might make final success possible by mid-1969. The war could not be lost, even without reinforcements, he emphatically repeated, but progress would unavoidably be at a crawl. The general admitted, in response perhaps to the president's scowl of evident displeasure, that his evaluation did not present "an encouraging outlook but a realistic one."

For nearly two years President Johnson had been listening to repeated Pentagon requests for more and more men. When North Vietnamese soldiers had first entered the South, MACV headquarters had estimated that 100,000 or so Americans would be quite enough to beat them back. That appraisal quickly leaped to 200,000. Then, in the wake of the bloody Ia Drang battles, Westmoreland asked for a 1966 authorization of 400,000, and warned that he may need yet another 200,000 in 1967. The White House had gone along with most of the requests, edging the actual authorization up to nearly 470,000 by the end of 1966. Nevertheless, as Westmoreland had predicted, the Joint Chiefs felt compelled early in 1967 to forward an application for a further increment of 200,000 men. (Their immediate reason for concern was the dangerously overextended deployment of American units. To find reinforcements to counter a grave threat to South Vietnam's northernmost provinces, Westmoreland had been obliged to thin his combat strength elsewhere, thus reducing his ability to secure other crucial areas of the country.) Watching what in retrospect had been a modest initial commitment spiral to a bid for two-thirds of a million men in just two years, with no end in sight, a perplexed president had finally called a stop and had summoned Westmoreland home to explain. That was what brought about the general's April visit to Washington.

"When we add divisions can't the enemy add divisions?" the unhappy political leader asked his field commander. "If so," plaintively, "where does it all end?"

"It appears that last month we reached the crossover point in areas excluding the two northern provinces," Westmoreland replied, rather indirectly. The crossover point he then defined as that moment beyond which enemy "attritions will be greater than additions," past which the Allies will kill more soldiers each month than Hanoi can infiltrate or recruit. From now on, in other words, the campaign of attrition will work progressively and irresistibly against the communists. It is only a question of deciding how long to take, which is in turn a function of how large our force is. In short, if you want victory in the next two or three years, I need the additional two hundred thousand troops.

The President offered no answer at that meeting. As he had done so often before, President Johnson once more put off making the tough decisions. General Westmoreland flew back to Vietnam. His war of attrition remained open-ended.

Disenchantment with the war's progress had surfaced early inside the Johnson administration—and had escalated ever since in tight lockstep with the war itself. In late 1965, only months after the U.S. build-up had begun, Secretary McNamara had first forecast "a military standoff." At the beginning of 1966 Department of Defense officials whispered nervously of "an escalating military stalemate." By the middle of that year Westmoreland himself was describing the conflict as "a protracted war of attrition." Following an inspection visit in October of 1966, McNamara penned pessimistically, "The prognosis is bad that the war can be brought to a satisfactory conclusion within the next two years. The large-unit operations probably will not do it; negotiations probably will not do it." He also wrote broodingly of "the spectre of apparently endless escalation of U.S. deployments." To finish the year off, Harrison E. Salisbury, assistant managing editor of *The New York Times*, went to North Vietnam and filed several sensational anti-war dispatches from Hanoi. From then on a raging, emotional public debate paralleled the intense arguments flaring within the administration. President and public both were becoming uneasily aware of the true, terrible meaning of attrition—that it is gruesomely costly, and achieves results with agonizing slowness if at all. In the White House and in the streets, as the months of 1967 passed by, people asked questions which should have been posed a year and a half earlier. How many men are we prepared to spend? How long will we be willing to continue? What is our objective? What is our strategy? What alternatives are open? A memo from a presidential advisor only stated the painfully obvious when it informed Johnson that "uncertainty about the future size of the war is now having destructive effects on the national will."

The policy of graduated response came under fire as a result of that barrage of questioning. The strategy had done precisely what its critics had always predicted it would—it had extended and confounded the war. General Maxwell Taylor, writing in 1967, said, "The graduated use of military force, which has been an essential characteristic of our strategy, had compounded the difficulties of explaining to our people what we are doing and why it takes so long." The policy's basic fallacy came home painfully to President Johnson when he asked Westmoreland at that White House meeting in the spring of 1967 to explain how increased enemy infiltration would influence U.S. combat operations. The best answer the general could offer was to depict the war as one of action and counteraction: "Anytime we take an action we expect a reaction." In blunt military terminology, Americans had forfeited the initiative to the enemy. One critic put it allegorically:

> Step on my toe and I'll kick your shin.
> Hit me in the thigh and I'll knee your groin.
> Smash me in the belly and I'll swat your spleen.
> Slash my throat and I'll . . .

That colorful description of the doctrine of graduated response was quite near the mark. Which side would back down first was indeed the question: Hanoi under the gradually rising military assault, or Washington under the similarly escalating dissent assault?

Senators and representatives joined the chorus of voices calling for a revised policy. Under probing from the Senate Preparedness Subcommittee in 1967, Army Chief of Staff Harold K. Johnson acknowledged that "military commanders have chafed continually under a relatively low rate of increase of the pressure." When asked if any war in history had been won by a policy of "graduated increase," he said:

> I think the only one that one might equate to the situation in South Vietnam could be our own Indian Wars. Even there, however, the actions taken within given areas had no restraint . . . So I would have to answer your question, "No." When force has been applied, generally it has been applied faster and in greater quantity.

Low opinions of the worth of graduated response seemed to be validated by intelligence estimates telling repeatedly of Hanoi's lack of respect for the policy. After eighteen frustrating months of experimenting with his concept, Secretary McNamara had to admit its unfortunate failure to impress the other side: "Enemy morale has not broken—he apparently has adjusted to our stopping his drive for military victory and has adopted a strategy of keeping us busy and waiting us out (a strategy of attriting our national will)." Half a year later the secretary's spirit had dropped lower still: "Hanoi shows no signs of ending the large war and advising the VC to melt into the jungles . . . [The North Vietnamese] believe the world is with them and that the American public will not have staying power against them . . . They believe that, in the long run, they are stronger than we are for the purpose." At bottom, the theory of graduated response rested on the assumption that the enemy, recognizing his inherent inferiority, would rationally pull in his horns at some point and simply fade away. In the event, however, communists took heart from the cautiously measured way power was brought to bear on them; victory would come, they stoutly believed, because they could absorb the American pressure for years while Washington could not continue meting it out. In that meat grinder war, those feeding the machine felt they could outlast those grinding it. In private, many of President Johnson's advisors agreed with that assessment.

A search for alternatives began. The military had theirs ready: unshackle Sharp's bombing campaign; free Westmoreland to attack enemy sanctuaries in Cambodia and Laos; prepare to enter North Vietnam if necessary to eliminate enemy troop concentrations near the Demilitarized Zone. ("Moderation in war is imbecility!" Admiral Fisher had thundered way back in 1905.) Moreover, that is what the Joint Chiefs of Staff had been recommending from the beginning, as General Earle G. Wheeler pointedly reminded McNamara, "rather than the campaign of slowly increasing pressure which was adopted." The chairman continued, "Whatever the political merits of the latter course, we deprived ourselves of the military effects of early weight of effort and shock, and gave to the enemy time to adjust to our slow quantitative and qualitative increase of pressure." Around the rings of the Pentagon and across much of the nation that "hawkish" stance found considerable support. After all, proponents argued, the inane policies dreamed up by civilian think tanks had utterly failed; it was high time to wage the war by proven military precepts.

Convinced of the futility in continuing the unproductive course of attrition, and appalled at the thought of adopting the military's even more aggressive recommendations, a significant segment of "dovish" policy makers within the administration sought some solution in between. Maybe the most imaginative and interesting of all their ideas—and certainly illustrative of their passive approach to the war—was the wall called "McNamara's Fence."

Through the centuries, from the Great Wall of China to the notorious Berlin Wall, palisades have always recommended themselves to men as methods for keeping others in or out of an area. They are not new to military history, nor to the history of insurgency warfare, nor even in Vietnam history. Three centuries ago a successful pair of walls was erected in Vietnam just a few miles north of the 17th Parallel. The purpose then, too, was to hold back invaders from the north. Other obstructions come readily to mind: Hadrian's Wall in England; British barriers in the Boer War; the De Lattre Line in Indochina; France's inglorious Maginot Line; the modern screen erected in Algeria to block infiltration from Tunisia. Some succeeded, some failed, usually according to the degree of wisdom displayed in constructing and defending them.

When it had first become apparent that Rolling Thunder was not turning off the stream of Northern reinforcements, Defense Department officials resurrected the idea of a wall. A study conducted by the Institute for Defense Analysis in the summer of 1966 included a detailed investigation of a highly sophisticated barrier reaching along the southern edge of the Demilitarized Zone from the South China Sea to Laos and thence westward to the Mekong River. The study proposed dividing the wall into three integrated sections. One, a rather conventional line of battlefield fortifications, defended by troops, would stretch from the sea to the steep hills near the Laotian border. The other two—an antipersonnel belt one hundred by twenty kilometers in area and an anti-vehicle strip of some one hundred forty kilometers—would be saturated with mines and electronic sensors. Aircraft would sow the mines initially and keep the fields constantly replenished thereafter. The sensors would do double duty, detecting hostile movement and guiding attack aircraft in reaction strikes. Although somewhat futuristic—many of the devices were still on the drawing board and were not expected to be available for a year or two—the study became the basic document for developing the wall.

In an October 1966 memorandum to the president, Secretary McNamara officially recommended construction of a barrier.

> . . . perhaps 10,000 [troops] should be devoted to the construction and maintenance of an infiltration barrier. Such a barrier would lie near the 17th Parallel—would run from the sea, across the neck of South Vietnam (choking off the new infiltration routes through the DMZ) and across the trail into Laos. This interdiction system (at an approximate cost of $1 billion) would comprise to the east a ground barrier of fences, wire, sensors, artillery, aircraft and mobile troops; and to the west—mainly in Laos—an interdiction zone covered by air-laid mines and bombing attacks pin-pointed by air-laid acoustic sensors.

He told the president that it could be quite effective in reducing the rate of infiltration and "would be persuasive evidence both that our sole aim is to protect the South from the North and that we intend to see the job through." Forming a top secret task force headed by Lieutenant General Alfred D. Starbird, McNamara began research aimed at building the barrier.

By mid-1967 engineers were erecting parts of the wall and scientists had designed most of the complicated gadgetry necessary to make it work. Nevertheless, although Secretary McNamara personally pushed the project, he never managed to convince his generals of its efficacy. "A jungle Maginot Line," they grumbled, a static defense which would tie down troops and could be by-passed through Laos. So long as Allied forces were denied entry into Laos, the generals said, enemy units could simply slip around their flank to strike at overextended strongpoints—such as Khe Sanh, one of the system's western-most posts. Events overtook the argument while the wall was still in embryo stage, making further debate entirely academic. As it turned out, "McNamara's Fence" never was completed, so it didn't undergo a valid test.

Another strategic option considered—and fortunately rejected out of hand—was the enclave theory. Authors of this concept, who were mostly men outside the government, espoused a rapid withdrawal of all forces to tiny areas near key seaports. There, where all the strength inherent in their superior air and sea arms could have been brought to bear, Allied troops would have been impregnable. In those enclaves they were expected to hunker down, secure behind a wall of wire and fire, the friendly sea at their back, while passively hoping and waiting for negotiations—and in the meantime relinquishing to the Viet Cong the remainder of South Vietnam. The stark military and psychological disadvantages of that plan are painfully evident. Such a situation would have been intolerable. If portions of the South were to be given up, it would have been better simply to hand over all the territory in the northern half of South Vietnam and concentrate on holding the area around Saigon and the delta. That is where the people were. The enclave proposal was, in essence, a camouflaged scheme for surrender forwarded by those who couldn't bring themselves to recommend outright acceptance of defeat, but who also couldn't envision any way to win.

Negotiations offered yet another path to termination of the war. The State Department expended untold effort to that end, all to no avail. The diplomatic history of the war belongs in another book, but suffice it to say here that diplomacy never has had and never will have more than a minuscule chance of succeeding unless both sides can see some possible advantage to negotiating a peace. The war aims of Washington and Hanoi were not in the least reconcilable—the latter's being to conquer South Vietnam, the former's to prevent that from happening. There was no way both could win, no middle ground where compromise could stand. So long as Ho Chi Minh believed he had a chance to outlast the United States, negotiations remained a pipe dream.

Pacification came to the fore again. Quite accurately, Secretary McNamara pointed out in late 1966 that political stability in Saigon had not "translated itself into political achievements at Province level or below. Pacification has if anything gone backward." However, pacification itself was not an answer, let alone a strategy. It was, to be sure, an indispensable ingredient for final success, but one depending first on military security to provide an environment in which it could flourish. No one ever phrased it better than the secretary himself: "The large-unit operations war, which we know best how to fight and where we have had our successes, is largely irrelevant to pacification as long as we do not lose it." Pacification was not panacea.

Some advisors, unable to devise a new strategy which

195

would attain the American objective in Vietnam, toyed instead with changing the objective in order to make the old strategy seem successful. That bit of cart-before-horsemanship failed for the simple reason that the American objective—to prevent a North Vietnamese take-over of South Vietnam—was itself so elemental as to allow no tinkering. The objective could definitely stand clarification, though, a fact McNamara recognized. "The time has come for us to eliminate the ambiguities from our minimum objectives," the defense chief wrote. "Indeed, at one time or another, one U.S. voice or another has told the Vietnamese, third countries, the U.S. Congress, and the public of 'goals' or 'objectives' that go beyond the...bare-bones statement of our 'commitment'." He was right on the mark in that regard. Years of bureaucratic double-talk and official equivocation had opened a major credibility gap between the Johnson administration and the American public. Distrust fed dissent. The people plainly did not understand their country's war aims—and they were vocally unhappy about it. A clearer comprehension of why we were in Vietnam might have helped cool the debate—if it had been possible to impart clarity at that late date. But clarification itself would do nothing to help discover a strategy.

In sum, after all the searching, distraught policy makers could find no viable alternative to the bellicose strategy proposed by the Joint Chiefs of Staff. Moreover, if Washington was unwilling to allow professional warriors to make war professionally, there was no option other than continuing the unpopular war of attrition.

Backed into that dialectic corner, the searchers switched tactics, launching an examination of Westmoreland's management of the ground fighting: was it as effective as he claimed it was and did he really need more troops? Both were penetrating questions which might profitably have been considered long before.

On the score of effective utilization of the manpower

on hand, MACV and General Westmoreland were indeed vulnerable to valid criticism. American soldiers have never been characterized as light travelers, and those who fought in Vietnam were no exceptions. They needed—or, more accurately, were permitted to have—refrigerators, movies, ice cream, PXs, Red Cross girls, air conditioners, tape recorders, their own television and radio stations, free flights to Asian resort areas, service clubs, Bob Hope Christmas shows, hobby shops, and a host of other fringe benefits not usually seen in a combat zone. Never in any war has any force been so munificently pampered. In large measure such an extravagant attempt to hold morale at high peak was necessary in order to counter the deflating impact of anti-war preachings from a growing number of the folks back home, including such traditionally respected members of the community as editors, doctors, teachers, men of the cloth, and elected representatives. It was also an effort to keep American dollars in American hands, an essential if the fragile economy of South Vietnam were to be buffered from an already explosive inflationary spiral. Nevertheless, the sheer size of the effort to furnish entertainment and provide creature comforts was staggering. Russell F. Weigley, in his excellent work, *History of the United States Army*, placed his sharp pen right on the obvious fact: ". . . the conclusion seems inescapable that the effort to maintain an approximation of the American standard of living in the Army and even in the combat zones diverted an excessive amount of manpower away from the essential combat units of the Army."

No one in the military establishment, and certainly no one who had been in Vietnam, could refute the charges of excess staffing and overplush conditions. For every man who lived in a grubby bunker on a remote firebase, four or five slept between sheets and, likely as not, in air conditioned rooms. One might excuse the higher commanders—who in the final analysis permitted the situation to exist—on grounds that

Washington's open-ended commitment never forced them to think in austere terms. Or the opulence could be dismissed as a casualty due to the imperative of maintaining morale. Or, as Westmoreland himself stated, it was a device to "keep American soldiers and their dollars on their bases and out of towns and cities." But the fact remains: the U.S. high command in Saigon was guilty of failing to obtain optimum results from troops on hand. Too many men were wasted on non-essential tasks, weakening Westmoreland's plea for reinforcements, and making the Vietnam War one of the least efficient in our history.

Critics of the war abounded, and some of their criticism inevitably spilled over on General Westmoreland. But the weight of opinion in 1967 was at least grudgingly complimentary of what he had achieved in the vexing predicament in which he had found himself. Generally, even antagonists were obliged to concede that the military had at the very worst muddled through. Overall, the president heard mostly optimistic assessments of the course of the war. His special assistant, Robert W. Komer, returned from a trip to Vietnam in February 1967 with a report typical of most the White House received from informed visitors:

> The cumulative change since my first visit last April is dramatic, if not yet visibly demonstrable in all respects. Indeed, I'll reaffirm even more vigorously my prognosis of last November [that we will in time just overwhelm the Communists]. Wastefully, expensively, but nonetheless indisputably, we are winning the war in the South. Few of our programs—civil or military—are very efficient, but we are grinding the enemy down by sheer weight and mass.

Another key assisant, McGeorge Bundy, wrote that preventing a communist victory had been "the great and central achievement of these last two years. The fact that South Vietnam has not been lost and is not going to be lost is a fact of truly massive importance in the history of Asia, the Pacific, and the U.S." What is more, Westmoreland himself was popular outside the government. *Time* had made him "Man of the Year" for his performance in the war; he had been selected as one of America's ten best dressed men despite his habitual appearance in jungle fatigues; the press praised his sincerity; the public acclaimed him. All told, President Johnson was well satisfied that his field commander had indeed achieved prodigious results under trying circumstances. So it was no surprise when the president decided to let the ground war continue on the course Westmoreland had set.

But how many more troops should he get? The general's spring request for another two hundred thousand men had raised a violent reaction in Washington, precipitating a debate which dragged on through much of the summer. Granting that request, argued John McNaughton, McNamara's influential assistant secretary, "falls into the trap that has ensnared us for the past three years. It actually *gives* the troops while only *praying* for their proper use . . ." The philosophy of the war should be decided now, McNaughton continued, "so everyone will not be proceeding on their own major premises, and getting us in deeper and deeper." He thought Johnson should give Westmoreland a limit, just as Truman had done to MacArthur, and tell him, "That will be all, and we mean it." McNaughton was absolutely correct. It is the job of the president to set national objectives and to prescribe the resources available to attain those goals. By leaving the commitment open-ended, Johnson in effect invited his generals to waste their energy arguing for increases when they should more properly have been getting the most out of assets at hand. McGeorge Bundy chimed in to support McNaughton, ". . . as a matter of high national policy there should be a publicly stated ceiling to the level of American participation in Vietnam, as long as there is no further marked escalation on the enemy side."

Closely related to the lavish American mode of living in Vietnam, and another factor strongly militating against an increase in force levels, was the rampant inflation racking South Vietnam. Westmoreland and the Joint Chiefs, fully recognizing the seriousness of this problem, worried constantly that the very troops needed to protect South Vietnam militarily would torpedo the Saigon government economically. MACV instituted extreme measures to curb the fiscal chaos, but they were never more than marginally successful. To understand the magnitude of the threat, imagine the United States with an agrarian economy severely strained by the pressures of a long, internal war. Then picture the impact if about seven million young men, each earning the equivalent of one hundred thousand dollars a year (tax free), were turned loose in the country. Now suppose the government of those young men should go on a building and hiring spree in the United States at a rate somewhere in the neighborhood of our entire gross national product. Even our mature economy would have difficulty withstanding the shock. The economy of South Vietnam barely did.

Then, too, there was a large body of opinion holding that the South Vietnamese were not doing all they could to help themselves. Sending still more men to South Vietnam when Saigon had not mobilized completely was patently unpalatable to a president who had campaigned for election on the promise that "American boys wouldn't do what Asian boys should do for themselves."

President Johnson had other factors to consider as well. The international situation cast a somber shadow across his desk, while the troubled domestic waters churned with economic, social, racial, and political whitecaps. In June the ever volatile Middle East erupted in the Six Day Arab-Israeli War, and that was the same summer in which Russian Premier Alexei Kosygin came to America. The dictates of international politics alone wouldn't let the commander in chief dispatch another two hundred thousand men, while national politics were even more demandingly restrictive. Johnson knew that another escalation in Vietnam would exacerbate all his manifold headaches at home.

For another thing, just finding a fifth of a million more fighting men was itself a problem of major proportions. Manifestly, sending another two hundred thousand men to Vietnam meant calling up the reserves. The regular army was neither organized nor prepared to wage a war on the scale of Vietnam—while maintaining its readiness elsewhere in the world—without at least a partial mobilization. The Joint Chiefs had asked for a call-up of nearly seven hundred thousand reservists in 1966, and had repeated their demand periodically. But, from first to last, the president refused to take that step. Politically it may have been feasible in 1965 or very early 1966. But, as the war and the accompanying debate waxed hotter, it became less and less acceptable to the public. Historian Weigley recorded the irony of the situation: "After all McNamara's efforts to heighten the readiness of the National Guard and the Army Reserves, when an apparently appropriate hour struck the Secretary of Defense hesitated to call upon them." Weigley went on to note the paradox of draftees going to Vietnam "while other young men long since trained and shifted into reserve components remained safely at home." Whether such a situation was fair or not, with an election year coming up the president simply did not dare mobilize in 1967. After all, the politician in Johnson admonished, even so drastic an act of mobilization, by General Westmoreland's very own estimate, would not bring a victory before the voting booths were scheduled to open in November 1968.

Hence, examined from every conceivable angle,

there was just no way President Johnson could even so much as seriously consider sending another two hundred thousand men to Vietnam. Inescapable realities around the world, inside America, and in Vietnam had done for him what he had never done for himself—had set a ceiling on U.S. involvement in the Vietnam War.

In July 1967, McNamara flew to Saigon to inform Westmoreland that reinforcements in the quantities he wanted would not be forthcoming, but that some lesser number was negotiable. Their discussions were interrupted by the death of Westmoreland's mother; after the funeral President Johnson told the general that he would get an increase of about fifty thousand troops, which raised the authorized strength to five hundred and twenty-five thousand. That figure was established solely as the total after adding another increment, not as an absolute ceiling. General Westmoreland's view had not changed since his April talk with the president: results attained would be a function of resources committed. To him it remained merely a matter of how soon Washington expected victory; the more men available, the sooner it would come. He still felt he needed two hundred thousand additional soldiers in order to finish the war in from two to three years.

Westmoreland placed no special significance to it at the time, but that number—two hundred thousand—would return painfully and with force early in the next year.

And that is how the search for a strategy ended. Policy makers had been unwilling from the beginning to execute the war with military decisiveness; they still demurred as 1967 faded. They had been unable, however, to discover an alternative course, which remained the case as American combat forces approached the end of their third year in Vietnam. The president had never clamped a lid on the level of involvement, letting the war remain open-ended, although the general no longer had *carte blanche* and events themselves seemed to be establishing a limit on commitment. Westmoreland's war of attrition, costly and time-consuming though it was, had reached the point where ultimate victory could be glimpsed. He got the green light to continue. The next year and the years after that were programmed to be reruns of 1966 and 1967. More of the same. Attrition. The search for a strategy had failed.

PART IV

THE CLIMACTIC YEAR

1968

MY YEAR

CHAPTER 19

The History Teacher

Hanoi's high command began changing its collective mind in 1967. In fact, providing one of the war's more curious coincidences, General Giap and President Ho were seeking alternatives in April in Hanoi at the same time General Westmoreland and President Johnson were huddling in Washington. But, while the Americans unimaginatively opted for more of the same, the North Vietnamese elected to strike out on an audacious, novel strategic course in a Herculean effort to win the war. That bold 1967 decision led to bitter 1968 fighting—which in retrospect proved to be the climax of the Vietnam War.

General Nguyen Chi Thanh, Hanoi's capable battle leader, had long been arguing staunchly though unsuccessfully against his nation's policy of vying with Americans in a macabre struggle of attrition. Time stood squarely on the side of the enemy, he thought. Living with his men in a Cambodian base area just beyond the South Vietnamese border, General Thanh had a stark, close-up view of Allied military might which was difficult if not impossible to transmit accurately to distant Hanoi. Thanh's countrymen far to the north saw firsthand only the oddly ineffective American aerial bombardment; Thanh himself knew the terrible weight of Allied tactical firepower and recognized the significance of American mechanized mobility. Seen from his ringside vantage point, it was evident that communist forces would never be able to fashion a battlefield victory over such a vastly superior enemy. What was worse, despite his sanctuaries in Cambodia and Laos, and regardless of the dedication or courage or agility of his troops, defeat after bloody defeat had been General Thanh's lot. Westmoreland's search-and-destroy operations had methodically, massively, irresistibly sliced into communist strength. To continue, the pragmatic Thanh believed, was utterly futile. Only losses and more losses and eventual defeat waited along the present path. The Ho Chi Minh Trail was a one-way street of death.

In 1966, General Thanh had been unable to sway his superiors in Hanoi. They had stubbornly insisted on pressing the protracted fight in the South. Gradually, though, as 1966 ended without a single victory over the hated Americans or their Saigon "running dogs," the politburo began to reexamine its strategy. Mounting battle casualties and a cascade of Allied successes in the first half of 1967 accelerated that reassessment. Too, continued pounding from the air, though still endurable, was beginning to have serious impact on the national nerves. And, most disheartening, unprecedented reverses in the process of the insurgency against the Southern regime contributed to the new search. Across South Vietnam, public sentiment had shifted visibly away from the Viet Cong as prospects for governmental stability in Saigon steadily improved. There had not been a coup or even a serious threat of one since Nguyen Van Thieu had become chief of state with Nguyen Cao Ky as prime minister some two years earlier. Ho's followers had less and less reason to hope for a gratuitous collapse in Saigon. The trends were definitely against it. Reluctantly, but realistically, a majority of the high command members swung around to General Thanh's view that a new strategy was indeed necessary.

But, having agreed to change, the individuals comprising the politburo promptly disagreed on the method. One faction wanted to escalate the fighting in an attempt to gain a decisive victory; another, strongly influenced by the sobering observation of General Thanh, urged adoption of a more prudent course. This cautious group thought that the war should be phased back to the initial stages of revolutionary warfare, that the communists should stop grappling with Allied forces in costly engagements, that negotiations could remove American planes from North Vietnamese skies and extricate Allied troops from South Vietnamese lands.

Essentially, the disagreement was over the key temporal question: for whom did time work? Giap and others of his ilk sensed that time was on the side of the enemy, that a continuation of the protracted war of attrition would lead inevitably to defeat. After all, the mushrooming death rate in the South was approaching the birth rate in the North. Some two hundred thousand youths reached the age of seventeen each year in North Vietnam, not all of whom were physically qualified to become soldiers. Of those, many were required to perform other essential tasks. Already the crossover point had been reached—each month about as many soldiers died in the faraway fighting as the North was able to train and send southward. In the long run, that baleful fact pointed to an obviously intolerable situation. No, Giap concluded, we cannot win over the distance—but we can achieve victory by shortening the length of the race, by mounting a "continuous, comprehensive offensive."

The opposition argument, articulated by Truong Chinh, claimed that time was actually the only thing favoring the communists. Never, he said, can we beat the Americans in a slugging match. Our only hope is in patience. They can be outlasted but not outfought, outwaited but not outmaneuvered. Victory will belong to the side which can endure the longest, not to the one winning a big battle, or even a dozen big battles. The answer, as Chinh, the long-time theorist, saw it, lay neither in a new offensive nor in a continuation of attrition warfare; rather, it could be found in the normal doctrine for revolutionary warfare—and that doctrine said to bend under pressure, to phase back to a lower level of intensity.

Although the last vestiges of internal dissent were not quieted until bombs from a B-52 killed General Thanh that summer, the politburo expressed its generally militant consensus in Party Resolution 13, approved in April 1967. Urging a quest for "decisive victory in South Vietnam in the shortest possible time," party leaders resoundingly rejected their previous concept of protracted warfare while advocating an adventurous, go-for-broke policy. Douglas Pike, a respected authority on both the Viet Cong and the North Vietnamese, termed that new policy a "regular force strategy." In essence, the regular force strategy shifted Hanoi's balance of emphasis in the war from political to military considerations, from a goal of undermining the Allies' position to one of seeking their outright defeat.

Important to note, in that regular force strategy resided an element of irrationality. Even years afterward, one finds it singularly amazing that Hanoi's leaders could realistically have contemplated defeating in battle the United States of America, the world's most powerful nation. Pike explains it as "the point where logic touches ego." For Ho and his contemporaries, the unification of Vietnam was more than a political struggle, it was a spiritual crusade. And, just as they had succeeded in the face of all odds before, they had faith in being able to do it again. Nevertheless, revolutionary zeal did not blind them to the inexorable march of the years. Ho Chi Minh was seventy-six, his cohorts not much younger. Being old men, they could no longer believe the calendar worked for them. Time, the staunch ally of their youth, was the implacable foe of their gray years. Ego said victory was possible; logic said it would be best to hurry.

On Friday, 7 July, the top dignitaries of the North Vietnamese government assembled for the funeral of General Thanh. Aides had taken his body from their blasted jungle headquarters to an airport near Phnom Penh, the Cambodian capital, from where it was flown to Hanoi. His burial signified an end to an era. Before the flowers had faded on his grave, the politburo had made its final decision to launch an all-out, win-the-war offensive early in 1968. It was expected to be the year of triumph, the year when North and South would become one.

While mourners in Hanoi listened to General Thanh's funeral eulogy, Secretary of Defense McNamara was arriving in Saigon to inform General Westmoreland of the Johnson administration's decision to continue the war of attrition at its then current level. As a disgruntled Westmoreland settled down to a continuation of his meat-grinder campaign, an eager General Giap geared up to launch the most spectacular offensive of his spectacular career.

Vo Nguyen Giap, portly, fifty-five years old, a revolutionary all his adult life, had become a self-taught soldier after he was thirty. From the very first he had been Ho Chi Minh's saber, a cool, ruthless fighter who had shrewdly conducted and won the national struggle to oust the French. His was the single most authoritative military voice within the politburo, which is to say in all North Vietnam. With the decision firmly made to strive for a military victory, it was no surprise that he should be appointed to command the grand effort.

An ex-teacher of history, and a life-long disciple of that discipline, Giap did not need to thumb very far through the pages of time in search of inspiration. He simply reread the narrative of his own climactic campaign against the French in 1953 and 1954. Finding himself unable at that time to defeat the technologically superior French forces massed about Hanoi and other population centers, Gaip had launched a peripheral campaign designed to scatter his foe into the hinterlands. His intent was to fall upon and annihilate a major force which might foolishly venture too far from support. Banking on the evident war weariness saturating France, he had calculated that wiping out a large enemy unit would be enough of a military catastrophe to collapse the will of Paris. The French commander had taken the bait, blundering into Dien Bien Phu and disaster. Shock waves from the fall of that fortress had secured the independence of North Vietnam, assuring the fame of General Giap.

Now, fourteen years later, he prepared to repeat his triumph. He would teach his foes a history lesson. If his strategy had worked against the French, it could work against the Americans. First, a peripheral campaign to distract attention and to draw troops away from densely populated areas and out of mutually supporting distance. Then a smashing victory akin to Dien Bien Phu. After that a caving-in of the American will to continue. It could work.

Giap was a bold but not a blind gambler. He calculated real chances for success. First, concerning the Americans, he formed three assumptions. He believed U.S. strength could not (or would not) be raised above the numbers already committed; he concluded that the Johnson administration would not loosen its strategic restraints on the American war machine; and he hypothesized that anti-war sentiment in the United States, especially in an election year, would force political leaders to throw in the towel following a communist victory. The first two were generally correct, and as events were to disclose, the third was not at all far-fetched.

As for the South Vietnamese, Giap formulated two assumptions, neither of which was illogical. To begin with, the ARVN, scathingly and repeatedly described as "the army that won't fight," could be expected to provide little serious resistance and might even disintegrate in the face of a sudden, fierce onslaught. Next, the people of South Vietnam, when confronted with a victorious communist army, would rise up as one to overthrow the remnants of the Saigon regime. Oddly, Giap had fathomed the American spirit more accurately than he had that of the South Vietnamese; his assumptions about U.S. reactions were remarkably accurate, while those pertaining to the people and army of South Vietnam turned out to be dead wrong. But, at the time, all five of his basic assumptions looked good. He therefore began energetically building for an offensive to open in January or February of 1968.

The first indication the rest of the world had that something different was brewing in the Vietnam pot was when Northern forces suddenly and inexplicably initiated a series of bloody battles in remote areas along South Vietnam's borders.

October opened with American attention drawn to a besieged marine base at Con Thien near the Demilitarized Zone. It took massive doses of artillery, tons of napalm, and waves of B-52 bombers to discourage the determined North Vietnamese attackers. Then communist shock troops streamed across the Cambodian border not far from Saigon to assault the district capital of Loc Ninh, a rubber plantation town on Highway 13 in Binh Long Province. A few miles to the east, Song Be came under violent attack. General Westmoreland had earlier in the year sent reinforcements scurrying to the Demilitarized Zone; he now promptly rushed reserves to the Loc Ninh and Song Be area. Bitter fighting continued there until November. Next, North Vietnamese units struck Dak To in Kontum Province, a strategically chosen target in the Central Highlands near the juncture of the Cambodian, Laotian, and South Vietnamese borders. For twenty-two days that battle raged, becoming a magnet attracting elements of the 4th Infantry and 1st Cavalry Divisions, as well as the entire 173rd Airborne Brigade and six ARVN battalions. December saw the largest battle fought up to that time in the delta. The widespread combat that autumn was characterized by unusually heavy casualties and a strange enemy persistence in mounting mass attacks.

The border battles had cost North Vietnam dearly. Human loss had been staggering. But Giap was not bothered by that. "Every minute, hundreds of thousands of people die all over the world," he once said. "The life or death of a hundred, a thousand, or of tens of thousands of human beings, even if they are our own compatriots, represents really very little." To him the important thing, the only thing, was results achieved. He had those. Many American forces were scattered all over South Vietnam, mostly in distant areas far from centers of population. Partly that was a result of the deliberate Allied plan to send U.S. units into enemy base areas, partly it was a result of the instinctive desire of American commanders to engage the North Vietnamese, and partly it was a result of Giap's peripheral campaign to pull them even further into remote stretches.

Using his sanctuaries skillfully, Giap had managed to prolong each of the bloody encounters, making possible a long run of sanguinary headlines in American newspapers. Beyond question, the border battles were excellent attention grabbers. Which was precisely what the North Vietnamese commander had intended. He had not really dispersed the Americans in any meaningful physical sense, for Westmoreland's ability to displace entire divisions by air meant that no unit could ever be left without assistance. And the overwhelmingly massive fire support always available was itself often able to destroy enemy attacks in the very act of staging. But, in a powerful psychological sense, Americans had indeed been scattered when their attention was riveted to the borders.

Several of Westmoreland's key staff officers gradually became uneasily aware of the haunting resemblance between the 1967 peripheral battles and those of 1953 which had led to Dien Bien Phu. General Giap had stoked their curiosity by issuing a statement in September explaining that his plan was to draw Allied forces to the borders, ostensibly to free guerrillas and local forces to attack unprotected populated regions. But that explanation was too pat. No believable picture emerged from the unusual enemy activity, which seemed more suicidal than reasoned. Puzzled intelligence analysts finally concluded that the border battles would fit a discernible, logical pattern only if a clash in the style of Dien Bien Phu should result. However, not only was no such situation at hand, there seemed no likelihood of one developing.

Then, as if by magic, overnight, one emerged. Khe Sanh, a marine base on a plateau near the corner formed by the Demilitarized Zone and the Laotian border, came under sudden siege. Two years earlier, Khe Sanh had been a tiny, bunkered fort manned by an American special forces detachment and some two hundred local mercenaries. Their purpose had been to keep tabs on enemy infiltrations from Laos. Then, in 1966, General Westmoreland and Lieutenant General Lewis W. Walt, the burly commander of marine forces in Vietnam, had flown together to the isolated post for a personal look. Intelligence sources had detected North Vietnamese troops massing only a few miles to the west where jungle-clad mountains climbed swiftly into the clouds. Overlooking Route 9, Khe Sanh sat astride the natural invasion path to the populous lowlands. Westmoreland and Walt decided to shift the irregular occupants and their special forces advisors to a base farther west, to enlarge the small, dirt airstrip, to bring in artillery, and to garrison Khe Sanh with U.S. Marines. Then, early in 1967, communist forces did in fact attempt to brush by the strongly entrenched post in an effort to link up with other elements for a combined assault on Hue, the ancient Vietnamese capital some fifty miles away.

They occupied the hills north and west of the airstrip. Walt quickly counter-attacked with the 3rd Marine Regiment. After heavy fighting, he retook the hills, successfully blunting the Northern drive. From then until the ominous build-up began in late 1967, Khe Sanh had remained quiet, just one more scarred site of a forgotten battle of the Vietnam War, not much different from any of a hundred other such locations.

Now, however, Khe Sanh awakened abruptly from its anonymity to become the most widely discussed battleground of the entire war. Two NVA divisions painstakingly worked into position to encircle the camp, while heavy artillery, hidden in caves in the nearby ring of hills, began to rain shells down on the leatherneck defenders. North Vietnamese artillerists pounded the base incessantly while infantrymen began digging approach trenches closer and closer to the American perimeter. The similarities between Khe Sanh and Dien Bien Phu, in terms of both terrain and enemy action, were eerily striking. American commanders were mulling that coincidence over when intelligence officers excitedly identified the two NVA divisions. The 325C Division was one, an ordinary outfit. But the other was an elite Hanoi guard division, the 304th. The 304th was renowned as the victor of Dien Bien Phu!

Public interest flared. The press leaped on the story. An Australian journalist wrote of the "Dien Bien Phu Gambit"—making a series of wide-ranging and seemingly disconnected attacks to dilute attention and divert reserves, all the while methodically preparing for a key battle at yet another location. American headlines bannered the fighting at Khe Sanh, television news programs reported on it nightly, columnists investigated all aspects of it. Enjoying an enigmatic private laugh, General Giap let out the word that he was in the field and in personal command of the siege. Public and official attention intensified.

President Johnson became virtually mesmerized by developments at Khe Sanh. In the White House situation room, the basement command post reserved for supreme crises, he had aides construct a minutely accurate photomural of the marine base. Lapping over several tables, the huge mosaic showed trenches, gun positions, bunkers, ammunition dumps, and other local details, as well as the latest activities of the encircling North Vietnamese.

By mid-January the president's war room also boasted a terrain model of the battle area and a memorandum on the marines' defensive plans prepared by the chairman of the Joint Chiefs of Staff. It is possible that the president in Washington had a better view of the developing battle than did anyone other than the commander of the Khe Sanh garrison himself, Colonel David E. Lownds. As Don Oberdorfer wrote in his vivid book, *Tet!*, "The President and [Presidential advisor Walt] Rostow were mentally in the trenches with the boys." And when the commander in chief mans the barricades, his entire entourage gets mental mud on their boots. It is hard to keep an eye on the big picture while hunkering in a bunker. For the administration, and for the nation, the war in Vietnam that fretful January of 1968 was seen through a microscope focused on Khe Sanh.

In the early hours of 21 January 1968, communist storm troops, following close behind a heavy artillery barrage, assaulted one of Khe Sanh's outposts, Hill 861. The attackers managed to penetrate the barbed wire entanglements, but were beaten back in fierce hand-to-hand fighting. That was the opening blow in a continuous encounter which would last for seventy-seven days. The long build-up was over; the long battle had begun. Having picked up the North Vietnamese gauntlet, having decided to defend the outpost in spite of its symbolic and actual likenesses to Dien Bien Phu, the United States could not, simply could not, permit the position to be taken. Reinforcements went in. Westmoreland began sleeping next to his combat operations center, keeping a round-the-clock vigil. He shifted electronic sensors from the Ho Chi Minh Trail to the approaches to Khe Sanh. He ordered the 1st Cavalry Division northward. And more marines. Devastating air raids, including repeated B-52 bombings, brutally punished the besiegers. In all, nearly one hundred thousand tons of bombs fell around the camp. Still the NVA persisted. Giap launched bombardment after bombardment, increased his anti-aircraft defenses, crept closer and closer with approach trenches and tunnels, moved tanks up to pose a frightening new threat, but held back the final rush. The beleaguered defenders waited anxiously for the big push while a fascinated America watched the entire, unfolding drama on television. It was the suspense thriller of the season.

The president harried General Wheeler for assurances that everything possible was being done to defend the base. "I don't want anybody coming back and saying if we had had this and that we would not have suffered so many losses," he said. With an election looming he was haunted by the terrible thought of a defeat in the style of Dien Bien Phu. The Pentagon's professional soldiers shared Johnson's concern, but not his fear. Khe Sanh in 1968 was not Dien Bien Phu in 1954. In just hours at Khe Sanh, for instance, Allied fliers could stagger Giap's troops with more tons of explosives than the French could in all the weeks of the siege of Dien Bien Phu. The American military felt supremely confident in its ability to protect Khe Sanh; in fact, the generals rather eagerly hoped Giap would go ahead and launch an all-out assault. Nonetheless, the president was not satisfied. In one of the most humiliating gestures any American political leader has ever inflicted on his military aides, Johnson extracted from the head of each military service a public pledge that he could hold Khe Sanh. That promise, "signed in blood" as he allegedly put it, served no practical purpose other than to set up the military establishment as the scapegoat should the six thousand men defending the battered marine base be overrun and lost.

Meanwhile, in Hanoi, General Giap was smugly satisfied with his handiwork. He had never had any intention of capturing Khe Sanh. His purpose there all along had been to divert Westmoreland's attention and resources. Khe Sanh was a feint, a diversionary effort. And it had accomplished its purpose magnificently.

While the rest of the world watched the extravaganza at Khe Sanh, Vo Nguyen Giap, perhaps one of the world's most brilliant generals, looked elsewhere. The history teacher had his eyes on a Dien Bien Phu all right, but a far larger and more decisive one than was represented by Khe Sanh.

CHAPTER 20

General Offensive— General Uprising

The idea of a general uprising was an article of faith. It was every bit as vital to the early revolutionary movement in South Vietnam as was, perhaps, the belief in the second coming of Christ to the early Christian movement in Southern Europe. It served to inspire the insurgent, to provide him a vision of victory, to enthuse him to battle, to bestow martyrdom on him should he fall. Viet Cong propagandists, according to Douglas Pike, grandiloquently described the general uprising as "that golden moment when the spirit explodes simultaneously in all the villages of the country." They portrayed it as the glorious spectacle of an entire people arising at once to thrust off tyranny. It was the orgasm of revolution.

From the very first, insurgents in South Vietnam had accepted as absolute truth the concept of a general uprising. It was the guiding principle of Viet Cong guerrillas from 1959 through 1963. By terror, sabotage, assassination, and selected military operations they aimed at sowing social anarchy across the land, at creating conditions favorable for the general uprising. A document captured in 1963, at the time when President Diem was tottering in the face of Buddhist unrest, spoke glowingly of the onset of a magnificent insurrection in which the cities of South Vietnam would rise in support of the rural areas as singing peasant masses marched against the urban centers. But it never came about.

By his 1964 decision to invade the South, Ho Chi Minh in effect had chosen to reach for a rapid military victory rather than to wait for the slow germination and ultimate blooming of the general uprising. Of note, though, he did not forsake the faith entirely, for it remained a very necessary trumpet summons for true believers. He had merely intended to achieve unification through swifter and more ordinary means. But, because of American intervention, success eluded the old revolutionary. By 1967 he had sorrowfully if belatedly conceded the failure of his military efforts and was earnestly searching for a method to break out of the resulting battlefield stalemate.

Having always hoped for the miraculous advent of the general uprising—which would unquestionably and quickly have ended the military deadlock of 1966 and 1967—Ho Chi Minh set out with determination to make it happen in 1968. He planned to nudge the inevitable.

That was Giap's secret, his new Dien Bien Phu. By sudden, stunning, large-scale assaults across the land—what he called a general offensive—the North Vietnamese commander planned to precipitate the long-awaited and much heralded general uprising. He code-named his plan TCK-TKN (the initials of *Tong Cong Kich—Tong Khoi Nghia*, or, "General Offensive—General Uprising").

Without doubt, Hanoi was quite right in its reasoning about the far-reaching, beneficial results of a general uprising. Should the people of South Vietnam suddenly unite in a spontaneous revolt to rattle the rule of Saigon, proclaiming their universal desire for peace under some convenient front organization, and indicating profound disdain for the economic and martial efforts of foreigners in their land, then America and other Allied nations would have but one recourse—to withdraw from the war. In the United States, Lyndon Johnson was finding the war exceedingly difficult to justify as it was; it would be patently impossible to do so in the wake of a general uprising. Being thus deprived of outside support, finding its population openly hostile, the government of Saigon could not stand. The revolution would be triumphant.

Basically, then, General Giap's grand strategy was to achieve his political ends by social means. Fortunately for him, the foundation for such a movement already existed in the deep-seated and widespread belief in the phenomenon of the general uprising. He started with that much accomplished. His problem, therefore, was to ignite the long-anticipated social upheaval, to find a catalyst to stir the emotions of a people.

While fabricating their strategy, in the late spring and summer of 1967, Giap and his fellow planners astutely recognized three limiting tactical realities: First, Allied forces, and especially the Americans, were unbeatable in a toe-to-toe slugging match; second, the people of South Vietnam would be quite unlikely to respond with the necessary spontaneity to an offensive conducted in the main by North Vietnamese troops and, third, surprise was absolutely necessary in order to shock the Saigon government into numbness and the Southern people into line. Accordingly, the plan which emerged called for avoiding enemy military strength, advocated using local units to the maximum, and established extreme measures to achieve deception.

As the grandiose scheme took final shape it split into three distinct parts. The first, to be fought mainly with North Vietnamese troops, was the peripheral campaign designed to distract and overextend the Allies. This was the deception phase. It would be waged in remote areas, far from population centers; that is, far from the people, the ultimate target. To be effective, battles during this phase had to be large, long, and costly. Eminently newsworthy. They had to grip the enemy's mind, to attract his attention and overpower his imagination. In sum, the border battles comprised a huge feint. There is no precise word in Vietnamese for that particular maneuver; they describe it as a "one point, two front" tactic. That one point, the people, never varied, but Giap purposefully kept the initial fighting far from the population. Meanwhile, as North Vietnamese soldiers died dutifully by the thousands at places like Dak To, Loc Ninh, and Khe Sanh, Viet Cong units infiltrated into positions around the cities. There, finding Allied units and interest drawn to the first front, they prepared methodically and clandestinely for the second. For TCK-TKN.

In areas close enough to the cities to permit rapid development, but just far enough away to avoid detection, Viet Cong units drilled carefully. They broke out and distributed new Russian AK-47 assault rifles and B-40 rockets. Massive shipments of those weapons had arrived through Cambodian ports late in 1967 and had gone directly to waiting guerrillas inside South Vietnam. Supply officers built stocks of food and medicine and ammunition to the highest levels ever. Local agents dropped covers which had concealed them for years to join and strengthen regular Viet Cong units. Leaders read and reread instructions. Propaganda teams prepared leaflets. The painstaking, incessant activity was clearly a sign of something unusual, something big. Everyone sensed a major event in the offing. Each one knew what his personal role was. But no one knew when it would happen or what the overall picture was. Just that it would be soon, that it would involve hard fighting, probably in several cities, and that the general uprising and final victory would follow.

At a propitious moment those waiting Viet Cong troops would surge into the unsuspecting and vulnerable cities, bypassing where possible all military units or positions which might provide serious resistance, to seize symbols of government such as radio stations, administrative buildings, police stations, bureau offices, and political headquarters. Once ensconced in the hearts of the towns, they would announce the fall of the Saigon regime, proclaim the establishment of a new coalition government, extend amnesty to all ARVN soldiers who might elect to join them, and coordinate the joyous uprising of the people, who were expected to be quick to express their natural antagonism to Saigon and intense hatred of Americans. For that latter purpose, to arouse the people, political agitators and organizers would enter the towns right alongside the soldiers. By thus breaking into every principal city in the country, all at once, the communists fully expected the resulting shock to trigger both the collapse of Saigon and an immense, popular swing of support to the Viet Cong. The ARVN would probably simply melt away through mass desertions, though it was entirely possible that large segments would switch sides to join the Viet Cong. Further, and of supreme importance, once inside the cities, sheltered amidst non-combatants, the attackers would be immune to the devastating Allied firepower. They would therefore be able to hold whatever they could grab.

The United States, faced with a *fait accompli* of major proportions—an evaporated South Vietnamese army, a crumbling government in Saigon, an aroused and hostile countryside, and communist occupation of every large city in the land—would have no option but to retreat ignominiously to coastal enclaves and prepare to debark.

Then, the final phase would commence. North Vietnamese troops, rested and refitted after the border battles, would storm out of their sanctuaries to help the Viet Cong wipe out any remaining pockets of resistance and to assure the final success of the entire campaign. (And, incidentally, to assure continued control by Hanoi.) In short order they would be able to consolidate all gains made during the general uprising.

North and South Vietnam would be reunited. The long war would be over. The revolution would be victorious.

Thus ran Ho Chi Minh's scenario. It was a complicated plan, a costly one, but also one entirely feasible. It depended for success on General Giap's genius at organization—and on the validity of Hanoi's five assumptions about the Americans and the South Vietnamese. Those assumptions, once made and accepted, had to stand or fall on their own. The organization of the drive for victory, on the other hand, required Giap's exclusive guidance, his unique touch. North Vietnam's first soldier assumed personal command of the entire operation.

In May and June of 1967, even prior to the politburo's final decision, Viet Cong leaders, acting on orders from Hanoi, had reorganized their territorial commands and tactical units into the configuration they would later employ to attack the cities. About that same time they formed another political front to display the banner of coalition. Replete with its own distinctive flag, the new front announced its christening as the "Alliance of National, Democratic, and Peaceful Forces."

After the decision in July, the Hanoi high command issued instructions permitting lower level cadres to be brought in on a part of the big picture. Carefully trained discussion leaders spread out in August to begin detailed indoctrination of Viet Cong officials. As North Vietnamese soldiers played their sacrificial role that autumn in the slaughterhouse battles along the borders, South Vietnamese insurgents labored diligently to master the meaning of a small booklet entitled, "For an Understanding of the New Situation and the New Tasks."

Although the pamphlet gave no specific plan or time of execution, it told the party faithful that the struggle would take the form of intense, large-scale attacks. In the first of its four sections, it announced that the ultimate Viet Cong objective was to seek an end to the U.S. presence in Vietnam through formation of a coalition government. Part three was an assessment of why the Americans were now more vulnerable than they had previously been, while part four was a candid and accurate accounting of communist shortcomings. The significant second section listed three tasks: 1) destroy the U.S. military and political positions; 2) cause the collapse of the ARVN; and 3) promote the general uprising. Outlining virtually everything except the precise scheme of maneuver and hour of attack, that booklet depicted the entire second portion of Giap's three-phase plan—the part he called TCK-TKN, and which has come to be known popularly as the *Tet* offensive. Americans captured a copy on 25 November 1967, two months and five days before the offensive began. Unfortunately, analysts interpreted it as just another propaganda tract.

While North Vietnamese units carried out the suicidal operations scheduled in the first phase, and their Viet Cong compatriots girded themselves for the nation-wide assault which would signal the beginning of the second, Allied headquarters remained wholly ignorant of Giap's overall scheme.

Not that there was any shortage of indicators. They abounded. Too many people in too many places knew the broad outline of the plan for it to be kept secret. Moreover, except for the crucial details of when and where, Hanoi made no unusual effort at secrecy. By late 1967, Allied intelligence maps showed large shifts being made by most major Viet Cong units. District and regional forces were known to be consolidating. Captured documents and other indicators provided almost constant warnings of pending attacks against cities. Prisoners corroborated the evidence, many of them willingly admitting that they fully expected to achieve total victory sometime in the next several months. Northern newspapers spoke rather freely of a coming campaign of historic dimensions. Giap himself had gone on record in September as predicting heavy fighting leading to ultimate victory.

Other kinds of indicators raised storm flags as well. The flow of Viet Cong soldiers voluntarily returning to the government, a torrent in 1966 and early 1967, had dried to a trickle by the end of 1967; clear evidence that communists were promising victory and their troops were believing it. Progress in the all-important pacification program, ever a true barometer of popular faith in the future of the government in power, braked almost to a halt—testimony that appreciable numbers of the pragmatic peasantry were taking a wait-and-see attitude. The rate of guerrilla and terrorist incidents in densely populated areas surged sharply upward; undeniable indication that increased numbers of a more aggressive enemy lurked amidst the people.

In what just might be the most ironic footnote to the war, the U.S. mission in Vietnam, on 5 January 1968, within a month of the approaching holocaust, published and distributed in the form of a press release a captured document which proved to be the general instructions for the *Tet* offensive. "Captured Document Indicates Final Phase of the Revolution at Hand," was the headline given the release. Translated in full and attached to the release, the enemy paper proclaimed that "the opportunity for a general offensive and general uprising is within reach." Although not saying when it was to occur, the communist author did explain how the general offensive should be conducted:

> Use very strong military attacks in coordination with the uprisings of the local population to take over towns and cities. Troops should flood the lowlands. They should move toward liberating the capital city, take power and try to rally enemy brigades and regiments to our side one by one. Propaganda should be broadly disseminated among the population in general, and leaflets should be used to reach enemy officers and enlisted personnel.

The press release pointedly called attention to the paper's mention of a general uprising and its announcement of attacks on major towns and cities.

Finally, after Giap began his theatrical siege of Khe Sanh on 21 January, field operators began picking up all sorts of unusual information. In Qui Nhon, for example, police arrested several Viet Cong agents on the twenty-eighth. Concealed among their belongings was a tape to be played over the Qui Nhon radio station after its capture, exhorting the populace to join in the general uprising. A communist offensive, the tape announced, had captured all key cities in South Vietnam, obliging the United States to agree to a coalition government in Saigon. Allied forces, in yet another instance, captured the actual Viet Cong operation order for the attack on Pleiku. The plan boldly and immodestly included provisions for a mammoth victory parade along Pleiku's main street.

A military history textbook, printed in 1969 and used by cadets at West Point in their study of the Vietnam War, says, "The first thing to understand about Giap's *Tet* Offensive is that it was an Allied intelligence failure ranking with Pearl Harbor in 1941 or the Ardennes Offensive in 1944. The North Vietnamese gained complete surprise." The cadets got the word straight and unvarnished.

But why should the Allies have been surprised? Why did commanders ignore the ample evidence available to them? The answer is more psychological than military, more emotional than professional. They were victims of their own sturdy optimism and of General Giap's shrewd staging of his deception campaign.

Ever since the turning point at the Battle of the Ia Drang, the fighting had been going well for the Allies. They had won every encounter. North Vietnamese and Viet Cong forces plainly were unable to overcome the firepower and mobility edge possessed by the Americans. By late 1967, Allied forces were near the peak of their strength while the communists were staggering noticeably, especially after their most recent maulings. It was inconceivable that the battered foe could bounce off the mat to deliver a punch capable of knocking out his opponent, incomprehensible that he should even want to try. Articulating the attitude of the vast majority of military men in Vietnam, a U.S. Army intelligence officer, who had seen and discounted all the evidence of an offensive against the cities, was quoted as admitting, "If we'd gotten the whole battle plan, it wouldn't have been credible to us." That Hanoi should launch an all-out assault was as unthinkable as if a chess player, about to be checked in a championship tourney, should suddenly send board and pieces flying with a sweep of his hand and leap across the table to grab his opponent by the throat. The Allied high command simply did not believe the evidence.

The other reason, of course, as presented in the previous chapter, was General Giap's superb execution of the first phase of his plan. By fixing his enemy's attention on the border areas, the North Vietnamese leader had splendidly masked his real intentions. Both Westmoreland and Washington, as a matter of fact, were so preoccupied with Khe Sanh that for several days after the *Tet* offensive began there persisted a strong fear that the attacks on the cities were diversionary, designed to divide Allied strength so that an assault against the marine base could be successful. Blinded by the ruse, officials could not see the reality. The deception plan had worked. Perfectly. Indeed, there exist in military history few examples of so effective a feint.

In mid-November 1967, President Johnson summoned General Westmoreland to Washington. Doubts concerning the war's progress had eaten deeper and deeper into the marrow of the country. On one hand the president and other officials announced repeatedly that everything was fine; on the other the war went interminably on and on and on, never really seeming to come under control. Habituated to thinking of warfare in terms of Patton's pursuit through France and MacArthur's turning movement at Inchon, Americans could not comprehend the tortoise pace of progress in Vietnam—which was in truth no more than the anticipated harvest of a non-strategy of attrition sown between the fencelines of a limited war. Westmoreland's difficult task was to help convince a dubious nation of the correctness of the American course in Vietnam.

In a series of interviews and addresses the dutiful general more or less successfully accomplished his mission. "We have reached an important point when the end begins to come into view," he said. Announcing the dawning of a new phase in the war, he told the American people what they wanted to hear: the fighting was progressing so well that it could soon be turned over to the South Vietnamese. Moreover, he added, the time to begin that turnover was not more than two years away. Claiming that he had never been so encouraged or optimistic at any other moment during the previous four years, he stated flatly, "We are making real progress."

At that time, most Americans wanted to support their president, but were troubled mainly by the unanswerable contradictions presented by dissenters to the war. What the erect, serious, straightforward career soldier said made sense to most people. He possessed credibility, which was enhanced when he honestly admitted the unpleasant fact that it would be two more years before American soldiers could start coming home. Okay. The public could accept that. The important things were that everything was all right, that we had the other side on the run, and that it would all be over at some predictable point. There was light at the end of the tunnel. That was certainly good news to hear straight from the mouth of the general who commanded all the boys over there. The public restlessness receded. General Westmoreland returned to the war zone leaving a somewhat mollified nation behind him.

But he had been wrong. The enemy tide had not yet reached its high water mark. The new year would usher in a new phase, true enough, but not the one he had described in Washington.

Not long after Westmoreland returned to Saigon, Ho Chi Minh read a poem over Radio Hanoi:

> This spring will be far better than any spring past,
>   As truth of triumph spreads with trumpet blast.
> North and South, rushing heroically together, shall smite
>   the American invaders.
>   Go forward!
>   Certain victory is ours at last!

Allied listeners in the South supposed it to be merely a propaganda message. Communists, however, heard it for what it was—Uncle Ho's personal order to launch a general offensive to spark the general uprising. The moment for TCK-TKN was at hand.

CHAPTER 21

Unexpected Callers

Tet is the Vietnamese holiday celebrating the arrival of the Chinese lunar new year. But it is much more than just that. Imagine the Christmas season in the United States, throw in Easter, New Year's Eve, All Soul's Day, then add the Fourth of July for good measure, and you are close to what *Tet* means. It is also family reunion time, a spring festival, a week-long national holiday—and everybody's birthday.

In 1968 the first and most holy day of *Tet* fell on 30 January. Beginning the evening before and lasting for the better part of a week, revelers would welcome the Year of the Monkey.

Historically, in all the years of the war, *Tet* had been a time of peace, an announced or assumed pause in the fighting during which antagonists on both sides laid aside weapons to visit their families with a reasonable assurance of immunity. For a few days people could almost forget the war. No one expected *Tet* of 1968 to be any different. No one, that is, in Saigon or Washington.

Now, to be sure, both of those capitals were on edge in the waning days of January. Giap's show at Khe Sanh had seen to that. Moreover, Allied intelligence analysts had not totally ignored the flood of data crossing their desks, they had only misinterpreted it. There were simply too many indicators to overlook entirely—the enemy was evidently preparing for something big. Everyone in the business tended to agree that the North Vietnamese had a major attack up their sleeve; and most of them concurred in the prevailing belief that Khe Sanh was the most likely candidate for such a blow. Assaults elsewhere were not to be unexpected, but they would probably be nothing more than diversionary efforts. A few months later, General Westmoreland would state that he and his staff had foreseen some kind of major enemy offensive near *Tet,* but he also honestly admitted, "... we did not surmise the true nature or scope of the countrywide attack." His claim, of course, was true; he fully anticipated an effort against Khe Sanh with scattered secondary attacks erupting at other points in the country. His staff agreed with him. Intelligence experts disagreed among themselves, however, on one important matter: half of them thought the offensive would fall before *Tet* while the others believed it would come afterwards. Military action during *Tet,* and particularly on the first day, was simply inconceivable. But that was precisely what General Giap proposed to do. D-day for the general offensive was set for early on 30 January 1968.

A closer reading of Vietnamese history could have helped analysts in this case. The greatest Vietnamese feat of arms, with the exception perhaps of Dien Bien Phu, was the epic surprise attack launched by Nguyen Hue against the Chinese occupiers of Hanoi during *Tet,* 1789.

According to Vietnamese custom, one's luck in the succeeding twelve months is determined by the personality of the first person to come calling on *Tet's* opening day. For most residents of most cities in South Vietnam, that visitor was slated to be a Viet Cong soldier, his calling card an AK-47 assault rifle.

Sometime after mid-January, Viet Cong cadres and

troops began drifting into the cities. They came by tens and by hundreds, bringing along arms and ammunition—and they completed that furtive maneuver virtually without detection. Weapons arrived in the beds of carts overflowing with flowers destined for the holiday celebration, mixed in with truck loads of vegetables and fruit, even in caskets carried in mock funeral processions. The men themselves were more open. They simply joined the hordes of legitimate *Tet* travellers. Some, dressed as ARVN soldiers, brazenly hitched rides on U.S. trucks returning empty from supply runs. GI drivers were known to be happy to help their likable little comrades—and policemen never thought to check troops being transported by Americans. Others openly entered towns riding motor scooters or bicycles. Buses brought more. Many, of course, slipped in by back ways during darkness. Not all made it. In fact, relatively large numbers, including a few rather high ranking officials, blundered into captivity. But that didn't strike intelligence officers as overly unusual; after all, *Tet* was the season to return home, to visit friends, to call on relatives.

Meanwhile, January saw a few key shifts in Allied troop dispositions as well. Reserves sent northward in reaction to the threat against Khe Sanh bolstered the cities in that area, of course, while weakening defenses elsewhere. The major move, however, was in the American defensive posture around Saigon.

Lieutenant General Fred Weyand, field commander in the sector, had grown increasingly uneasy as he studied the incoherent pattern of enemy activity in the vicinity of the capital. Charged with the responsibility of protecting the approaches to Saigon, he took more literally than most the communist boasts of occupying the sprawling city. On 10 January he called on General Westmoreland and convinced him that something unusual might be afoot. After their conference, Westmoreland issued an order redeploying several American combat battalions from their forward positions on the

Cambodian border and near base areas. For the time being they were told to fall back nearer to Saigon. That last-minute shift of about fifteen battalions represented one of the most critical decisions of the war. On the eve of *Tet* there were, as a result of Weyand's worry, some twenty-seven U.S. maneuver battalions close around Saigon. That fact might have been what saved the city. It certainly was a prime factor in the fighting which followed.

Hanoi had one last card to play in its deception phase. Holiday cease-fires had become more or less an accepted feature of the war, especially at *Tet* time. Far in advance, and with great fanfare, Viet Cong headquarters had announced a seven-day truce to last from 27 January to 3 February. Then, just four days before they intended to kick off their offensive, National Liberation Front spokesmen publicly, piously appealed for a scrupulous observance of the stoppage. They enticingly hinted that the truce might even be extended. The bait of a permanent armistice, implicitly contained in the plea, was all the more credible because diplomats wanted to see it there. For their part, the Allies would play it straight—they expected the other side to do the same.

Past cessations had always been marked on the communist side by frenzied, logistical activities and scattered minor breaches, but never had either side conducted major military maneuvers. Allied generals didn't like the idea of granting truces, for it gave the enemy a free opportunity to resupply. But they didn't object so vociferously on grounds of the threat posed to local security. Saigon announced its own pause, which was to run only 36 hours from 29 to 31 January. An exception was made in the area near Khe Sanh, where no respite was programmed.

A significant clue to enemy intentions passed without note. North Vietnam changed the date of *Tet* by government decree. Instead of beginning on Tuesday, 30 January, the holiday opened in Hanoi on Monday, the twenty-ninth. Ostensibly, the reason had to do with the relative positions of heavenly bodies; actually, it was a means to allow Northern families a chance to celebrate *Tet's* most sacred day, a chance which was to be denied Southerners. Ho Chi Minh fully expected retaliatory bombing of his own urban areas for the damage he was about to inflict on Southern cities, and he didn't want his people to be caught unprepared in the midst of a holiday.

As *Tet* approached, Allied operations gradually tapered off. Most troops looked forward to a few days' rest. About half the men in South Vietnam's armed forces received passes. Diplomats wondered wistfully if the temporary truce might not lead to something more permanent. The American public happily contemplated a brief vacation from casualty reports. But, even as Allied soldiers relaxed, the bloodiest battles of the entire war were almost upon them; while Americans were standing down from operations, Viet Cong units grimly eased into attack positions.

South Vietnam's cease-fire went into effect at 1800 hours on 29 January. Except at Khe Sanh, Allied soldiers went to bed anticipating their first restful sleep in weeks. Not counting the persistent popping of firecrackers, the night was quiet at first. Then, shortly after midnight, slumber was shattered by the thunderclap of Hanoi's most imaginative and most nearly successful campaign. The *Tet* offensive had begun.

Fortunately, something had gone wrong with Giap's coordination at the final moment. Until the very last, he had withheld from most of his subordinates the crucial data concerning the date of the offensive and the nation-wide nature of the attacks. To assure surprise, he had not dared publish that information prematurely. His secretiveness did in fact guarantee surprise, but it cost him that degree of close coordination upon which success also depended. Making the problem even worse, it became necessary for him to order a few late changes in objectives and timing. Not everyone got the word. Instead of a simultaneous blow, therefore, the assaults came piecemeal over a period of several days. Poor communications, the necessity during the days before *Tet* to hide from Allied reconnaissance elements, weak leadership in several instances, and a lack of overall understanding combined to disrupt his ambitious scheme. Had all battles commenced as planned that first night, the outcome might well have been different. As it turned out, most Allied forces were granted from a few hours to a few days to brace for the storm. And, in view of their vast technological superiority, a few hours were all they needed.

Still and all, it was a near thing. To harried staff officers attempting to piece together a pattern from the spate of alarming reports suddenly flowing in, it appeared that all South Vietnam had exploded. During that first night and for the next several days, furious fighting erupted in nearly every population center. It was a rare airfield or headquarters complex which did not sustain at least a mortar bombardment. Many suffered serious attack. Surfacing within the defenses they had managed to infiltrate successfully, or savagely assaulting from without, Viet Cong elements broke into just about every important provincial capital and large city in South Vietnam. Startled defenders, unprepared and at reduced strength, frantically sought to recover from the shock to organize hasty defenses. Initial casualties were heavy.

In full-scale ground assaults, on that first day of *Tet*, communists struck five provinces in the center of South Vietnam—Kontum, Pleiku, Binh Dinh, Darlac, Khanh Hoa—and one farther north, Quang Nam. The next night they assailed Saigon and seven more provinces—Quang Tri, Thua Thien, Quang Tin, Quang Ngai, Binh Thuan, Vinh Long, Phong Dinh. After still another day, eight additional provinces felt the sharp sword of the general offensive—Tuyen Duc, Binh Duong, Kien Tuong, Bien Hoa, Dinh Tuong, Kien Hoa, Vinh Binh, Kien Giang. Thereafter, attacks trailed off sporadically, with Bac Lieu being the last province hit a full twelve days after the opening blows. The general pattern was from center to north and back again to the far south. All told, the Viet Cong attacked or fired upon 36 of 44 provincial capitals, 5 of 6 autonomous cities, 64 of 242 district capitals, and 50 hamlets. Additionally, they raided a number of military installations, including almost every airfield. A total of about 70,000 determined shock troops conducted the initial attacks. Thousands more stood close by to reinforce.

Anticipating being hailed as liberators, and expecting to see the ARVN tuck tail and run, Viet Cong leaders were sorely disappointed on both counts. The ARVN, taken unawares, operating at half-strength or less, fought as it had never fought before. Rather than causing Saigon's forces to disintegrate, the massive incursion had quite the opposite effect. It rallied them. Fighting in defense of their homes and towns, South Vietnam's soldiers showed a spirit and toughness surprising to most observers, especially to the North Vietnamese. The general uprising proved to be a complete myth. The people of South Vietnam took not the first step to assist their unwelcome *Tet* callers. They rose, but in revulsion and resistance to the invaders.

The *Tet* Offensive

CHAPTER 22

The Battles of Tet

The Viet Cong failed in most towns to carve out a defensible niche. Bloodily repulsed, the would-be conquerors retired to the hinterlands just days—in some cases, hours—after the offensive began. However, in several locations they were initially more successful. They snatched at least partial control of ten provincial capitals and caused severe damage elsewhere. At Hue, die-hard attackers clung to the ancient capital until 25 February, forcing South Vietnamese and American troops into some of the fiercest city fighting seen since World War II. Parts of Dalat remained in hostile hands until 9 February, while other units, isolated in the Cholon suburb of Saigon, were not eliminated until mid-February.

The battles of *Tet,* all going on at once countrywide, provide an overall picture of Allied technology and tenacity overcoming communist surprise and offensive spirit. The military panorama is one of a fighting Allied recovery from the initial astonishment and an unhappy Viet Cong reaction to the abrupt failure of its win-the-war offensive. But that is in the big picture. Each separate battle was a special vignette, differing from all the others in style and tone. The tale of three—Saigon, Hue, Dalat—will present at least a partial view of all.

Saigon had not been hit on the first day. Celebrations continued uninterrupted. So secure did everyone in the city feel, moreover, that the startling attacks against several provincial capitals farther north caused scarcely a ripple of nervousness. Allied officials duly noted the unexpected offensive and took perfunctory steps to increase their local levels of security, but, deep down, they didn't really expect to become involved. During that second night the streets were thick with happy people. The war, as always, was a long, long way from Saigon.

But, in the midst of that carnival atmosphere, a small group of men—not more than twenty—made final preparations for an attack which would shock the world. In a garage a few blocks from the new American Embassy, those men, members of Sapper Battalion C-10, quietly loaded weapons and explosives into a battered taxi and a small truck. They tensely received their mission: to break into the embassy of the United States of America. It didn't matter what they did once inside; theirs was not a military objective. The purpose was simply to make a psychological gesture. Driving slowly toward the embassy grounds, at 2:45 A.M., they knew their chances of survival were slim.

As the vehicles approached the large front gate, a gunman in the taxi opened fire on the two U.S. military policemen guarding the entrance. The soldiers returned the fire, leaped inside the compound, swung shut the heavy iron gate and locked it. At 2:47 A.M. they radioed an emergency code to announce the raid and summon help. Working rapidly, the sappers exploded a plastic charge against the wall, blowing a hole three feet high. Squirming quickly through their new entranceway they entered the compound, guns blazing. Before they were killed themselves, the two military policemen shot two or three of the sappers, most importantly the platoon leader. The sappers were inside the compound. Hastily getting their bearings, they raced for the embassy building, reaching it just as the huge teak doors slammed shut in their faces.

Guards in the building, alerted by the gunfire, had reacted in time to bolt the door and seal themselves inside. The frustrated sappers poured a fusillade of rifle and B-40 fire into the lobby, but decided against blasting their way into the building. Without precise orders from that point, and leaderless, they milled around in the courtyard, exchanging desultory fire with the few Americans in the six-story structure, and waiting for developments. Some were already dead. Several others were incapacitated with wounds. All were doomed. Military police reinforcements arrived about dawn to rush the front gate while airborne troopers landed by helicopter on the rooftop chopper pad. The last sapper was shot to death at about 7:00 A.M. Their foray had lasted all told some four hours. They had killed five Americans, had caused minor damage to embassy property, and they had been wiped out. However, they had been hugely successful, probably even beyond their wildest dreams.

Confused and inaccurate wire reports reached the United States just in time for the evening news on television. With no time to verify the facts, broadcasters put out a garbled version. Astounded viewers heard that communists had captured the U.S. Embassy. Consternation is the only word to describe the immediate public reaction. An American Embassy, supposedly secure in downtown Saigon, had been captured! Incredible! "What the hell is going on?" an amazed Walter Cronkite, the dean of newscasters, is said to have roared. "I thought we were winning this war!" It mattered not at all that the misleading reports later were corrected. By then the fuller realization of the entire extent of Giap's general offensive had crowded retractions out of the public consciousness. All that registered was that Vietnam was aflame, that our embassy had been captured, that a war reportedly won now wobbled on the perilous edge of being lost. The Viet Cong were to suffer thirty thousand dead in the first ten days of the *Tet* offensive—none would achieve as much as the twenty who blew a hole in the embassy wall and survived inside the compound for four hours.

Although the embassy attack initially occupied the lion's share of news coverage, it was actually a very small part of the enemy's attempt against Saigon. In all, some eleven local force Viet Cong battalions marched against various objectives in the capital city. Reserves waited outside, poised to rush in to exploit any success attained by the storm troops. But there was no success to exploit. Assailing Tan Son Nhut Airbase, the presidential palace, the Vietnamese Joint General Staff compound, the giant airbase at Bien Hoa, and numerous other targets, that first wave was almost uniformly repulsed. In addition to the American Embassy grounds, enemy soldiers penetrated the headquarters complex of the Vietnamese high command and the back side of Tan Son Nhut Airbase. They were quickly ejected from both. In Cholon, the Chinese sector of Saigon, enemy units set up headquarters in a race track and entrenched themselves among the hovels of that teeming part of town.

American and South Vietnamese units moved rapidly to clear the entire city and its approaches. By the end of the first day, General Westmoreland had committed five American battalions to the task inside the city. He sent in two more on the second day and ordered others to block highways leading in to the battle area. By 6 February fewer than a thousand attackers remained in isolated pockets of resistance, mostly in Cholon. As their compatriots in the embassy grounds had been, they were leaderless and lacking instructions. There had been no plan of retreat, nor any consideration of alternatives. They had been so sure of victory that defeat had been incomprehensible, unmentionable. In the next few days all of them either died or donned civilian clothing to fade into the population. The battle of Saigon was over for the time being.

It was fortunate for the people of Saigon that communist political commissars had no opportunity to remain in their midst more than a few hours. They had arrived with a license to kill. In their packs they carried sheaves of official NLF death certificates having blanks for date, name, and crime. All that was required was to insert a person's name; he could then be summarily executed in the name of the revolution. That the forms were intended to be used was demonstrated at Hue, where the communists remained long enough to begin a blood bath.

Hue, like Saigon, was not attacked until the second night. Like Saigon, too, it was unprepared despite a full day's warning. Hue's defenders, though, were not able to beat off the city's assailants. Communists, gaining a firm foothold, accomplished their aims there.

Hue is actually two towns. The interior city, called the Citadel, is a walled fortress patterned after the Imperial City at Peking. A rough square, about two miles on a side, built on the banks of the Perfume River, the Citadel once served as the residence for Annamese emperors. It contains many ancient and revered structures, including the imposing Palace of Peace. One of the few cultural shrines the Vietnamese have, the Citadel is protected by an outer wall sixteen feet high and varying in thickness from sixty to over two hundred feet.

Brigadier General Ngo Quang Truong, commander of the ARVN 1st Division, held a special flag raising ceremony at his headquarters in the Citadel on the morning of 30 January to mark the arrival of the Year of the Monkey. Right afterwards, he received the disturbing news of the first wave of attacks elsewhere in the country. Cautiously, but not showing undue concern, General Truong heightened his division's alert status and decided he and his staff would sleep that night in the Citadel headquarters. That precautionary step saved Hue by keeping intact Truong's command setup and by preventing the 1st Division from being surprised. The general did not know it, but sappers were already inside the city. Having sneaked in two days earlier, they were anxiously awaiting the arrival of two Viet Cong regiments.

Those regiments, the 5th, commanded by Lieutenant Colonel Nguyen Van, and the 6th, commanded by Lieutenant Colonel Nguyen Truong Dan, were moving stealthily toward Hue even while General Truong was holding his New Year's ceremony. In all, the eight battalions of the two regiments had seventy-five hundred men, including both Viet Cong and North Vietnamese soldiers.

About 2:00 A.M. Colonel Dan's men, aided by dense fog and guided by accomplices inside the city, slipped undetected into the outskirts and headed directly for their objective, the Citadel. At 3:40 A.M. they surged into one section, surprising sentries and gaining an immediate bridgehead. Colonel Van's 5th Regiment, meanwhile, having been delayed by a South Vietnamese ambush, hurried to join them. Failing to coordinate their operation, and encountering unexpectedly ferocious ARVN opposition, the two regiments had occupied only a portion of the Citadel when dawn came. They found themselves sharing the sturdy fortress with General Truong's stubbornly resistant ARVN troops. Perhaps two full Viet Cong battalions held the crucial central part of the Citadel. As they consolidated their newly conquered position, other battalions fortified sectors of the outer city, particularly the area south of the Perfume River. At 8:00 A.M. unhappy Allied officers saw a huge Viet Cong flag fluttering defiantly from the main flagpole in front of the Palace of Peace.

Straightway, Allied forces counterattacked. American marines, South Vietnamese paratroopers, and South Vietnamese armored troops tried to root out the invaders. They failed. That first attempt set the pattern. Day after day Allied units endeavored to shove the obstinate communists out of the Citadel and to loosen their bulldog grip on the adjacent part of the outer city. But they found the positions too tough to take without absorbing prohibitive casualties. They were extremely reluctant, also, to damage the highly valued cultural center by bringing heavy weapons to bear on the entrenched foe. As a result, the fighting was largely house-to-house, hand-to-hand, bloody, and quite drawn out.

Because the Allies had insufficient forces at hand to seal the penetration completely, the Viet Cong commanders retained an ability to evacuate casualties, reinforce, and resupply. Strength enough was available nearby to cut them off, but it was not committed. Still fearful that Giap would attempt to overrun Khe Sanh, Westmoreland held a string on his strategic reserve in that area for a couple of weeks after the *Tet* offensive began. With opposing sides so evenly balanced, the battle lasted a week, then another, then yet another. It was easily the longest of the *Tet* battles.

Having uncontested control of a good portion of the population for nearly a month, Viet Cong political leaders had an unusual opportunity to display the style of liberty entailed in communist "liberation." Brutally but efficiently they murdered some three thousand persons who might have had any influence in the city. Drumhead courts sentenced the unfortunate victims, many of whom had been selected for death ahead of time. Executioners then lined them up in groups by hastily dug mass graves where they were shot, bludgeoned, bayoneted, or merely buried alive. The slain included intellectuals, local officials, civil servants, policemen, priests and nuns, teachers, businessmen, whatever foreigners could be found, and not a few women and children. Entire family units were eliminated in an effort to purge the old social order. Execution, of course, was a communist solution of long standing, but never before had it affected so many people for so long a time.

Frustrated by the snail's pace of the fighting, and worried by the rumors of unhindered slaughter of civilians, the South Vietnamese government finally decided to commit heavier firepower. Starting on 7 February, planes began bombing everything outside the Citadel walls. On 14 February, jets struck the Citadel itself. From then on it was just a matter of time. At last, when elements of the U.S. 1st Cavalry Division managed to sever the enemy supply line, communist commanders began to plan a withdrawal. On the night of 23 February they launched a counterattack to cover their departure. Next morning, for the first time since 31 January, the Viet Cong flag did not fly above the Palace of Peace. The beautiful city of twenty-five days ago was a shattered, stinking hulk, its streets choked with rubble and rotting bodies.

Hue was a costly struggle for all sides. American and South Vietnamese units together lost over 500 killed, while Viet Cong and North Vietnamese battle deaths may have been somewhere between 4,000 and 5,000. Civilian casualties, in addition to the 3,000 or more murdered by political agents, were surely higher than the 2,000 tallied. A whopping 116,000 were made homeless. The clash there also had a markedly adverse impact on public opinion in the United States. Because of the major role played by U.S. Marines, and the grim scenery, evoking ghostly memories of shattered European towns during World War II, television camera crews had a prolonged bonanza. Day after day viewers saw American fighting men locked in bitter battle with a foe who just weeks before was supposedly beaten. It didn't look like a war that was won.

The fighting in Dalat had none of the shock effect of combat in Saigon. Indeed, few people outside of Dalat were even aware of events there. Nor did it produce the casualties and devastation witnessed in Hue. But, for those very reasons, it was perhaps more representative of the battles of *Tet* than either Saigon or Hue.

Dalat, sitting amidst pine forests on a stream-laced plateau nearly a mile high, is a cool, mountain resort city. It is more like a French Alpine village than a Vietnamese town. Remote, surrounded by verdant peaks, the quiet city was a haven for educational institutions, tiger hunters, and honeymooners. It had been untouched by the war, a tranquil backwater whose residents felt wholly removed and totally secure from the turmoil ravaging the rest of their country. When the first day of *Tet* brought news of aggression in several nearby provinces, the people of Dalat hardly knew, or cared. When the attacks spread over the country on the next day, they were alerted, curious, but remained unworried. After all, theirs was a resort town, not a battleground.

Colonel Philip J. Erdle, head of the Department of Engineering Mechanics at the United States Air Force Academy, had arrived in Dalat on 26 January. He was on brief loan from the Air Force Academy to help the fledgling Vietnamese National Military Academy prepare a four-year course of study. Sleeping soundly on the second night of *Tet* in a sprawling villa which had been occupied by U.S. advisors ever since Diem had deposed the emperor, Erdle had no dreams of combat. The crisp night air was just like that which he was accustomed to in Colorado; the peaceful environment, as well, was snugly familiar. About 1:45 A.M. another officer banged excitedly on his door. "Get up! We're being mortared!" Groggily the academician muttered, "What do you mean—I'm here to write a curriculum." Before the professor would put pen to a new curriculum, though, he was scheduled to log a few unscholarly combat missions.

Under a barrage of mortars, the 186th Viet Cong Battalion crashed past weak outposts to occupy the southwestern sector of town. Fortuitously, one self-defense squad detected their preliminary movements in time to alert the provincial headquarters, permitting the province chief a few precious moments in which to man all his defenses and to repulse enemy efforts to overrun his complex. A local force Viet Cong company of perhaps a hundred men, entering from the north, raced quickly for the center of town, the Hoa Binh Square and market. Reaching their objective with no opposition, the marauders stopped, waiting—in vain as it turned out—for the rest of their battalion to join them. Communist political agents with the company began organizing for an election designed to establish a facade of legality of NLF claims of a complete takeover of the town.

The province chief, finding himself invested at multiple points, had no uncommitted forces to counter the unit in the market. His few troops were already tied down defending key installations around town. Anxiously, he turned to the superintendent of the military academy for help. Although he had troubles enough of his own, the superintendent recognized the pressing need to clear the city center before the Viet Cong could stage any sort of an election. He sent two understrength regional force security companies, having about forty men each, and a company of freshmen cadets (the other classes were gone on holiday). The cadets dropped off at a large French school building to occupy a blocking position while the regional force companies rendezvoused with their newly designated commander, Major Dao Mong Xuan, the deputy province chief.

Major Xuan, his force of two weak companies and two armored cars in hand around noon, surveyed his tough mission. Communist defenders outnumbered him, and they had been barricading their positions for hours. Worse, many friendly civilians were caught in the area, meaning Xuan could not use heavy weapons. On the plus side, however, the local people had absolutely refused to assist the unwanted visitors. Many slipped out to give information on enemy dispositions; others resisted passively. Further, Viet Cong soldiers were more or less disoriented in their strange surroundings while Major Xuan and his men knew the area intimately—Xuan's home was located there. Finally, and most fortunately, the enemy company had no outside means of assistance. The remaining forces on the northern side of town had stopped in the outskirts where they had dug themselves in. They would be able to defend their positions stoutly, but were beyond supporting distance of the troops in the market. All in all, Xuan had the advantage. Using loudspeakers to warn the people and to urge Viet Cong soldiers to surrender, he started his operation shortly after noon. There would be no communist election in Dalat that day.

The Modern Hotel, overlooking the market area, was a large, multistory building catering to the American GI trade. Establishments of that sort invariably sprang up on the fringes of every concentration of U.S. troops in Vietnam. There one could relax from the rigors of war with massages, steam baths, stateside steaks, and sex. The Modern had an especially erotic reputation placing it high on the soldiers' list of places to visit in Dalat. Hence, despite the ban on military movement during *Tet*, several Americans were spending the night there when the Viet Cong moved into Hoa Binh Square. Having planned to escape from the war for at least a night, they woke up to find themselves right in the middle of the melee by the market. Which was another lucky break for Major Xuan. From their high perch on the roof of the Modern, they set up a steady sniper fire against any Viet Cong who exposed himself. Combat they had not bargained for, but, in a way, doing battle from a bordello was in itself a new thrill. Discovering that they could still use the city telephone system, the Americans, showing commendable initiative, kept the South Vietnamese commander abreast of enemy activities in the streets below them.

Those men, though missing from their own units, were certainly invaluable throughout the day, and deserved high praise, but when Major Xuan later tried to get their names in order to decorate them he was quite surprised at their modesty. Not one cared to be cited for his service.

Around 1530 hours, a lone American helicopter gunship flew over to help. Xuan contacted it by radio, forbade the pilot from using rockets, and directed him to pin down the enemy with machine gun fire. With that skimpy support, he kicked off his final attack shortly before four o'clock. Using the two armored cars, he broke past the hostile barricades and knifed through the enemy position. Then, from house to house, he methodically dug out the Viet Cong company. By dusk Dalat's business center was once again in friendly hands. Major Xuan had lost only one man killed and two wounded; the enemy left twenty-two bodies.

Expecting the 145th Viet Cong Battalion to reinforce him momentarily, the commander of the 186th ordered his men to fortify the high ground they had occupied near the Pasteur Institute, a modern industrial complex for the manufacture of vaccines for all Southeast Asia. Having failed to overrun the city, but lacking authority to withdraw, the Viet Cong waited. A standoff developed. The attackers had insufficient strength to grab more of the city, but the Dalat defenders were too weak to throw them out. On 2 February the antagonists mostly just watched one another. On the third a motley collection of regional force companies, led by Major Xuan, fresh from his success at the Hoa Binh Market, tried to dislodge the Viet Cong. Xuan pushed the enemy away from the Pasteur Institute, but fell back in turn in the face of a counterattack. That was the pattern of fighting for the next several days; five times in all Major Xuan liberated Pasteur Institute, only to lose it each time. The very tardy 145th Battalion arrived, but too late to do much good, for Xuan's strength had also increased. Had the battalion's commander shown more initiative and come sooner, the two units combined could conceivably have overwhelmed the almost defenseless city.

In the meantime, Colonel Erdle had found all the excitement he had missed during his years in the academic world. Observation planes were parked at a nearby airfield, but, in the confusion of the city fighting, the pilots could not be located. Knowing Erdle was a flyer, an American officer who was helping coordinate the defensive efforts sent him aloft to direct fire. Flying a small, single-engine spotter plane, and working with a very unfamiliar radio, the erstwhile professor directed jet air strikes on hostile positions, controlled attacking helicopter gunships, and even helped out with artillery adjustment. He was a long way from a sedate classroom at Colorado Springs.

Unable to exploit their initial successes, the Viet Cong could endure the unequal exchange of fire for just so long. When the South Vietnamese assaulted again on 6 February, led once more by the redoubtable Major Xuan, they encountered a much less determined foe. Main force units began a withdrawal during the night of 7 and 8 February, leaving only local force elements holding the northern sectors of the city. Friendly forces massed against them, forcing their retirement after another two days. By 10 February, Dalat was secured. Of the thousand enemy soldiers who had entered a week earlier, most had become casualties. Over two hundred bodies lay amid the wreckage they left behind.

Major Xuan had eaten only bread for a week. Haggard but happy, he sat down to a big dinner. Colonel Erdle returned to his curriculum study.

At that point only Saigon and Hue still had any resisting enemy elements.

Casualties in Dalat had not been especially heavy—fewer than fifty deaths—and, for the most part, fighting had not been hard. Considerable damage had been done to a part of the city, mostly by air and artillery strikes, but even that was acceptable. There were, when all the accounting was done, only two great results of the affray in the resort city. To begin with, the previously complacent citizenry was for the first time made to feel involved in the war effort. From then on the people had a recognizable stake in success. Second, the local insurgency movement suffered a devastating loss when it surfaced to assume the leadership of a general uprising that never materialized. The clandestine shadow government, years in the building, was thus in a trice largely destroyed.

In a hundred different variations, what happened in Dalat happened almost everywhere the communists struck. Each incursion, sooner or later, failed.

The reasons for Hanoi's crushing lack of military success in the battles of *Tet* are several. Strategically, by attacking everywhere Giap had superior strength nowhere. Simply put, he failed to mass his forces, a strategic error which he committed knowingly, but an error nonetheless. Military victories are not won by violating military principles. Furthermore, according to the communists' own reckoning, they committed far too many tactical blunders to have had a hope of winning. Eleventh hour announcements of timing and objectives threw insurmountable obstacles in the path of the inflexible Viet Cong command and control system. Communications proved to be faulty at best, further aggravating the already delicate coordination problems when changes were required at the last moment. Leadership, too, was less than outstanding in all too many instances, as the total commitment had required Giap to utilize every available commander in decentralized fashion. Thus, there was no slack, no way to stiffen weaker officers with proven leaders. But that is just one side of the story—communist errors are half the tale, Allied actions the other.

A document captured some time after the offensive noted wryly that the time of the campaign had really not been propitious because Allied units were too strong. Westmoreland's late shifting of American battalions to positions nearer the cities placed reserves right by the action and served also to block enemy reinforcements from aiding their comrades once they were locked in combat inside the towns. Allied reconnaissance activities complicated communist preliminary movements, thus disrupting Giap's timetable and exacerbating his coordination headaches. Finally, as always, there was the Allied technological superiority, an awesome edge which the Viet Cong could not overcome. A group of South Vietnamese marines, for instance, flew to Hue on 12 February after having first resisted the offensive in two other locations, initially in the delta and then in Saigon, an exploit of strategic mobility Giap could in no wise match. In all, the Allied response to the *Tet* offensive was a military feat of the first order.

Most significantly, however, Giap's general offensive failed because his two initial assumptions about the South Vietnamese proved to be erroneous—the people were not on the verge of a general uprising, and Saigon's armed forces refused to fold. The citizens of the South, however apathetic they may have appeared toward their own government, turned out to be overwhelmingly anti-communist, while the army of the South totally reversed its previously flaccid image by a courageous, tenacious stand. In all, it was South Vietnam's proudest hour.

Another widespread flurry of attacks on 18 February, mostly by fire, raised fears again, but that second surge was nothing more than the convulsive tremor of a dying offensive. By the end of February, the battles of *Tet* were over. A total of about eighty-five thousand Viet Cong and North Vietnamese troops had participated in the initial onslaughts and the follow-up attacks. Maybe half or more had been slain. The general offensive had run its course; the general uprising was evidently not going to happen.

CHAPTER 23

Of Victory and Defeat

The *Tet* offensive was the most disastrous defeat North Vietnam suffered in the long war. Paradoxically, it was also the North's most resounding victory during the years of American military presence.

To find explanation for that strange turn of events one must explore not only the military and political aspects of the war, but the psychological as well. The clash of fighting forces on the battlefield produced a tactical, military result—defeat for North Vietnam—quite the opposite of its strategic, psychological harvest in Washington—victory for North Vietnam.

In the first, heady surge of success, the communist press waxed ecstatic. "The once-in-a-thousand-year opportunity had come," declared the party's official paper, *Nhan Dan*. "The trumpet has sounded victory." Applauding "brilliant victories," Peking's *People's Daily* crowed: "The East Wind has brought us happy tidings!" But that initial elation soon shifted to caution as the offensive's failure became apparent. "The closer the victory, the more difficult the problem," Ho Chi Minh warned just a day after *Nhan Dan* printed its exultant victory notice. Surviving Viet Cong leaders immediately began rationalizing the results. To their questioning followers they explained that the general offensive was in truth a prolonged campaign designed to achieve victory after several months, not just in days. A captured secret Viet Cong message admitted that "to a large extent our successes were limited." Another confidential report lamented that "the people's spirit for uprising is still very weak." Towards the end of February, NLF headquarters indirectly recognized failure by ordering Viet Cong forces to revert to less grand offensive actions, explaining that further large-scale attacks were for the time being impractical. In a notebook, captured near Hue much later, a disillusioned North Vietnamese officer spoke for many of his compatriots when he wrote, "After the general offensive [of 1968] our organizations were shaken to the roots..."

The picture in the enemy camp at the beginning of March, one month after the *Tet* offensive began, was indeed bleak. At no single point was the Viet Cong flag flying, nowhere had attacks been more than temporarily successful, not in so much as one isolated instance had the people attempted a general uprising. The scorecard was entirely negative. Moreover, the cost had been appalling. Up to forty-five thousand Viet Cong soldiers had died in the attacks, other thousands had been captured, one could only guess at how many tens of thousands had been disabled. Worse, even, than those stark, raw statistics was the fact that the fallen included the bulk of the irreplaceable infrastructure of the insurgency, the Viet Cong political leadership. The revolution, which had been nourished so painstakingly ever since 1956, had been nipped off right at the ground. If it were not in fact destroyed outright the insurgency had absorbed such a telling blow that it could not be a major consideration for years to come— if ever. Bright expectation in January turned to bitter dejection in February. Evidently, 1968 would not be the year of triumph after all.

Yet, before March was out that gloomy picture would reverse itself completely. Always supremely opportunistic, the politburo would find ample reason to portray the 1968 *Tet* offensive as its brightest moment, its grandest ploy. Typical of the light in which the campaign came to be viewed in the North was a statement issued by Prime Minister Pham Van Dong three years later, on 18 May 1971. The climax of the "continuous victories scored by the Army and the people throughout the country," he said, "was the spring 1968 general offensive and uprising of the South Vietnamese Army and people."

How that astounding turnabout happened is a study in the abject frailty of the Johnson administration's war management apparatus. Military historian S.L.A. Marshall described the phenomenon as "a potential major victory turned into a disastrous retreat through mistaken estimates, loss of nerve, bad advice, failure in leadership and a tidal wave of defeatism." Giap's original, uncomplimentary assessment of the likely American reaction to his general offensive proved to have been uncomfortably close to the mark. Washington panicked.

The disintegration of Washington's will began with that erroneous but startling newscast announcing the capture of the Saigon Embassy building. It continued under the deafening drumfire of criticism from all sides as the general offensive unfolded. Knocked off balance by the very unexpectedness and sheer audacity of General Giap's campaign, neither President Johnson nor his close advisors ever quite recovered their equilibrium. Their surprise, if not their open-mouthed reaction, was understandable, for they had been genuinely convinced that the communists were reeling. Reinforcing that euphoric feeling, Westmoreland's summary of 1967 had reached Washington just four days before the *Tet* offensive began. Like nearly every official, the general was optimistic. He confidently reported:

> In many areas the enemy has been driven away from the
> population centers; in others he has been compelled to
> disperse and evade contact, thus nullifying much of his
> potential. The year ended with the enemy resorting to
> desperation tactics in attempting to achieve military/psy-
> chological victory; and he has experienced only failure in
> these attempts.

The government had not deliberately misled the American people. With the possible exception of Khe Sanh,
the president and his entourage truly believed their
own assurances. Which was why they were so stunned.

As the fighting spread and casualties mounted, a
mood bordering on hysteria permeated the halls of the
White House. One high-ranking insider thought the
atmosphere in the city on the Potomac was similar to
the one described in history books just after the shattered Union army fled in panic from Bull Run, when
defeat and despair stalked the streets, when everyone
looked for someone else to blame. The trumpet summons gave way to a Cassandra chorus.

Meanwhile, all across the country, people were asking pointedly how such an attack could have been carried out by a foe who had been reportedly on the ropes.
There was no ready answer. Throughout the month of
February, the fighting monopolized headlines, keeping
the subject uppermost in the public mind. On the thir-
teenth, the Pentagon announced the airlift of 10,500
reinforcements to Vietnam; on the seventeenth, MACV
posted a grisly high in U.S. battle casualties for a single
week—543 killed and 2,547 wounded; on the eighteenth
the second thrust of the communist offensive sent 122-
mm rockets thundering into Saigon; on the twenty-
third, the Selective Service announced a new draft call
of 48,000, the second highest of the war; also on the
twenty-third, Khe Sanh absorbed a bombardment
of over 1,100 high explosive rounds; on the twenty-
seventh, influential news commentator Walter Cronkite avowed that the war was in a hopeless stalemate

from which only negotiations could extract the United States.

On the final day of that painfully long February, the Pentagon staged a military ceremony to honor departing Defense Secretary Robert S. McNamara. Ever since 1961, when he and President John F. Kennedy had decided to send more advisors and equipment to bolster Saigon, McNamara had been increasingly enmeshed in the web of Vietnam. For seven years it had been "McNamara's War." His cybernetic strategy of graduated response, and his scarcely concealed disdain for military advice, had inexorably brought the fighting to its present unquantifiable situation. Unable to fathom the emotional response of his human adversaries in Hanoi, and unwilling to wage the war the way his generals wanted to, McNamara in frustration simply gave up. The defense secretary had been deeply disenchanted with the war for months. It was most ironic—and somehow rather fitting—that he should depart at its climactic moment.

The windy month began in the White House with the study of a report tendered to President Johnson by General Earle G. Wheeler, the chairman of the Joint Chiefs of Staff. Wheeler had gone to Saigon late in February to discuss strategy requirements with General Westmoreland. The situation in Vietnam, he reported to the president, although still developing, was "fraught with opportunities as well as dangers."

Though he carefully described the initial enemy failure, General Wheeler warned that Hanoi had nevertheless not decided to quit. Because Allied forces were in a defensive stance around the cities, communists were "operating with relative freedom in the countryside, probably recruiting heavily and no doubt infiltrating NVA units and personnel." The ARVN was "in a dilemma as it cannot afford another enemy thrust into the cities and towns and yet if it remains in a defensive posture against this contingency, the countryside goes by default." American forces were not much help, for fully half of the U.S. maneuver battalions had been sent to defend the area near Khe Sanh and Hue. Given their degree of freedom of action, possessing adequate supplies and a determination to persevere, the North Vietnamese could be expected to continue their offensive, Wheeler concluded.

Nonetheless, Westmoreland and Wheeler both saw splendid opportunities in the situation. The enemy had taken enormous losses in his traumatic defeat at *Tet*. Having gone for broke, and failed, he was exposed to being broken completely. The military leaders unequivocally espoused a more aggressive strategy at this point. Here was the opportunity to deal the enemy a lethal stroke, they felt. By virtue of our soundly defeating Hanoi's offensive, Wheeler reasoned in his report, "the situation overall will be greatly improved over the pre-*Tet* condition." Attacking in such strength so far from their sanctuaries, enemy units had recklessly exposed themselves to destruction. The American generals believed this to be the golden moment to lean heavily on Hanoi in a strong effort to end the war. At that juncture they were not yet fully aware of the enormous wastage of Viet Cong leadership in the *Tet* battles, nor of the cataclysmic impact those losses would have on the insurgency movement. But they sensed that something of the sort was within reach, that both the Viet Cong movement and the North Vietnamese invaders were ripe for a fatal counterblow. Closeted in Saigon, the two generals had devised an offensive strategy which they believed would end the war quickly and decisively. They wanted to go for the jugular. It was high time to break out of the attrition strait jacket, to go after the enemy in his sanctuaries. Both thought Washington would be receptive. General Wheeler's task was to present to the president their proposal for an increased military involvement and a "win" strategy.

American forces then in Vietnam, and on the way, totalled 525,000 men, not counting about 25,000 more

Westmoreland had asked for to help contain the *Tet* offensive. In addition, there were 61,000 other Allied troops and 600,000 South Vietnamese. But those were "inadequate in numbers to carry out the strategy and to accomplish the tasks described," Wheeler advised the president. He then relayed the bombshell. The new strategy would require up to another 206,000 men! That meant a total of 731,000 Americans. And Westmoreland wanted them all to be ready within ten months, in time for the next dry season. A year earlier he had asked in vain for an additional 200,000 troops so he could end the war sooner. Now he was in effect repeating his request, but on the basis of the new opportunity presented by the North Vietnamese willingness to exchange blows.

This ground had already been fought over. The sides were already chosen. A hot debate erupted immediately within the Johnson administration—but it was almost as quickly pre-empted by a press leak. A disgruntled official told the *New York Times* of the military's request for 206,000 reinforcements, although failing to mention that it was to support a proposed change in operations. The news broke in headlines spread across three columns of the Sunday edition of 10 March 1968. For all intents and purposes, that story ended the debate—and killed Westmoreland's plans for a dynamic new strategy.

Looked upon erroneously but naturally by readers as a desperate move to avert defeat, news of the request for 206,000 men confirmed the suspicions of many that the result of the *Tet* offensive had not been depicted accurately by the president or his spokesmen. If the communists had suffered such a grievous setback, why would we need to increase our forces by 40 percent? For years officials had been uttering rosy public statements; for years the war had dragged on. Just three months before, in fact, the commanding general himself had returned to America to assure the public that all was well, that the end was in sight. Now the war had exploded and that same general was asking for still more men to wage a still wider war. It was too much. The public rebelled. From that moment on the majority of Americans no longer supported the president in his conduct of the fighting. In the election year of 1968 there could be no further escalation of the conflict, not if the Democrats hoped to retain the White House.

On 12 March, two days after learning of the request for reinforcements, voters in New Hampshire went to the polls in the nation's first presidential primary. Senator Eugene McCarthy, an all but unknown peace candidate, won an astonishing 42 percent of the vote in the Democratic Party. Four days later, the popular Senator Robert Kennedy, sensing a pacifist swing, announced his candidacy to oppose President Johnson for the Democratic nomination. The president saw his party and his country rent by internal division over a war which wouldn't go away and which he didn't know how to win. His own cabinet, too, had split acrimoniously on the issue. The final blow, though, might have been the "wise men" episode. A group of eminent men, all from outside the government, who were called together that month specifically for the purpose of advising the president on the Vietnam issue, frankly informed him of the country's disenchantment—and recommended disengagement. Beyond any doubt, the nation had lost confidence in the commander in chief and his leadership of the war effort. The president was clearly unable to find a solution; the people as clearly would not tolerate more of the same.

In a television address on 31 March 1968, President Johnson announced, as a bid for peace, a partial cessation of the bombing of North Vietnam. He also took himself out of the race for a second term.

The nation and its president had received a wrenching psychological setback, had suffered a galling defeat of the very soul. That the defeat was largely self-inflicted made it no less real or crippling.

Militarily, and to a lesser extent, politically, events in Vietnam did not justify the breast-beating in Washington. Indeed, as the dust settled and Allied generals began to realize the full consequences of the *Tet* offensive, they became in many ways more optimistic than ever.

In February, when General Wheeler had visited Saigon, Westmoreland had credited the communists with more strength than they actually possessed. Gradually, however, in March, a truer picture emerged. Enemy losses had been far more severe than originally estimated while the South Vietnamese had displayed a most remarkable resiliency. Under those circumstances, even without the extra 206,000 men, a counteroffensive was possible. Having less fear of another assault against the cities, Allied forces began an aggressive, concerted campaign to destroy the remnants of Giap's forces.

The 1st Cavalry Division, aided by the 1st Marine Regiment and ARVN airborne and ranger troops, attacked overland and by air assault on the first of April to raise the siege of Khe Sanh. Encountering unexpectedly light resistance—Giap had begun withdrawing his divisions at least ten days earlier—the relieving column linked up with marines from the garrison on 6 April. The battle of Khe Sanh was history. The maps in the basement of the White House disappeared.

Elsewhere throughout South Vietnam the tide of combat flowed similarly against the communists. American airborne brigades swept enemy survivors from the environs of Hue. General Weyand's units, in search-and-destroy operations, scoured the crucial area around Saigon, killing several thousand enemy soldiers in the process. Far to the north, the 1st Cavalry Division and the 101st Airborne Division, reinforced with a regiment from the Vietnamese 1st Division, invaded the A Shau Valley, a major base area not entered by Allied troops since 1966. From that safe haven enemy forces had previously staged their attacks against Hue and Da Nang. In the Mekong Delta, too, clearing operations added to the mounting toll of communists killed. Everywhere the story was the same. Militarily, Allied units had not enjoyed such successful hunting since 1965.

But Hanoi was no longer looking for a military victory. That possibility had evaporated in the first few days of *Tet*. Northern newspapers stopped speaking of the general uprising or of impending success. The situation had changed and the pragmatic politburo was quick to shift gears, to pursue new opportunities. Ho Chi Minh now sought political leverage. He readily accepted President Johnson's invitation to enter into direct negotiations, but wanted to approach any talks from a position of strength. Fully cognizant of the pervasive end-the-war sentiment in the United States, Ho Chi Minh determined to continue applying all the pressure his bleeding units in the South could muster, regardless of price. "Blood in May, Peace in June," was his new rallying cry.

Starting about 5 May and lasting into June, communists conducted another country-wide series of attacks, mostly by fire, giving the general appearance of a sustained offensive, but with a level of intensity not even closely approximating that achieved during *Tet*. Their aim was to avoid direct confrontation with military units while spreading maximum confusion and despair everywhere. Lacking the element of surprise, that much vaunted effort was doomed from the outset, although U.S. bases came in for their share of the pounding this second time around, which kept American casualties high. Except in Saigon, where determined units did penetrate and fight savagely, the most the enemy managed to do was to maintain an active presence, mainly by indiscriminate shelling of populated areas. For that dubious success they paid a terrible toll in both lives and morale. Retreating once more to sanctuaries beyond the borders to lick ragged wounds, they promised yet another offensive in August.

In those first six months of 1968, Hanoi's forces had probably lost over one hundred thousand fighting men, or about half their entire strength at the beginning of the year. In terms of combat organizations, that is the equivalent of ten entire divisions. By comparison, fewer than twenty thousand Allied soldiers died in the same time frame. It was a higher human price than many of the remaining commanders were willing to continue paying. Considering also the appalling losses incurred in the border battles of the preceding autumn, one can readily understand the cumulative, morale-shattering impact on communist leaders and troops alike of the year-long blood letting. From May through the summer, disillusioned enemy soldiers began increasingly laying down their arms. High-level defectors came over in significant numbers for the first time in the war, while ordinary troopers surrendered by the thousands. Entire units capitulated. Despite fervent exhortations from Hanoi, the attack in August never got off the ground. The general offensive had simply run out of men. The campaign of 1968 was over. It had been an unmitigated military disaster for Hanoi.

Politically, the results were more mixed. On the credit side of Ho Chi Minh's ledger, the bombing of the North had been curtailed, the political scene in the United States had been scrambled, negotiations were to begin, the pacification program inside South Vietnam had been flattened, refugees by the tens of thousands comprised a new and crushing burden for the Saigon government, and the ever delicate economic situation had been knocked askew. Damage in many places had been unusually severe, a result of the intense fighting needed to root out Viet Cong elements clinging stubbornly to fortified positions inside the towns. In the densely populated Delta, for instance, whereas there had been only 14,000 refugees in the entire area in January, after *Tet* some 170,000 were homeless. The requirement to respond to such immense human dislocation and misery would seriously inhibit national recovery efforts by diluting Saigon's always creaky and already overtaxed bureaucratic machinery.

In the debit column, however, was an impressive list of facts unfavorable to Hanoi. Most importantly, the offensive had united South Vietnam in solid opposition to the North, had galvanized the urban population against the insurgents. The people properly blamed the widespread killing and destruction on the communists. Many, particularly the city folk who had previously remained largely indifferent to the progress of the war, were catapulted into commitment. Of the Vietnamese effort in their own behalf, Secretary McNamara had written despairingly back in 1966, "But the discouraging truth is that... we have not found the formula, the catalyst, for training and inspiring them to action." Giap's general offensive provided the impetus American advice had been unable to give. General mobilization, which would have been political suicide in a splintered South Vietnam, became possible in the aftermath of *Tet*, letting President Thieu place all segments of his country on a total war footing and enabling the armed forces nearly to double in size.

As for the ARVN, "the army that won't fight," it showed that it would and could, gaining thereby a well-deserved sense of self-respect, confidence, and pride. It came of age during the 1968 fighting. At year's end it was bigger, more reliable, better equipped, and more strongly motivated.

Finally, the credibility of communist claims to be of and for the people was irretrievably lost. Mass murders at Hue and elsewhere disclosed the true nature of Red liberation, while rocket attacks against densely packed civilian areas removed once and for all the possibility of popular support for the insurgency. Never again would Viet Cong agents be able to recruit effectively in the South without using force; never again

266

would guerrillas receive voluntary sustenance from the people.

And that is how the *Tet* offensive ended for General Giap: a military defeat; a psychological victory; and more lost than gained politically.

Manifestly, 1968 was the climactic year of the Vietnam War. It was the turning point which saw the virtual elimination of the Viet Cong as a viable movement, the apex of United States involvement in Southeast Asia, the final North Vietnamese attempt to gain a military victory in the face of American ground forces, the uniting of South Vietnam, the emergence of the ARVN as a mature fighting force, and a shift in the entire thrust of the conflict. Both sides, despairing of winning militarily as things stood, decided to explore other avenues to end the war or to change the balance of power.

Old faces changed that year, too. The nation elected a Republican, Richard Nixon, to replace Democrat Johnson; McNamara stepped down as defense chief, to be followed after an interval by Melvin Laird, a former congressman more comfortable with people than with computers; Westmoreland returned to the United States after four and a half years in Vietnam to become Army Chief of Staff, leaving General Creighton Abrams, his West Point classmate and MACV deputy since 1967, as the commander in Saigon.

At year's end the four principals—South Vietnam, North Vietnam, the Viet Cong, and the United States— were in Paris ready to begin negotiations. The Allies, obviously, wanted to end the struggle in some honorable fashion; the communists, as obviously, hoped to gain at the negotiating table what they had been unable to win on the battlefield. Political power, Mao Tse-tung once proclaimed, grows out of the end of a gun barrel. In 1968 Ho Chi Minh's gun had not been very effective, but it had been strong enough to bring America to a peace conference. And peace, like war, can be won or lost.

PART V

THE SEARCH FOR A PEACE

1969–1973

CHAPTER 24

Nixon Takes Command

One year after the *Tet* offensive began, Richard Milhous Nixon stood in the crisp January air to take the oath of office as the thirty-seventh president of the United States of America. Precisely eight years before, occupying a nearby seat on the same honor platform, he had heard John Fitzgerald Kennedy's clarion call for the American people to answer the summons of the trumpet. Now, in one of those peculiar quirks of fate so often spicing the tale of human events, it was up to Nixon, the defeated candidate of 1961, to conclude the crusade begun so long ago by the victor. Formalities over, the new president turned deliberately to the podium to deliver his own inaugural address, to make his first statement as commander in chief of the nation's armed forces.

1961 was more than just eight years before 1969. It was an entire era away. The confidence and crusading zeal so much in evidence previously were now dormant, if not missing altogether. National will and pride had wilted to an alarming degree; long hot summers of racial strife and a long, long, hot war had sapped the people's spirit. America suffered from a malaise of the soul. It was ill at ease with the world and unable to find peace with itself. Not for a hundred years had such divisive winds blown across the country; not for nearly two hundred had revolution been so openly and seriously discussed. The reasons for the restless mood were many and complex—but forming a somber backdrop to all, and foremost in the public mind, was the Vietnam War.

In January 1961 fewer than a thousand American servicemen worked in Vietnam and the entire combat death toll consisted of a single soldier; now well over half a million fought there and three hundred of them died each week. Time and again America had seemed to be standing firmly on the shore of victory, only to have unforeseen waves wash the beach away. Each escalation, promising victory, brought a widened war instead. Incongruously, incredibly, the conflict in that small part of the world had burgeoned into one of the country's bloodiest and most expensive wars—and its longest. In January 1969 the new president knew he could not ask the nation to heed that particular trumpet call anymore.

He didn't. He announced the opening of an era of negotiations rather than confrontation. He pledged himself to seek peace in Vietnam.

Easier said than done. It is a sad commentary on the human ability to manage human affairs that wars always prove easier to get into than out of; man invariably leaps to arms but creeps to peace. The Vietnam War followed this apparently inviolable law of social behavior. Even as Nixon was speaking, diplomats in Paris were beginning the search for a peace, a quest fated to endure for years. In the meantime, the fighting continued.

No American president before had ever faced so complex a war situation with so few options remaining. President Johnson had already escalated the fighting quite beyond the point of public tolerance, so an increase of U.S. strength on the battlefield was out of the question. Similarly, Johnson had previously agreed to stop bombing the enemy homeland and had arranged to enter into negotiations with the enemy, so both of those powerful levers were denied to Nixon. Even negotiations, for that matter, were an uncertain tool because of their erroneous implication, for Americans at least, that the end of the war was near. Communists, as every neophyte Marxist can quickly quote, negotiate for one of three reasons: to consolidate a victory; to stave off defeat; or to open another front. It was that last reason which had brought Ho Chi Minh to a conference table after the *Tet* offensive.

On the surface, all the new administration had inherited from the old was a bankrupt strategic concept, half a million men fighting a thankless war with no visible way to win it, and a nation on the shaky edge of mutiny. Americans were bone-tired of the war. Even staunch proponents no longer had much stomach for it. The desire for peace was pervasive—but, even so, not in the form of outright or even disguised surrender. Despite everything, both Hanoi and Washington still embraced their original, basic objectives. Hanoi's was to acquire South Vietnam; Washington's to prevent that from happening. Like everything else in that unhappy war, the search for a peace would be neither simple, easy, nor rapidly attained.

Among his very first acts after moving into the White House, Nixon ordered a top-to-bottom study of the entire Vietnam question. Handing the project to Dr. Henry A. Kissinger, his advisor on national security, the president asked for an unvarnished report on all aspects of the conflict. He also told Kissinger to explore every possible course of action between the two extremes of abject American surrender and the total destruction of North Vietnam. Kissinger, the ex-college professor, did his research well. The results were revealing.

To begin with, there was no consensus in official circles on most major facets of the war. Various agencies differed sharply on the impact of the bombing campaign against the North, on the efficacy of B-52 strikes, on the validity of the "domino theory", on prospects for providing security and prosperity to the Vietnamese peasants, on the possibilities for isolating Hanoi from outside aid, and so on.

There were, however, at least three areas in which all advisors agreed, Dr. Kissinger reported. Alone, the South Vietnamese armed forces "cannot now, or in the foreseeable future, stand up to the current North Vietnamese and Viet Cong Forces." Nor was the South Vietnamese government strong enough to be sure of surviving without continued assistance. And, lastly, the strategy of attrition, as it was being applied, was wholly futile. Kissinger surmised that "under current rules of engagement the enemy's manpower pool and infiltration capabilities can outlast Allied attrition efforts indefinitely." Attrition was not a way to win after all. America would not pay the price to make it work. Attrition, Kissinger said, might forestall a victory by North Vietnam but it would not bring one to the United States.

Clearly, the road to success began with three corrective steps: strengthen Saigon's military arm; bolster nation-building efforts inside South Vietnam; and adopt a strategic underpinning other than attrition. But was attaining success worth the price of continuing?

When President Kennedy had ordered his aides to survey the Vietnam situation in 1961 they had come up with five primary reasons to justify American involvement in that distant land: containing communism; retaining influence in strategically important Southeast Asia; maintaining the international credibility of the United States; meeting the challenge of "wars of national liberation"; and avoiding a third blow to Kennedy's crumbling personal prestige brought about by the Bay of Pigs and Berlin Wall episodes. President Nixon discovered that time and events had markedly altered those issues. Kennedy's first-year difficulties were obviously not a consideration, containment was no longer so absolute an imperative in view of internal ruptures in the communist world itself, and the threat of a global epidemic of Red-led insurgencies had diminished, thanks in great measure to the prophylaxis of America's stand in Vietnam. On the other hand, Southeast Asia remained strategically crucial—perhaps even more so in 1969 than in 1961—and the credibility of the United States was more on the line than ever.

Not surprisingly, then, precipitate withdrawal was one option discarded early. Explaining why he had rejected that course, the new chief executive said:

> When we assumed the burden of helping defend South Vietnam, millions of South Vietnamese men, women, and children placed their trust in us. To abandon them now would risk a massacre ... Abandoning the South Vietnamese people ... would threaten our long-term hopes for peace in the world. A great nation cannot renege on its pledges. A great nation must be worthy of trust ... If we simply abandoned our effort in Vietnam, the cause of peace might not survive the damage that would be done to other nations' confidence in our reliability ... If Hanoi were to succeed in taking over South Vietnam by force—even after the power of the United States had been engaged—it would greatly strengthen those leaders who scorn negotiation, who advocate aggression, who minimize the risks of confrontation with the United States. It would bring peace now but it would enormously increase the danger of a bigger war later.

Nixon, like Eisenhower, Kennedy, and Johnson before him, was determined to meet the communist challenge in Vietnam. The difference would come in how he would try to counter it.

Aware of the errors of his predecessors—Kennedy was prone to lunge impulsively without due consideration for future effects, while Johnson tended to crest from crisis to crisis without full benefit of long-range planning—Nixon determined to move cautiously but surefootedly in accordance with a carefully developed master plan. He did not unduly hurry the completion

275

of that plan, nor did he leave to chance the quality of information placed on his desk. He formed, under the chairmanship of Dr. Kissinger, a Vietnam Special Studies Group, whose membership included representatives from the State Department, Defense Department, the CIA, and the Joint Chiefs of Staff. Essentially, the purpose of that body was to direct studies aimed at determining the factual situation in Vietnam. He turned, as well, to independent sources. For instance, Sir Robert Thompson, the respected British authority on insurgency warfare, agreed to make a candid personal appraisal for the new American president. Thus, overall, Nixon came to be far more objectively informed than was Johnson, and he received his advice in a more dispassionate, academic fashion through the intellectual filter of Dr. Kissinger's office.

Gradually a picture emerged which was quite different from the dismal view prevalent around official Washington in 1968. Every indicator had the same story to tell regarding the devastating losses inflicted on the Viet Cong movement during the *Tet* offensive. Such Viet Cong units as were still operating were manned largely and in some cases entirely with North Vietnamese soldiers. The insurgency, while not eradicated, was in itself no longer an immediate danger. It had been virtually reduced to the status of being a police problem. The North Vietnamese regulars were effectively denied access to population centers by the armed shield of Allied forces. Having been obliged to revert to a form of protracted warfare while licking its grievous wounds, the NVA nevertheless still constituted a serious threat, but one generally contained in or near the border sanctuaries.

As for the South Vietnamese, their own situation had steadily improved. Mobilization had placed the entire nation on a war footing. Having seen how emphatically the people had rejected communist blandishments during the *Tet* battles, Saigon for the first time had felt confident enough to arm almost the entire countryside, a move placing much of the burden of local defense on local forces. In the words of General Cao Van Vien, chief of the Joint General Staff, the tables were thereby turned on the enemy: "With one million, then two million, and even more men given the means to resist the communist rule of terror, the conflict became a people's war—on the South Vietnamese side." Thanks largely to *Tet*, there was new spirit and new promise. The seeds of victory, wrote Maxwell Taylor, had been implanted in the soil of Vietnam for cultivation and harvesting by Mr. Nixon—if he could somehow "hold the country together for the time required for the reaping."

CHAPTER 25

Vietnamization

Heartened by the definitely improving security situation in South Vietnam, keenly aware of the political limitations imposed on his range of options, and in keeping with the doctrine he would announce at Guam, President Nixon set his long-range course in Vietnam. He called it Vietnamization. It was a half-way house between the narcotic of full military commitment and the trauma of total withdrawal.

At Guam, in a major foreign policy address on 25 July 1969, the new president told the world that the United States would thereafter look more carefully to its own national interests before becoming militarily involved in local wars. America would still "furnish military and economic assistance when requested and as appropriate. But we shall look to the nation directly threatened to assume the primary responsibility of providing the manpower for its defense." Just as South Vietnam had become the testing ground for Kennedy's campaign against wars of national liberation, so would it be the testing ground for the Nixon doctrine. The new trumpet blew "Recall."

To Congress and the country Nixon explained his concept as "a program to strengthen the ability of the

South Vietnamese government and people to defend themselves." Vietnamization reversed a de facto policy of "Americanization" which had held sway ever since 1961. It now appeared that American predominance had tended to weaken rather than strengthen the South Vietnamese capability to stand alone. As late as 1969 the Chief of the General Staff could admit to a delegation of the National Assembly, "As long as the conduct of the war remains an American responsibility, we have no doctrine of our own." Interestingly, General Giap had seen the need for Vietnamization long before. "The more the war of aggression is Americanized," he said in 1967, "the more disintegrated the Saigon puppet army and administration become." Implicit in the awkward but descriptive term was the understanding that Allied forces would gradually leave South Vietnam as the South Vietnamese themselves made the transition to a posture of full self-defense.

The idea was not new. General Matthew Ridgway, the renowned field commander in the Korean War, had recommended such an approach in March 1968. He told President Johnson that Washington should provide Saigon with modern arms and equipment and give the ARVN two years to take over the combat mission. Built into his plan was a fixed rate of American withdrawal to spur the South Vietnamese. This was the essence of Vietnamization. But it was left for Johnson's successor to act on the recommendation.

Saigon, responding to the Nixon concept, established a national goal, titled *Ba Tu*, which translates roughly to "Three Selves"—self-recovery, self-powering, self-sustaining. General Creighton Abrams called *Ba Tu* "the reciprocal action of Vietnamization." Outlining the two principal components of Vietnamization, President Nixon concisely summarized the new American policy: "The first [component] is the strengthening of the armed forces of the South Vietnamese in numbers, equipment, leadership and combat skills, and overall capability. The second component is the extension of the pacification program in South Vietnam."

The first was relatively easy to achieve. Mobilization had already swelled ARVN ranks; providing better equipment was merely a matter of funding and transportation, while a vigorous training program could develop the necessary skills and techniques. Indisputably, accomplishing all of that would strengthen the overall capability of Saigon's armed forces. But time was a problem. Improvements could not be made overnight. To produce a helicopter pilot, for example, required months of English language training even before the candidate could travel to a flight training school in the United States, where he would then spend months more learning the intricate skills needed to fly the chopper in combat. General Ridgway's estimate had been remarkably accurate—some two years would be consumed in preparing the enlarged South Vietnamese armed forces to handle their own defense. That meant, in President Nixon's timetable, that American fighting forces would continue shouldering a portion—though a steadily decreasing portion—of the ground role until sometime in 1971. At that point they should be able to step back completely and hand the combat mission over to the ARVN. It was envisioned that a degree of air and naval support would continue for some time after that.

Pacification, the second component, posed the real challenge. Though often displayed in fancy clothing, pacification was nothing more or less than an overall program to remove the reasons for revolution. It was benevolent governmental action in areas where the government should always have been benevolently active. It was developing a stronger economy, removing corruption, providing security and essential services, creating a spirit of national unity, promoting better health standards. In the now trite phrase, it was winning the hearts and minds of the people. Often called "the other war," pacification was far less responsive to American efforts than was the shooting war, for it had always been an area in which we could only advise, never act. Moreover, the problems of nation-building are markedly more complex than those of nation-defending. Winning the hearts and minds of a people is often more difficult than securing their bodies. But doing both was necessary if Vietnamization were to work.

Being both sociologist and soldier is a trying role, and one for which few American military men are either temperamentally suited or professionally trained. In Vietnam it was not enough for the soldier to content himself with seizing a ridge or killing enemy troops; he had to be equally adept at controlling inflation or electing an honest village chief, at building bridges or raising pigs. However, based on the record, not enough American leaders were able to comprehend the requirements of "the other war." The story of U.S. and South Vietnamese attempts to pacify the countryside is not a bright one.

The French once started a program—typically too little, too late, and too French—which they called *pacification*. To this day that word has a stigma attached to it in the Vietnamese mind. It reeks of colonialism. But we used it, nevertheless. It translated so easily into English. Therein lies an indication of the degree of sensitivity with which Americans all too often approached the rather delicate task of nation-building.

President Diem's 1962 Strategic Hamlet program, copied largely from the Malayan experience, was basically a good concept pushed too far too fast, and executed with too little real feeling for the human beings involved. It failed. In its wake came a succession of new schemes. Actually, the fundamental concepts were not new—only the timing, location, and administrative systems differed. Pundits claimed that the greatest changes were in nomenclature, that "new" programs were merely old failures with revamped names and a higher paid hierarchy. "Rural Reconstruction" followed Strategic Hamlets; but that smacked of a return to the old ways, so the title became "Rural Construction." The Vietnamese phrase for Rural Construction was *Bo Xay Dung*. Later, taking a cue from the Madison Avenue penchant for marketing tired products in shiny new boxes, American officials decided to select a more dynamic name than Rural Construction. "Revolutionary Development" was the ornate package they chose. Advisors promptly pressed the Vietnamese to adopt the new title. Compliantly, the then prime minister, Nguyen Cao Ky, issued a decree stating that henceforth the phrase *Bo Xay Dung* would be translated into English as "Revolutionary Development." Which says something about both the Americans and the Vietnamese.

American officials also had a hard time deciding who should be responsible for pacification, civilians or soldiers. At first both worked at it, more or less in competition with one another. Then civilians received the total responsibility, but, for a variety of reasons, were unable to manage the program. Finally Washington shifted the entire burden back to the military, giving General Westmoreland a high ranking civilian deputy to run an integrated operation comprising both soldiers and civilians. At least in part, that organizational vacillation was a result of the initial tendency to separate pacification from purely military actions. Splitting the two functions was an error. They are at most two sides of the same coin. There is no "other war." Against an insurgency movement, pacification can never succeed without military security, while military operations are a waste unless they lead to pacification. Considering one aspect without the other is in the same category as planning to stockpile ammunition while forgetting the guns.

By any name, under whatever authority, pacification is simple to discuss, difficult to apply. This component of President Nixon's Vietnamization policy manifestly threatened to be the burr under his strategic saddle. However, by the end of 1968, both Washington and Saigon had learned much about pacification—by trial and error, to be sure, but they had learned nonetheless. Both capitals knew its importance to achieving long-range success. Both had redoubled their pacification efforts. Indeed, after years of stubborn evasiveness on the matter, Saigon even initiated a land reform program which held out real hope to the long-suffering peasantry. In 1966, Secretary McNamara had concluded that successful pacification would depend in large measure "on the extent to which the South Vietnamese can be shocked out of their present [indifferent] pattern of behavior." *Tet* of 1968 had been the shocker; Vietnamization was the prod. It was quite optimistic, perhaps, but not illogical to anticipate having most of the Vietnamese countryside pacified by mid-1971.

Having decided upon its course, the Nixon administration lost no time in setting sail. Ships and planes carrying new weapons and supplies for the South Vietnamese armed forces passed others laden with American fighting men heading home. Troop reduction was the first and most visible result of Vietnamization— some one hundred thousand men returned in the initial year. It was also one of the most cautiously orchestrated steps in the Vietnamization schedule. President Nixon fully agreed with Sir Robert Thompson's warning: "American troop withdrawals must be balanced against a declining enemy capability and a rising South Vietnamese capability; they must not be so fast that they allow the North Vietnamese army to stage an all-out offensive before the South Vietnamese are ready to cope with it; they must not be so slow that they encourage the South Vietnamese to think that American combat forces will be around forever." From a peak reached early in 1969 of nearly 550,000 men, the troop figures went down steadily and methodically to 475,000 at the end of 1969, to 335,000 a year later, and to 157,000 at the end of 1971. Most Allied forces, as well, withdrew during those years. The world could not doubt President Nixon's intention to turn the fighting over to President Thieu. But it could question Saigon's ability to pick up the gauntlet.

Should the Southern government prove unable to do so, Washington was determined that it would not be for lack of materiel. Nearly a million M-16 rifles, twelve thousand M-60 machine guns, and some forty thousand M-79 grenade launchers were enough to provide new small arms across the board. Over two thousand heavy mortars and howitzers provided fire support. Hundreds of armored vehicles and thousands of trucks afforded tactical and logistical mobility. New radios filled gaps in battlefield communications. Helicopters, close support jets, cargo aircraft, and high-speed gun boats bolstered the air and naval arms. All South Vietnamese forces, for the first time, had weapons equalling or bettering those employed by Northern units.

The training program was, perforce, enormous. In 1969 alone, almost one hundred thousand men graduated from special schools set up inside South Vietnam, while over a thousand select individuals received advanced training in the United States each year. Other tens of thousands passed through regular basic training centers and officer training schools. Every established combat unit was programmed for a several-week refresher course. Much of the South Vietnamese army was engaged for a good part of the year either in teaching or learning. It was an army at school.

Fortunately, South Vietnam had a respite in which to accomplish the comprehensive refitting and retraining program. The communists, recovering from the battering of 1968, were unable to launch a single offensive in all of 1969. Held at bay in their border sanctuaries by vastly superior Allied forces, Hanoi's units were helpless to interfere in any significant way with the Vietnamization program. Combat was for the most part small-scale, far from population centers, and initiated more often than not by Allied patrolling and reconnaissance elements. General Abrams kept his forces constantly on the move, never giving the enemy a breather. An American general described the Allied actions as windshield wiper tactics. "We just kept going, going, going back and forth to keep the countryside clear." American officers, returning to Vietnam in late 1969 or 1970 after a previous tour sometime between 1965 and 1968, were astounded at the difference. "In 1967," one said, "it was practically impossible to avoid a battle. In 1970 you had to really search to find someone to fight." His comment was typical. The Allied military victory in the *Tet* offensive had earned a year or more in which to build a rejuvenated South Vietnamese army.

Additionally, the death of Ho Chi Minh on 3 September 1969, just as Vietnamization was shifting into high gear, further widened the cushion of time. An inevitable gap in high level direction of the war effort occurred while the politburo readjusted itself to the revised leadership arrangements. "Uncle" Ho's passing also removed one of the remaining barriers to acceptance of the Saigon government by the South Vietnamese people. Even though most of them had strongly disagreed with his attempts to annex the South by force, not a few had continued to admire and respect Ho as a charismatic, nationalist leader. After all, he had ejected the French, had lifted the hated yoke of colonialism. But now he was gone. And the old, emotional ties could not be transposed to his successor.

Results of Vietnamization appeared rapidly. The most spectacular year of the war, in the opinion of Sir Robert Thompson, was 1969, "when there was the accelerated pacification in the countryside." The success of Vietnamization, he wrote in mid-1970, was reflected in the fact that three hundred thousand foreign troops were gone or going and South Vietnam was not falling apart. By his figures, Saigon controlled and provided complete security for 70 percent of the nation's villages and a "reasonable degree" of control and security for another 20 percent. Thus, he reasoned, the resources of South Vietnam were going to the government, not to the Viet Cong—a group which he saw at that point as being only a minor threat.

Outsiders could discern the remarkable results most easily on the roads. Freedom of movement has always been among the most reliable of pacification indicators—for disproportionately small effort, guerrillas reap grand dividends by cutting transportation arteries. After 1963, highways in South Vietnam were travelled only in convoy, and even then at some peril. In 1966 and 1967 a modicum of security returned as Allied forces pried enemy units away from population centers and worked to reopen the roads. At the height of the *Tet* offensive that security all but disappeared, but it quickly returned after the communists retreated. Then, with the enemy in full disarray and Allied units striking back with a vengeance, full freedom of the roads became a fact. In 1969, every careful observer shared the opinion of reporter Bert W. Okuley, who over the years had spent nearly forty months in Vietnam. He reckoned the highways were as safe as they had been in 1956 when the insurgency began. In mid-1971, only three routes in the entire country were considered dangerous: Highways 9, 14, and 19, all in remote areas. Transportation—economic, military, and private—was both reliable and safe.

Its leadership decimated in the *Tet* battles, the Viet Cong insurgency had suffered a dramatic decline in the ensuing Allied counterattack, a decline which quickened sharply in the face of Vietnamization. Each province had its own tale of success, differing only in degree from one to the next. In Kien Hoa, for instance, the birthplace of the National Liberation Front, a rice-rich and densely populated province in the Mekong Delta, Viet Cong strength fell from over twelve thousand in 1967 to about nine thousand after 1968, and plummeted to under two thousand in 1971. An ex-Viet Cong official, who surrendered to government forces out of intense frustration and dejection, reported that recruiting became next to impossible after pacification began in earnest in 1969. Throughout the teeming delta, the monthly rate of insurgency incidents in 1971 was reduced to the neighborhood of two or three per one hundred thousand of population. Many American communities would welcome a comparable crime rate.

An enhanced security situation, along with increased peasant ownership of property and steadily improving economic conditions, certainly constituted major dampeners to communist appeal, while the plainly diminishing chances of success likewise abetted defections in insurgent ranks. However, MACV and Saigon did not simply wait for time and events to remove the insurgents from the scene. They organized an ambitious program to root out the Viet Cong infrastructure. It was called "Phoenix." Though its methods were sometimes questioned as being unnecessarily ruthless, Operation Phoenix was quite successful. Ambassador William E. Colby, MACV deputy for pacification between 1968 and 1971, told a congressional committee that Phoenix had reduced the insurgency by 67,000 persons in those years. Of them, some 21,000 had been killed. The remainder had either surrendered or been captured. A healthy insurgency would have been staggered by such losses; one already hobbled could only have been virtually eliminated.

Hanoi did not remain ignorant of its declining strength in the South, but revolutionary warfare theoreticians had no ready solution. Exhorting the Viet Cong to remain faithful to the cause was about the best advice they could muster. That they recognized and feared the very real dangers of Vietnamization is evident in their writings and speeches from 1969 on. It was a diabolical scheme of the imperialist Nixon, a plan laced with "vicious aspects," a dastardly stroke aimed at perpetuating American influence in Southeast Asia. Having for years called loudly for American withdrawal, Hanoi's writers were impaled rather painfully on dialectical horns of their own making as they strove to explain just why that very departure was now some-how unfair, was a blow beneath the belt. As Vietnam-ization gathered steam, the diatribes from Hanoi and at the conference table in Paris increased apace. The communists were being hurt. "The pacification pro-gram," wrote Douglas Pike in 1969, "which previously had not been taken seriously, gradually assumed major significance for the communists. A full scale attack on it is now underway . . ." Finally, in 1971, Hanoi's lead-ers officially listed as their primary task: "Frustrate the Vietnamization plan."

Pacification was working. The enemy himself pro-vided ample proof. From the private notebook of a Viet Cong colonel: "If we are winning while the enemy is being defeated, why have we encountered increasing difficulties? . . . Last year we could attack United States forces. This year we find it difficult to attack even puppet forces . . . We failed to win the support of the people and keep them from moving back to enemy controlled areas . . . At present, the enemy is weakened while we are exhausted." From an official document captured near Saigon: "[Pacification] caused some per-sonnel losses to friendly units, destroyed some of our agent networks, and created difficulties for our per-sonnel to hold the ground and to operate in these areas. The movement has decreased to a certain extent." From an enemy report prepared in Binh Dinh Province, where the insurgents were strong and the rate of pacification lagged way behind the rest of the country: "[our] troops were confused to the point where they could hardly distinguish friends from foes. Many read enemy leaf-lets, listened to enemy radio broadcasts, kept enemy [free passage] letters, and even supported enemy prop-aganda themes . . . Mass defections were also recorded among troop units and included battalion and company political cadres." From private notes taken during a high-level conference held to discuss means to defeat Vietnamization: "We did not strictly follow orders. We displayed poor discipline, irresponsibility, and an absence of efforts to improve ourselves." From a Viet Cong physician who defected to the government after six years as an insurgent: "I have had enough. I want to go home to my wife and four children."

Indicative of the reduced American military role, in 1971 MACV appointed a civilian to head the entire advisory effort in Military Region II, one of four territorial sub-divisions of South Vietnam, each commanded by a Vietnamese lieutenant general with a U.S. two- or three-star general as senior advisor. The man selected was John Paul Vann, whose military career had ended unhappily with the Battle of Ap Bac in 1963. Vann had left the army, but had returned to Vietnam as a civilian pacification expert. Over the ensuing years he had developed a reservoir of experience matched by no other American, and had earned an outstanding reputation for getting things done. Though he had never managed completely to cloak his abrasive mannerisms, he had acquired a degree of wisdom and tact which had been missing in the angry lieutenant colonel at Ap Bac. Mr. Vann's appointment was personal vindication for him and an official milestone for Vietnamization.

About the same time, in an interview in Washington, General Westmoreland said South Vietnam was "now a viable country. It has a political stability that did not exist in 1964-65. The degree of pacification, now over 90 percent, is very high. The Viet Cong, which used to be a threat to the free Saigon government, is now but a nuisance."

CHAPTER 26

Cambodian Incursion

Saigon had two enemies—the Viet Cong and the North Vietnamese. Both had to be defeated or dissuaded before peace could return to Vietnam. By late 1969 it was evident that, with care, the Viet Cong would be reduced to "but a nuisance." On 3 November of that year President Nixon first referred optimistically to "Vietnamization of the peace." He was already looking beyond the war to a time when the search for a peace would have succeeded. But he was premature. The North Vietnamese had not been dissuaded, merely quiescent. Hanoi was by no means ready to throw in the towel. Pacification of the countryside and the rearming of ARVN had effectively ended the Viet Cong insurgency; it had not eliminated the threat posed by Hanoi's regular forces coiled just beyond the South Vietnamese borders with Laos and Cambodia.

There stood the snag in Vietnamization. So long as Hanoi persisted in aggression, so long as the NVA enjoyed sanctuaries within easy striking distance of Saigon, so long as Moscow and Peking continued to provide materiel support permitting Red divisions to retain an offensive capability, then so long would war or the threat of imminent invasion cast a dark shadow across South Vietnam. Though the hostile formations were no serious danger while Allied defenses remained strong, the continuing departure of combat organizations pointed inevitably to a day in the future when communist armies would again constitute a critical threat to the ARVN and whatever Allied troops remained.

Something else was needed. The security of American forces as well as the stability of South Vietnam demanded further action. The withdrawal of U.S. combat elements could not safely continue in the face of the menace beyond the borders. A withdrawal is the most hazardous of military operations. One risks debacle by trying it without first knocking the opponent off balance. President Nixon's solution was both military and diplomatic. Through the labyrinth of international politics, he labored to limit outside assistance to Hanoi and to pressure that stubborn capital into calling off its forces. Those efforts were destined to bear results, but not until 1972. In the meantime, military pressure was the other tong of his forceps.

Attrition had proved to be a no-win strategy. Replacing it was one of the imperatives facing the United States in the first year of the Nixon Administration. The search for a peace rested on three legs: a strengthened South Vietnamese Army, a solidified South Vietnamese government, and an effective operational strategy. The first two were easy to conceive if difficult to achieve; the latter had from the beginning eluded Washington's "best and brightest," as one writer caustically labelled America's Vietnam policy makers. Actually, a solution had been there all along, but it had been laid aside in favor of the concept of graduated response. The solution was to carry the war to the enemy, to hit him in his vulnerable and vital sanctuaries. Attrition had merely deferred a North Vietnamese victory, it had destroyed neither the will nor the capacity of Hanoi to continue the war. A different approach was needed. Planners began to look anew at communist bases beyond the borders of South Vietnam.

Two-thirds of South Vietnam's population lived in the southern two military regions, both of which bordered Cambodia. Fourteen major North Vietnamese bases stood inside Cambodia, three neighboring the Fourth Corps area and seven by the Third Corps. Some were within 35 miles of Saigon. As long as they remained "off-limits" to Allied forces, it was as if a loaded and cocked pistol was being held to the head of South Vietnam.

For years MACV and the Joint Chiefs of Staff had itched to cross the borders to raid the enemy sanctuaries, but political restraints had kept them back. Now, however, military leaders had a commander in chief more prone to listen to military advice. President Nixon, recognizing the irrefutable logic in making such a move, was willing. In fact, with tacit approval from Phnom Penh, American warplanes had begun bombing the bases as early as March 1969. General Abrams thought it was necessary to protect the withdrawal of combat forces from Vietnam. But bombing could never do the job—only a physical occupation by ground elements would disrupt the bases sufficiently. However, Cambodia was still ostensibly neutral. Washington remained reluctant to violate the territory of a neutral nation, even for the grand prize of busting the big bases there. That same dilemma had long bedevilled Lyndon Johnson.

But luck rode with Nixon.

Prince Norodom Sihanouk had been sailing Cambodia on a hazardous course between the shoals of neutrality and the reefs of war ever since casting off his diplomatic lines with Saigon in 1963. While he pointedly looked the other way, Viet Cong units had established snug sanctuaries in the belt of Cambodian territory adjacent to South Vietnam. Later, as the nature of the war changed, North Vietnamese soldiers occupied the bases, too. That border area was an all-important refuge for hit-and-run attacks into South Vietnam, invaluable because Allied search-and-destroy operations could not touch it. Then, after American navy and coast guard vessels had sealed the South Vietnamese coast, Hanoi also made a reluctant but compliant Cambodia its forward supply base. Although Sihanoukville (Kompong Som) had long been used by Hanoi, the port then became the primary logistical center for the support of all communist activities in the southern half of South Vietnam. By October 1966 it was in full operation. North Vietnamese truck convoys ran daily up Route 4 from Sihanoukville to two major depots at Kompong Speu. There supply officers broke the materiel down for distribution to the border camps. Not actively engaged in the war, Cambodia was nonetheless an important if unwilling accomplice—protected by neutrality.

But, as the fighting built to its 1968 crescendo, the North Vietnamese became too pushy to suit Sihanouk. They pressed Cambodian peasants into labor, grabbed an increasing portion of local rice crops, confiscated transportation and shelter, even closed segments of the border areas to Cambodian officials. In essence, North Vietnam clamped a military occupation on parts of Cambodia. Angered by such high-handed treatment, beset by internal difficulties, and emboldened by Hanoi's reverses in 1968 and 1969, Prince Sihanouk began in mid-1969 backing away from his support of the communists.

Long-simmering internal problems, exacerbated by Cambodia's growing entanglement in the Vietnam War, finally overflowed. The economy faltered, corruption flared. Cambodians, who are mostly ethnic Khmers, harbor a deep, historic dislike for Vietnamese, whether Northern or Southern. Resistance to Sihanouk's involvement with Hanoi was therefore strong to begin with, and it spread as domestic problems worsened. It ballooned when one core of corruption turned out to be a gang led by Sihanouk's fifth wife, Monique, her mother, and her half-brother. That trio reportedly ran the country's largest volume of business in illegal land sales, smuggling, and black market operations. Sihanouk, though not understanding all the causes, sensed that events were getting out of hand. In a desperate effort to correct the nation's ills, he formed a "Salvation Government" in August 1969. General Lon Nol headed it as prime minister. The general's crusading efforts were doomed to failure, largely because of "Monique's Mafia," but he thereafter had a position of power which the super-cautious Sihanouk had never before bestowed on any individual.

When he went to Hanoi to attend Ho Chi Minh's funeral that September, Sihanouk reached tenuous agreement with the North Vietnamese on their use of his country as a supply and staging base. He thus averted a showdown with Ho's successors, but he incurred the wrath of a growing segment of his own followers. His days were numbered.

The prince left his palace in Phnom Penh for a prolonged visit abroad on 6 January 1970. Unrest spread rapidly in his absence. Anti-communist demonstrations erupted. On 11 March 1970, angry crowds sacked the North Vietnamese Embassy, burning its furniture in the streets. Premier Lon Nol took that occasion to tell the NVA and Viet Cong to get out. On 18 March the National Assembly voted to oust Sihanouk, who was at the time in Russia. Lon Nol formed a new cabinet dedicated to removing foreigners from Cambodian lands.

Reacting to the coup in Phnom Penh, North Vietnamese commanders launched operations on 1 April to secure for themselves a safe strip of Cambodian territory ten to fifteen kilometers wide all along the South Vietnamese frontier. In short order they eliminated every Cambodian border post south of the Mekong and all but the very large ones to the north. Then, on 13 April, they began clearing lines of communications leading into their zone. The tiny Cambodian army, experienced only at ceremonial and guard duties, was all but helpless in the face of the hardened Vietnamese campaigners.

Lon Nol asked Washington for help. From then on, Nixon no longer had to be concerned over Cambodian neutrality. Cross-border operations, always militarily necessary, at least appeared to be politically feasible. South Vietnamese forces tested the waters on 14 April with a three-day raid into Cambodia. Riding with surprise, they scattered the unsuspecting Northern garrisons, inflicting heavy casualties and burning stacks of supplies. Political reaction abroad and within the United States was quite mild; the White House flashed the word to go.

General Abrams flew to the corps-level headquarters of Lieutenant General Michael S. Davison on 24 April to tell him to start planning for an attack into Cambodia six days later. The time was not as short as it might have seemed because the Allies had begun contingency planning for the operation at least as early as January of 1970. The rugged MACV commander pointed to an area on the map where the Cambodian border made an irregular indention into South Vietnam. Known locally as the "Fishhook," that salient and the area behind it were to be Davison's objective. It was a major base area, laden with supplies of all kinds and laced with important enemy installations. Moreover, intelligence officers estimated that some seven thousand NVA soldiers were in the vicinity of the Fishhook, which was about a third of the total North Vietnamese troop strength in the Cambodian borderland sanctuaries west of Saigon. Finally, somewhere in there, hidden by triple-canopied jungle, was COSVN, the National Liberation Front's Central Office for South Vietnam, the shadowy headquarters of the Viet Cong. Abrams ached to capture it. There were to be several other operations into other border bases, he told his staff, but this one held forth the promise of gaining the most glittering trophies.

A lightning stroke would be required if there were to be any hope of cornering the illusive enemy command center. Consequently, General Davison put together a force built around the concept of mobility. The 1st Cavalry Division, veteran of the 1965 Ia Drang campaign in the Central Highlands and of the 1968 fighting around Hue and Khe Sanh near the 17th Parallel, was now to participate in yet another key campaign in yet another area. The U.S. 11th and the ARVN 1st Armored Cavalry Regiments provided rapid and powerful ground reconnaissance and assault capabilities, while the ARVN 3rd Airborne Brigade comprised a substantial airmobile element. The U.S. 25th Division contributed the mailed fist of armor in the form of a tank battalion and a mechanized infantry battalion. Over ten thousand Americans and nearly five thousand South Vietnamese made up the assault echelons. Altogether, it was a most powerful and mobile force. If COSVN were indeed in the objective area, General Davison had the tactical mobility needed to eliminate it; if that intelligence should prove faulty, though, he still had sufficient strength to destroy the base itself.

The officer chosen to command the assaulting forces was Brigadier General Robert Shoemaker, an astute, low-key native of Michigan, called affectionately by his men "Handsome Bob." General Shoemaker had fought twice before in Vietnam, as an advisor in the early 1960's and with the 1st Cavalry Division in the mid-1960's when he had participated in the Ia Drang campaign. His greatest concern as he planned the operation was to keep security, to prevent leaks or telltale movements from revealing the time or location of his attack. He, himself, expected his attack to be merely a week-long raid; not until the third day after crossing into Cambodia, when he saw a newspaper quoting President Nixon's statement that Americans would withdraw by 30 June, a two month stay, did he realize the full magnitude of the undertaking.

On 29 April, South Vietnamese forces, in approximately division strength, jumped off in a major attack into a sanctuary in the "Parrot's Beak," that point where Cambodia knifes to within just thirty miles of Saigon. Shoemaker's troops were originally scheduled to have assaulted on the 30th; but, for reasons not related to the battlefield situation, Washington delayed the attack a day. That gap between the attacks, as well as the 14 April raid, gave the North Vietnamese ample warning that Cambodian bases were no longer sacrosanct. If there had been a chance to utterly surprise the foe in his lair, it was lost, no matter how hard members of General Shoemaker's task force tried to gain tactical surprise.

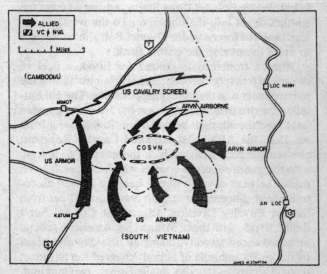

Operation *Toan Thang 43*

Designated Operation *Toan Thang 43*, the cross-border foray against the Fishhook began in darkness on 1 May 1970 with heavy pounding from B-52 bombers. Intensive tactical air strikes and artillery bombardments followed at dawn. Helicopters of the 1st

Cavalry Division entered Cambodian skies to screen north and west of the objective. Receiving ground fire immediately, gun ships from Troop B, 1st Squadron, 9th Cavalry became engaged in the operation's first skirmish. They reported destroying a truck, damaging four tents, and killing five North Vietnamese soldiers—a killing typical of scores which were to be racked up by the wide-ranging air cavalrymen.

Hoping to surround the enemy before he could escape, Shoemaker had planned to attack simultaneously from three directions. The ARVN 3rd Airborne Brigade was to occupy blocking positions north of the base area while the U.S. 11th Armored Cavalry Regiment, led by Colonel Donn Starry, advanced from the south straight into the objective. To the west, American tank-led forces under Colonel Bob Kingston were to drive to envelop the enemy flank.

After a troublesome ground fog lifted, a fleet of dozens of transport helicopters began air assaulting the paratroopers into their blocking positions. The 5th Battalion swirled in at mid-morning, the 3rd thirty minutes later, and the 9th right behind them. Rolling west from An Loc, the ARVN 1st Armored Cavalry Regiment crossed the Saigon River with the mission to link up with the paratroopers, a contact which the cavalrymen made the next day. To assure celerity as well as coordination, Shoemaker sent an American officer from the 1st Cavalry Division, Lieutenant Colonel Scott Smith, to ride with them. Meanwhile, American ground units advanced steadily, taking all first-day objectives by dark. An umbrella of aircraft covered the advance; tactical airstrikes that day totalled nearly two hundred. Resistance was sporadic and surprisingly light. Despite the early warning that tipped the communists off to the fact that their base was liable to attack, they had not detected the gathering of General Shoemaker's forces and were unprepared to make a determined or coordinated stand. Allied efforts to gain tactical surprise had been successful.

On 2 May an American armored column cut the road east of Mimot and the net was closed. But, disappointingly, most of the enemy was gone. Aerial reconnaissance that day detected widespread troop movements to the north—the delay of a day had been enough. COSVN, if it had been there, had escaped. However, the hastily retreating soldiers had been unable to evacuate their depots. Allied commanders devoted the next few days probing for new enemy positions and digging out camouflaged supply dumps.

Even veterans of operations against the largest base areas inside South Vietnam were astounded at the scale of the supply complex north of the Fishhook. They dubbed it "The City." Far more extensive than had been imagined, it yielded great stores of ammunition, weapons, rice, and every other sort of war materiel used in the South. While soldiers searched for the limits to the great cache, engineers built temporary roads connecting Highways 7 and 13 in order to remove as much of the treasure as possible. That recovery operation lasted until the raiders withdrew from Cambodia weeks later.

Meanwhile, combat elements pushed beyond Mimot and aircraft continued pounding hostile positions deeper in Cambodia. In mid-May communist defenses stiffened as the North Vietnamese got themselves more organized. Their recovery was made possible by a politically imposed Allied tether of about twenty miles. Washington, apparently shaken by an unexpectedly violent reaction within the United States over the expansion of the war to Cambodia, refused to extend the limit of penetration. The matter was somewhat academic anyway, for Allied troops had been racing against the weather all along. The southwest monsoons were due to begin about the first of June. By 1 July they would effectively end any fighting on the scale of *Toan Thang 43*. Whatever was accomplished had to be done before then.

Recognizing that he would not capture COSVN or

eliminate sizable numbers of the NVA, General Davison turned his energy to the destruction of the enemy base. "The City" would get the same treatment as had the Iron Triangle in 1967. The 11th Armored Cavalry Regiment, which had also been involved in busting the Iron Triangle, received the mission. To assist the cavalrymen, two specially designed land clearing companies arrived in June. Before they left at month's end they had cleared 1,694 acres of heavy jungle and had destroyed more than eight hundred reinforced bunkers. Finally, after all friendly troops had departed, *Toan Thang 43* ended the way it had begun—with a hammering by air and artillery. The Fishhook and environs would not be usable during that monsoon season.

In two months U.S. and ARVN forces had completed twelve cross-border operations, including the clearing of the Mekong River all the way to Phnom Penh. Despite bitter denunciations by anti-war spokesmen in the United States, the thrusts had been a distinct military success—though falling short of delivering the enemy a decisive blow. Communists, long accustomed to complete safety in their border bases, had been rudely dispossessed. Several thousand Northern troops had been killed. Elements operating inside South Vietnam no longer enjoyed the pressure vent of a nearby refuge, and stockpiles built up with so much effort over so many months were gone. Allied forces captured enough crew-served weapons to arm thirty-three communist infantry battalions, enough individual weapons to outfit those thirty-three and twenty-two more. They removed or destroyed mortar, rocket, and recoilless rifle ammunition sufficient to permit Red gunners to make ten thousand attacks by fire, each averaging fourteen rounds. At a time when North Vietnam sorely needed a victory, it received instead a jolting setback.

Just as important were the positive benefits accruing to Saigon. The South Vietnamese armed forces had taken the offensive against Northern units—and had beaten them at every turn. National pride glowed. Simply going on the offensive after so many, many years of fighting defensively was a magnificent tonic to the military, sending morale soaring. The Cambodian incursion was a benchmark in the maturing of ARVN, the point where confidence and spirit caught up to ability. For South Vietnam itself, the Cambodian victories spelled still more time to prepare and train its army as well as additional months to extend pacification. In short, a vital buffer before Vietnamization would be put to the test. Enemy pressure was, for all intents and purposes, removed from the III and IV Corps areas, the two regions comprising the bulk of the South's population. The enemy could not return until the end of the monsoon period, and even then they would need months more to reestablish their bases. Up to a year had been bought. That ran to the spring of 1971—a significant point on the calendar of Richard Nixon's withdrawal schedule.

The remainder of 1970 was more or less uneventful, either on the battlefield or at the negotiating table. In retrospect, the Cambodian incursion had splendidly attained three of Washington's four objectives in launching it: to lower Allied losses; to permit the withdrawal to continue on schedule; to enhance Vietnamization. But the fourth—to stimulate a negotiated settlement—was not realized. Hanoi remained as obdurate as ever.

CHAPTER 27

Lam Son 719

Four men had emerged after Ho's death to share the politburo leadership: Le Duan, first secretary of the Lao Dong party; Truong Chinh, chairman of the Standing Committee of the North Vietnamese National Assembly; Pham Van Dong, premier; and Vo Nguyen Giap, defense minister. They ruled without serious disagreement, at least in one important aspect—all four were steadfastly resolved to continue the crusade to unite North and South. Although a faction headed by Truong Chinh would have preferred to concentrate first on strengthening the North, a majority of the politburo persisted in viewing unification as Hanoi's ultimate imperative. The governing group was therefore adamantly opposed to any settlement short of a Northern victory. The long war would continue; Hanoi's negotiators in Paris would press for propaganda advantage only.

Deprived for the time being of sanctuaries in Cambodia, Giap began to reinforce those units operating from bases in Laos. Also, now having no line of communications other than the Ho Chi Minh Trail, the NVA exerted enormous energy to improve and fortify it.

In the final month of 1970, Allied intelligence analysts reported unusually heavy stockpiling in Base Area 604, an established sanctuary west of Khe Sanh and centering roughly on the Laotian town of Tchepone. From that position Northern regiments threatened Quang Tri, the northernmost province in South Vietnam. They were also but a short march from the city of Hue via Laotian Base Area 611 (which was just south of 604) and the A Shau Valley in South Vietnam, both of which were well developed redoubts. All indications pointed toward a pending assault against the northern two provinces of South Vietnam, a venerable plan which had been blocked before only by the sturdy presence of Allied forces. Now those forces were departing, leaving the difficult defense of the area to the South Vietnamese alone.

The situation was worrisome in the extreme. Should Saigon simply wait, it would forfeit the initiative to Hanoi. Moreover, each month of delay saw the continued steady departure of American fighting elements, which meant the rapid dwindling of Allied defensive strength in the threatened area. Attacking, on the other hand, would be a most difficult and possibly costly undertaking. The enemy bases were well defended by both nature and man; the terrain was wickedly broken, a forbidding, verdant fastness over which the communists had wisely and energetically superimposed a superb, in-depth defensive system. Offensive operations would be fraught with danger, might well lead to disaster—but, on the other hand, sitting tight almost surely would. President Thieu decided to take the bolder course which, in war, is more often than not the wiser one. He named the proposed operation Lam Son 719. (Lam Son, a village located in North Vietnam, is the site where Le Loi, an almost legendary Vietnamese national hero, inflicted a resounding defeat on an invading Chinese army in 1427.)

Since dictates of weather prescribed that supply bases along the Ho Chi Minh Trail would bulge at their fullest in February and March, Allied planners set early February as the target date. The spoils would be greatest then.

Lieutenant General Hoang Xuan Lam, commander in the I Corps area, secretly established a small planning group to preclude security leaks. Without surprise, he knew, his task would be much harder. That group did its work quickly and well, and Saigon approved the finished product on 16 January, two weeks before execution time.

Lam Son 719 was to be a spoiling attack, a sortie directed not so much at gaining terrain objectives as in upsetting the foe's plans and forestalling future enemy attacks. Allied aims were threefold: interdict Northern supply and infiltration routes; destroy hostile logistical facilities; inflict losses on NVA units. Saigon restricted General Lam to a corridor no wider than fifteen miles on either side of Highway 9 and to a penetration no deeper than Tchepone.

Allied commanders envisioned four phases to their scheme of maneuver. The first, executed by American forces, called for seizure of approaches inside South Vietnam leading to the Laotian border. Next the I ARVN Corps would attack along Highway 9 to Tchepone in a series of leap-frogging air assaults and armored advances. In the third phase, the South Vietnamese would conduct search-and-destroy missions throughout Base Area 604. The final phase, kept flexible to take advantage of openings of opportunity, was seen to be either a retirement along Highway 9 back to South Vietnam or a continued attack into Base Area 611 and then return.

Two significant factors were to make Lam Son 719 different from previous operations. For the first time since 1965 there was to be no thought of assistance from American combat troops; U.S. units were forbidden to enter Laos, meaning General Lam's ARVN forces would be completely on their own once they stepped beyond the border. Perhaps even more note-

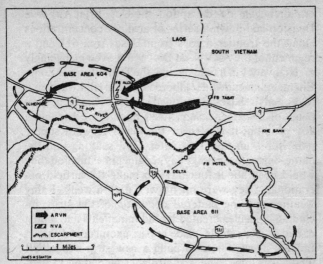

Operation *Lam Son 719*

worthy, neither could advisors accompany their counterparts. Not in a decade had South Vietnamese units gone into battle without American advisors. This was a big step in the weaning process of Vietnamization. American helicopters and tactical air would work in Laotian skies, and U.S. artillery would assist for as far as it could reach from fire bases along the border, but, on the ground, it would be entirely up to ARVN.

On the other side, put on guard by the Allied incursions into Cambodia, the NVA was ready. Hanoi had over twenty thousand men in the area, including thirteen thousand first line combat troops. Ammunition was pre-stocked, defensive positions were set, counterattack plans had been completed and rehearsed, high speed routes into the area had been improved, antiaircraft defenses were heavily bolstered. Base Area 604 would be defended. There would be no running away as there had been in Cambodia.

At one minute past midnight on 30 January the operation began. For deception, the U.S. 101st Airborne Division laid down a series of artillery concentrations along the frontier across from Base Area 611 and a regiment of the ARVN 1st Division moved menacingly up Highway 1 in a feint against the Demilitarized Zone. Engineers, meanwhile, labored to clear Highway 9 and to reopen firebases abandoned after the Khe Sanh campaign of 1968. Khe Sanh itself once more became a key position; it was to be the major forward supply point for Lam Son 719. After air assaulting into the battle-beaten base on D-day, engineers estimated they would need about four days to make the airfield operational. They were off by well over a week. Rainy weather and the battered condition of the strip, including obstacles created by old minefields and a host of dud artillery shells, made repairs excruciatingly slow. Indeed, it was faster to build a new strip altogether, which was done. The first airplanes landed on 15 February. Meanwhile, the operation could not wait—General Lam opened the second phase on 8 February, sending two divisions leaping past the Americans into Laos.

At first the going was easy. Deceptively so. Southern forces advanced methodically, establishing firebases as they went. Then, on the twelfth, enemy reinforcements arrived in the form of the NVA 308th Division. Resistance stiffened. Many small fights flared, including tank battles. At some points Northern and Southern soldiers grappled in bitter hand-to-hand combat. Allied air support, although concentrated more than ever, was less of a help than planners had foreseen. Always before U.S. advisors on the ground had coordinated the airstrikes—now those advisors were not there, leaving a crucial gap which had not been discovered in time to be filled. Additionally, the enemy air defense system was far denser and more effective than any the pilots had previously encountered, and NVA troops purposely hugged ARVN units and firebases in order further to minimize the impact of Allied air support. Thus, Lam's ground forces were even more on their own than he and his American advisors had envisioned in their most pessimistic moments. Still, as the struggle grew grimmer and tougher, ARVN units continued to push deeper into Base Area 604.

South Vietnamese forces took Tchepone on 6 March, a bloody month after beginning the operation. They stayed ten days, scouring the area for supply dumps and destroying enemy facilities. So far, though hardly to be classified as an exercise in swiftness, the raid had to be chalked up as successful. The base area had been seriously damaged, nothing had moved south on the temporarily severed Ho Chi Minh Trail, and the enemy had suffered heavy casualties. But so had ARVN units absorbed a mauling. Several of the thirty-four battalions committed had been decimated, were no longer effective fighting units. And Lam still had to extricate his tired troops over a long, narrow path lined with aroused defenders. The moment of truth was at hand. He started his run down that fiery gauntlet on 16 March.

General Giap threw everything he could into a furious effort to annihilate the raiding force. Political and psychological gains reaped from such a victory would be so great as to justify sacrifices of whatever magnitude. Victory would, for one thing, bury the viability of Vietnamization. It would be a belly blow to the confidence of ARVN, a stroke from which the Southern army might never recover. The NVA pulled out all stops.

At the peak, some 36,000 North Vietnamese, including two armored regiments equipped with Russian T-34 tanks, hammered at the outnumbered and fatigued Southerners inside Laos. Some ARVN units crumbled, but most maintained a precarious cohesiveness which saved them. A few fought magnificently. Attacking at times in human waves, sticking suicidally close to ARVN positions to escape bombing, NVA units bled horribly. It is likely that over ten thousand died; perhaps fifteen thousand, maybe more. But, as always, Northern leaders appeared oblivious to losses.

Thanks to massive air support, General Lam managed to extract most of his men, many by helicopter. In all, American pilots flew over 160,000 sorties (losing 107 choppers to the intense enemy fire), tactical aircraft made more than ten thousand strikes, and B-52s dropped some 46,000 tons of bombs. Even so, the outcome was in doubt time and again. Southern losses in men and materiel were very heavy: Saigon reported a casualty rate of nearly 50 percent, or about seventy-five hundred men, of whom over two thousand were known or presumed dead. The number may have been higher.

On 24 March the last ARVN troops returned to South Vietnam. Two weeks later U.S. units evacuated Khe Sanh. Lam Son 719 was over.

The results were a mixed bag. The South Vietnamese performance had not been up to expectations, but the opposition had been much more rigorous than anyone had anticipated. Friendly losses had been severe, but enemy casualties had been even greater. Despite numerous glaring errors along the way, all objectives of the spoiling attack had been achieved. Weaknesses in command and control had cropped up, especially those caused by the absence of advisors, but, once identified, they could be corrected. The most far-reaching result of Lam Son 719 was to delay for nearly a year the possibility of an invasion by North Vietnam. Replacing men and equipment chewed up in the futile effort to wipe out the Southern column would take Hanoi the remainder of 1971. Saigon had gained still more time to develop and prepare. Vietnamization would not have to face its test that year.

The cross-border operations of 1970 and 1971 were moves on the strategic chessboard which should have been made in 1966 and 1967. But, whereas they would have been strategically proper in the earlier period, in the latter they were strategically imperative. Only with the overwhelming presence of American ground forces to guarantee security could the South Vietnamese afford the strategic luxury of maintaining a completely defensive stance behind their own borders. As that American shield diminished it became absolutely necessary for Saigon to change its untenable situation by obliging Hanoi to adopt a defensive posture in Cambodia and Laos. Troops and resources consumed in defensive roles would significantly reduce the communist strength available for offensive operations. Thus, those who railed at the spoiling attacks missed the point. The American withdrawal itself made the Allied cross-border operations necessary. They were a rational, calculated step toward Vietnamization.

In his search for peace, President Nixon was required to do what President Johnson had refused to do in his search for a strategy. The study of peace begins with a study of war.

CHAPTER 28

The Test

A test was in the cards. Hanoi, thwarted so often, so gallingly, by U.S. and other Allied forces, was bound to have at least one last try after the foreigners left. Vietnamization would know its hour of truth. On that foreordained fact everyone agreed. The only questions were when and how.

The politburo didn't really have a tough time setting a time gate. Their assault must of necessity wait until most American combat elements had departed and should obviously begin before the South Vietnamese were strong enough to repulse them unaided. Because of the undeniably successful progress of pacification and the concurrent professionalization of Saigon's military arm, Hanoi had to strike as soon as possible. Each day delayed saw South Vietnam grow stronger. By the end of 1971, the Northern army would have recovered from the wounds of Lam Son 719 and, as General Giap knew by listening to U.S. announcements, Americans would no longer have a significant ground fighting capability in Vietnam. Which meant his offensive could be launched in the early months of 1972.

Another factor entered into Hanoi's calculations: 1972 was a presidential election year in the United

States. The communist leaders could not forget the impact of their *Tet* offensive on American politics in 1968. They saw themselves with special leverage in the spring and summer of 1972, leverage which they would not possess after the November elections. President Nixon, having promised to seek peace in Vietnam, could be expected to have far less strength and substantially fewer options while campaigning for reelection than he would possess after securing a second and final term. He would be at his most vulnerable in mid-1972, hence would be less prone to recommit American power and more likely to accept a bad bargain at the negotiating table. Besides, political repercussions should the Vietnamization strategy fail its test might well lead to a victory by the Democratic candidate— and all of Nixon's potential opponents seemed to be more or less inclined to drop Saigon. Both militarily and politically, then, 1972 shaped up as the year of the test.

The politburo reached that conclusion early in 1971, probably about the time Lam Son 719 ended. But the vote was not unanimous. As in 1967, in the debate conducted before the *Tet* offensive, a group led by Truong Chinh opposed the more militant members headed by Le Duan and General Giap. Truong Chinh wanted to concentrate on building the North while postponing unification. Le Duan, a Southerner, insisted that completing the revolution by conquering the South was the only ideologically proper path to follow. Giap, perhaps still smarting over the failure of his 1965 and 1968 offensives, sided with Le Duan. Invoking the memory of Ho Chi Minh, the "fight-now" faction won out.

After the debate, Le Duan went to Moscow to request—and get—artillery and tanks and other heavy equipment needed for a major, conventional push. One of the long conflict's final ironies is that Hanoi intended to launch in 1972 the kind of invasion American planners had prepared for in 1956, but which had never come.

Having decided to continue pressing the war, Hanoi had no good choice but to launch a conventional invasion of the South. The insurgency movement, emasculated by the success of Saigon's pacification program, could by no means be rejuvenated in the foreseeable future, if at all. Nor did pursuit of the protracted war promise greater gains than losses. Even though Giap still had the Ho Chi Minh Trail and numerous bases along the South's western border, his reach had been severely shortened by events in 1970 and 1971. He was unable to bring full power to bear where it counted, against the populous southern part of South Vietnam. Cambodia was no longer a primary satellite for Hanoi's warmaking machine, while the growing strength and aggressiveness of Saigon's forces posed a threat to the entire infiltration and basing system. Whatever course Hanoi decided upon, it could not be more of the same. Which left only the option of conventional attack.

As always, the pragmatic Giap had maximum and minimum objectives in mind. The maximum would be complete, classic military victory—the Southern army beaten decisively on the battlefield, much or all of South Vietnam occupied by triumphant North Vietnamese invaders, and the capitulation or flight of the Thieu government. A decision by force of arms. To that end he was willing to commit his entire army. His minimum aim, which would still translate into a Northern victory, was something quite less—discrediting Vietnamization. By administering a sound drubbing to ARVN, inflicting serious casualties and smashing its newly won confidence, Giap's forces could kick the Southern army back into the abyss of inefficiency from which it was emerging. That would take care of one arm of Vietnamization. At the same time, by dealing a searing blow to the pacification program—say, by occupying several provinces and establishing a NLF capital to govern the conquered territory—the invaders could severely damage that second vital half of Vietnamization. Any result between discrediting Vietnamization and total victory would constitute a Northern success, would place Hanoi in a superior bargaining position, and could logically be expected to lead to coalition government in the South, if not an outright communist takeover.

Twice before General Giap had launched an invasion of South Vietnam. His plan in 1965 had been to halve the country by slicing from the southern tip of Laos across the Central Highlands to Qui Nhon. That sundering stroke, he had quite correctly estimated, would probably have caused the collapse of an already insecure government in Saigon. In all likelihood his strategy would have succeeded but for the commitment of American troops. The Ia Drang campaign and the ensuing years of stalemate followed. Unable to overcome the Allied shield, Giap had next attempted in 1968 to execute a unique variant of a strategic turning movement to strike at the population hiding behind the military screen. The *Tet* offensive came close, but ultimately failed because Hanoi had wildly miscalculated the mood and will of the people of South Vietnam. The revered general uprising had been a propaganda pipe dream.

In devising his third plan, the 1972 test, Giap considered elements of both previous efforts. The forecast for 1972 showed no opposing American ground forces, as had also been the case in 1965. And, given all that had happened, it was nearly a certainty that this time the United States would not intervene. Committed irrevocably to withdrawal and Vietnamization, President Nixon could hardly, by any stretch of political legerdemain, reintroduce ground combat elements. Unlike 1965, however, in 1972 Giap faced large and powerful South Vietnamese armed forces aided by considerable numbers of American warplanes and at least a division of Korean troops; his foe would therefore be more of 1968 caliber than of 1965. Finally, there

313

would be little if any help from an atrophied Viet Cong movement. In both 1965 and 1968 Hanoi had counted heavily on effective and massive support from the insurgents. But in 1972 it would have to be done almost entirely with Northern resources.

The blueprint which evolved was a collage of fragments from the first two invasions pasted on the fabric of 1972. Typically, Giap divided his campaign into phases. In the first he intended to draw his opponent to the borders by attacks on the periphery of South Vietnam. The three primary areas he selected were eerily reminiscent of the 1967 border battles—Loc Ninh, Dak To, the DMZ. In meat-grinder battles, the Northern commander would tie down and batter Saigon's reserves at scattered sites far from the population and from one another. Meanwhile, infiltrated regiments would surface in populous and weakly pacified Binh Dinh Province to eject local defenders. By the end of his initial phase, Giap hoped to have control of Kontum and Pleiku in the Central Highlands, Binh Dinh on the coast, the cities of Quang Tri and Hue in the north, and the area around An Loc, a provincial capital not far from Saigon and near the "Fishhook" in Cambodia. In the second phase, he would rush units from the northern front to the central to reinforce for an advance from Pleiku to link up with elements in Binh Dinh. At that point, he would have realized his goal of seven years earlier—the severing of South Vietnam. The third phase was to be the consolidation and annexation of the northern half of the country, and the fourth he set as the destruction of remaining resistance in the southern half. That, in essential concept if not in precise detail, was Giap's four-step masterplan for conquering South Vietnam in 1972.

Preparations were intensive, on a scale never before seen in North Vietnam. Throughout 1971, draft teams scoured the countryside to raise the tens of thousands of new troops needed. Thinned severely by previous calls, the villages were hard pressed to meet demands.

Prisoners taken later in the South told of entire districts being stripped of able-bodied men from fourteen to forty-five. Even elements once considered too unreliable to serve in the army—devout Catholics, for instance—were caught up this time around. The precise number of new men raised is not known, but it was rather close to the maximum available and just enough to fill up the North Vietnamese armed forces, including the twelve combat divisions poised to launch the invasion.

While those recruits were training, new equipment poured in from Moscow, modern weapons expected to give the NVA a technological edge over ARVN. Nearly 350 Soviet ships brought a million tons of cargo to North Vietnamese ports in 1971. Foremost among the equipment delivered were scores of heavy artillery pieces and hundreds of main battle tanks. The artillery, 130-mm long-range cannon, provided Northern units a stand-off capability quite surpassing the South's, while Russian medium armor was a match for the U.S. M-48 tanks used by the South Vietnamese. What's more, in the overall amount of heavy equipment at hand, Northern troops would have a frightening superiority.

Throughout the year, new men and their new weapons flowed into staging areas just north of the Demilitarized Zone or at the exit points of the Ho Chi Minh Trail. Such massive movements did not completely escape detection. Allied intelligence analysts accurately predicted an invasion, saying it would begin early in 1972, and even pinpointing the three areas of maximum danger. They also guessed that the major effort would come in the Dak To-Kontum-Pleiku area. They failed, however, to detect enemy plans to spearhead attacks with armor. Once again Hanoi's skill at infiltration left the Allies a step behind. By slipping hundreds of tanks undetected down the Ho Chi Minh Trail, Giap set the stage to spring a surprise on his foe.

Beginning in January 1972, officials in both Washington and Saigon warned repeatedly and publicly of a pending offensive. Moreover, they hedged predictions of the outcome. In the fierce fighting anticipated, they said, the ARVN should not be expected to win every encounter. The Nixon administration intended to sidestep the kind of psychological shock created by the 1968 offensive by preparing the people and press for what was coming. The president wanted no repeat performance of some commentator demanding, "What the hell is going on?" There was to be no surprise element to the 1972 offensive.

That public information campaign in America was accompanied by a readiness campaign in South Vietnam. Saigon deployed its troops and set a high state of alert. Allies, too, were ready. *Tet* came, and everyone braced. Nothing. Then March neared its end. Still nothing. Listeners heard hopeful talk of a change of heart in Hanoi. The lack of hostile activity seemed to be a tip-off. Communist units along the western borders were holding in staging areas rather than moving forward, a fact meaning they couldn't attack for a matter of days at the soonest, and indicating a possible change in plan. President Nixon had made a much publicized trip to Red China and had one to Russia programmed just around the corner. Speculations abounded. Maybe Moscow and Peking had held Hanoi back? Maybe Giap had been overtaken by second thoughts? Everyone relaxed a little. Ambassador Ellsworth Bunker left for an Easter visit with his wife, the U.S. ambassador to Nepal, and General Abrams flew to Thailand to spend the holiday with his family there. But Giap, ever methodical, was simply waiting for each small item of preparation to fall into place. Everything was finally ready by late March, at the beginning of the Easter weekend.

Despite all preparations, the Allies were surprised. First, on 29 March, Giap sent armored columns crashing straight across the 17th Parallel, a blow not requiring tell-tale movements beforehand. Only then did his other divisions began shifting forward from their staging areas. Such a direct assault had been recognized as being within the NVA capabilities, and reconnaissance elements had long ago discovered Northern divisions deployed along the Demilitarized Zone, but a 1968 "understanding" connected with the halt to Rolling Thunder had ostensibly precluded attacks from that direction. Allied leaders had felt the assault would debouch from the mountains to the west. Thus, the best South Vietnamese units faced in that direction, toward Laos, while a newly organized and not much respected outfit, the 3rd Division, occupied firebases overlooking the DMZ. The suddenness and the unexpected direction of Giap's first move therefore gave him a considerable degree of initial surprise. In this case, the "indirect approach" was actually the most direct one.

Even more significantly, from the standpoint of surprise, Allied intelligence had also failed to predict either the scale of the offensive or the method of attack, a failure giving NVA assault echelons the inestimable benefit of shock effect, a crucial psychological edge over defenders who had expected something quite different.

Hanoi had fifteen combat divisions in the spring of 1972, counting two Viet Cong divisions comprised mainly of Northerners. Of that total, two were deployed to Laos and one was stationed inside North Vietnam as a reserve. The other twelve, with a total of some 150,000 men, joined in the offensive against South Vietnam. Giap felt justified in leaving his nation thus denuded of a strategic reserve due to the fact that North Vietnam itself remained a sanctuary, protected from counter-invasion by the political ground rules of the war. He knew that the South Vietnamese could not attack his homeland and that the Americans would not. By massing almost his entire army against the South and leaving the North undefended, he was taking an insignificant risk, if any at all. Nevertheless, Allied commanders had not anticipated such a convulsive effort on Hanoi's part; the very magnitude of the offensive, then, was itself a sharp surprise rocking the Allied high command back on its heels.

Communists had always before eschewed conventional tactics, probably as much from necessity as from conviction, for firepower and technology had always belonged to the other side. They had relied on dispersion and infiltration, on stealth and deception, on agility and surprise. Only rarely did they stand and fight. Ambush, hit-and-run, attack by fire—those were the traditional tactics. Theirs was a game of slaying the giant by a thousand razor nicks rather than with the single blow of a broadax. Mounting an offensive had merely meant increasing the frequency and ferocity of those razor slashes. But, in 1972, thanks to the munificence of Moscow, Giap found himself with the capability of unleashing a standard offensive using tactics of fire and maneuver. His powerful artillery arm could batter defenders dizzy while columns spearheaded by armor tore through the weakened positions. Mobile anti-aircraft batteries would keep enemy air at arm's length long enough for the racing tanks to reach their objectives. Giap reckoned that South Vietnamese units, unaccustomed to withstanding concentrated artillery fire and untrained at stopping massed armor assaults, would panic in the face of his blitzkrieg.

American and South Vietnamese officers had been surprised when Giap did not launch a standard invasion between 1956 and 1960; they were astounded when he finally did it in 1972. In fact, with quite embarrassing timing, just as the offensive began, the office in MACV charged with advising all training activities of Saigon's armed forces issued a directive urging every training advisor to "shift emphasis to small unit tactical operations—eliminate concentration on 'U.S. pattern.'" Future combat, MACV believed, would comprise even more of the razor nick variety; the day of big unit battles was seen as over. Giap's armor-tipped offensive caused quick reconsideration.

By attacking in such strength and out in the open, General Giap hoped to knock his opponents off balance and to achieve his goals quickly before they recovered. He risked ghastly losses, though, should his advances fall short. In the event his tank-led columns should stall, Northern forces would stand exposed and vulnerable to murderous Allied airpower, the one arm in which Hanoi remained totally inferior. In an interview a week after the offensive opened, General Creighton Abrams predicted that Giap's gamble would "turn out to be a big mistake—a terrible, horrible thing." He was right, but the matter hung in the balance for several weeks.

At first everything seemed to go Hanoi's way. Under intense pressure from artillery and armor, and outnumbered three to one in manpower, the 3rd ARVN Division fell back in considerable disorder from its line of firebases along the DMZ. Rainy weather during the first few days reduced the ability of airpower to slow the oncoming Northerners. An ARVN armored regiment checked them temporarily north of the city of Quang Tri, but at great cost and to little avail. That town fell when panic swept its defenders back to the gates of Hue. There, blocking routes to the ancient capital, the 1st ARVN Division, a good unit by any standards, established a new defensive line and contemplated methods of stopping tanks.

The battle was soon joined on the other three fronts. North Vietnamese infantrymen, closely supported by tanks, raged out of the hills to overrun the outer defenses of Kontum City, threatening the town itself. On the coast, communist regiments stormed outpost after outpost to wrest control over huge chunks of Binh Dinh Province—but quick reaction by the Korean division prevented the taking of Highway 19, which, had it been successful, might have led to an early link-up of enemy elements in Kontum with those in Binh Dinh. Farther south, assault troops, again with tanks, swarmed over Loc Ninh and pushed down Route 13 ("Thunder Highway") to besiege An Loc, a provincial capital of considerable symbolic value. Other elements cut the main road between Saigon and Phnom Penh, putting intense pressure on the struggling Cambodian army.

President Thieu, announcing a national emergency, told his people that the decisive battle of the long war was at hand. He rushed every reserve he could muster to the threatened areas, thus weakening his control over other parts of the country—a risk, but one he had to take. In the weeks ahead, while regular forces were undergoing the test of battle with Northern formations, the pacification program would also stand test in a crucible of its own—that of maintaining countryside harmony and prosperity even without sufficient security. The stakes were high: for President Nixon, the success or failure of his Vietnamization program rode on the outcome of Giap's offensive; for Saigon, survival itself.

And the scales were all too evenly balanced. South Vietnamese troops, helped by all-out American air and sea support, rallied to halt the offensive just shy of its phase one objectives. But ARVN was stretched taut, out of reserves. The situation was tense. If Giap could resupply and restore momentum, he had at least a decent chance of seeing his strategy work. His final reserves started southward. But President Nixon, short of sending in American ground units, was determined to apply what pressure he could to dampen the offensive. That meant air. "The bastards have never been bombed like they're going to be bombed this time," he said, his words being recorded by the taping system built into his desk.

As soon as the weather permitted, B-52 bombers plastered targets inside North Vietnam near the city of Vinh, a major supply area supporting operations in the South. Later the big bombers returned to strike at the port city of Haiphong. Then, in a dramatic step in early May, Nixon authorized the mining of Northern harbors, including previously untouchable Haiphong Harbor. (Still, though, diplomacy was not ignored. Washington wanted no direct confrontation with other powers over the aerial campaign. Warplanes began mining the approaches to Haiphong Harbor early on 9 May, but timers in the mines delayed activation until late on the 11th, giving any vessel that desired to leave three days to do so. What happened after then to those that decided to stay would be their own fault.) The air war, dormant since the demise of Rolling Thunder in 1968, was on again.

But this time it was different. The campaign's very name—Linebacker—conveyed a new purpose and determination. Airmen had the elementary military mission of eliminating Hanoi's ability to continue the offensive, which was a far cry from Rolling Thunder's graduated arm-twisting task. If a facility had military value, chances are it showed up on a target list, without undue restrictions on how it should be destroyed. Hanoi soon felt the full fury of a less restricted bombing campaign. Bombers closed the ports, blocked overland routes from China, seriously disrupted the internal highway system. In June pilots unleashed over 112,000 tons of ordnance, setting a new high for the war. The dismayed politburo watched its supplies dwindle dangerously, its factories and power facilities go up in smoke one after another. Linebacker was not Rolling Thunder—it was war.

Much of the effectiveness of the new campaign was due to a technological advance, the so-called "smart bombs." Guided unerringly to within five or ten feet of their targets by computers reading signals from laser beams or television cameras, each "smart bomb" did the work of a hundred "dumb bombs." For instance, on 13 May, twelve F-4 Phantom jets turned the Thanh Hoa Bridge into a heap of tangled wreckage rusting in the chasm below. A combination railway and highway bridge over the Song Ma River, known as the "Dragon's Jaw," that span had been a key link in Hanoi's supply line to the Southern fronts. Never before had it been cut. Exacting a terrible toll of twenty-nine airplanes, it had survived repeated efforts to knock it out between 1965 and 1968, becoming a symbol of invincibility for North Vietnam, of frustration for pilots. Combined with properly construed military policies—that is, a "smart campaign"—the technological advance embodied in the "smart bombs" allowed the air force and navy rapidly to remove North Vietnam's ability to support the full-scale invasion of South Vietnam. When supplies and equipment already stockpiled in the South were used up or destroyed, there would be precious little more. The Southern battle area was as nearly isolated as it ever had been.

For the type of battles Giap was waging, enormous amounts of fuel and ammunition were necessary. He was no longer fighting a bargain basement war. The bombing campaign therefore ended Hanoi's hopes of continuing the offensive into its programmed second phase—even should the first be successful.

President Thieu, in a move intended to bolster the backbone of his fighting forces, sacked the commanders of I and II Corps. That step, one not taken lightly in a country where military leaders have such considerable political clout, was indicative of the seriousness with which Saigon viewed the situation. The new commander in I Corps was Lieutenant General Ngo Quang Truong, who had led the 1st ARVN Division at Hue during the 1968 *Tet* offensive. A dynamic combat leader, he was ideally suited for the task. He quickly began kicking some discipline back into dispirited defenders around Hue, and lost little time before organizing a counteroffensive.

With ARVN dug in stubbornly and even starting to mount local counterattacks, points of constant contact between opposing forces began to take on the grim visage of World War I battlegrounds. Both sides shelled each other incessantly and Allied warplanes, working round-the-clock schedules, hammered the NVA mercilessly. Fighting was fierce, continuous, and exceptionally bloody, even by North Vietnamese standards. Northern soldiers died by the tens of thousands. It was worse than *Tet* of 1968. Abrams had used understatement when he said it would be "a terrible, horrible thing."

Early in May the initiative began shifting to the Allied side. Giap's storm troops, woefully undertrained in the complex tank-infantry tactics required by their new mode of attack, could not sustain their initial successes. On all fronts the NVA offensive bogged down from faulty coordination and stiffening ARVN resistance. Most Northern tanks, something quite beyond four hundred or five hundred of them, were soon destroyed or captured. South Vietnamese troops using hand-held rockets—issued after the offensive started—accounted for many of the kills, while aircraft, notably helicopters armed with antitank missiles, flown hurriedly to South Vietnam, took out most of the rest. Surviving tank crews soon viewed their task as suicidal, which it was. In several instances, enemy tanks were captured intact, engines running, having been abandoned by badly frightened crewmen. In not a few cases Northern leaders chained crew members to their positions to encourage fealty. Meanwhile, huge C-5 jet transports flew in replacement tanks to refurbish South Vietnamese armored units, changing the balance greatly in favor of Saigon's side. The story was about the same with regard to artillery. A concentrated program to locate and destroy the fearsome 130-mm pieces had resulted over the weeks in the suppression if not the elimination of those weapons. At that point, with Hanoi's forces halted and weakened, both in manpower and materiel, Saigon shifted to the offensive to regain territory lost at the outset of the invasion.

In the overall view, April had been a month of communist advance and Allied withdrawal, May a period of equilibrium, June and July a time of ARVN counterattacks. The first surge of the great NVA offensive had been its last. It had failed. Perhaps up to half the invasion force had been lost for nothing more than temporary control of chunks of South Vietnamese territory. In all, Hanoi's dead may have mounted to over one hundred thousand; Saigon's to some twenty-five thousand.

Vietnamization had passed its test—not making a 100 percent score, but clearly emerging with a solid grade. To be sure, there had been battlefield reverses and heavy losses—enough, in fact, to paint the first several weeks in cliff-hanger hues. Undeniably, in several instances ARVN's performance had fallen short of expectations, had been a good bit less than professional. Pacification had suffered, too, quite seriously in those areas where the invaders had penetrated deeply into the country. To help turn the tide, Nixon had felt compelled to summon massive American air and naval support—more massive than anyone, especially Hanoi, had predicted. General Giap had indeed managed to mar the image of Vietnamization. But one must give the devil his due. Giap's grand offensive, striking with such power after months of careful preparations, was no mere probe. It was not to be denied some initial successes. Besides, the failure of Allied intelligence to discover Hanoi's infiltration of hundreds of tanks down the Ho Chi Minh Trail was in large measure to blame for the early ARVN defeats. However, as soon as they had recovered from the initial shock, the South Vietnamese pulled themselves together, held with remarkable tenacity, and eventually ejected the invaders. Saigon's armed forces once again proved to be tough and resilient; the people once more rallied to their government, rejecting as they always had the blandishments of communism. Withal, a fine performance. Vietnamization was a fact.

Although American troops did not participate in the ground combat, advisors fought with their units. The conflict had come full circle—it was an advisory war again. Actually, it had never stopped being an advisory war. Ever since the first combat death in January 1961, Americans had been fighting and dying with South Vietnamese units. Their sacrifices and achievements had simply been monumentally overshadowed by the more newsworthy operations of U.S. combat units after they entered in 1965. Advisors fought a largely ignored war. But they had always been there, the steel reinforcing rods keeping the concrete from crumbling. (Lam Son 719 gave perceptive observers a glimpse of what might happen when they were no longer around, but that time and that eventuality were off somewhere in the future.) Somehow it seemed almost nostalgic that, although American fighting elements had departed, advisors were still at work.

Marking that completed cycle was the death in June of John Paul Vann. Vann had participated in the earliest advisory battles, had watched the U.S. build-up and the grisly years of attrition, had survived the *Tet* offensive, had labored first for pacification and then Vietnamization, and then had fought in the final advisory battles. When his helicopter crashed during a night flight to beleaguered Kontum, killing everyone aboard, it signalled the end of an era.

CHAPTER 29

Exit America

With no lasting results to show for his costly offensive, Giap reverted to razor-slash tactics in order to conserve strength, and extended his efforts to include scattered attacks on the Delta. Hanoi switched emphasis to the bargaining table. Actually, President Nixon had jerked the propaganda platform away from the communists by ordering his negotiators to boycott the Paris talks just before Giap's invasion wheeled across the DMZ. Hanoi, deprived of a forum for its favorite gambit—"talk, talk; fight, fight"—was quite openly upset. The president steadfastly refused to return his negotiators until he had some assurance that the other side had something more than propaganda in mind. Meanwhile, he energetically pursued his long-standing attempts to reach an understanding with Moscow and Peking. The intricate diplomatic maneuvering of this period will one day make a fascinating tale. The result was, though, that negotiations in Paris resumed in July.

Nothing happened at first. Hanoi's representatives found themselves facing a surprisingly intractable United States delegation. In spite of the Democratic party's selection of George McGovern, alleged to be a peace-at-any-price candidate, President Nixon let it be known that he would continue the bombing of North Vietnam until Hanoi either backed off or came to terms. That attitude shocked the politburo. Remembering how panic had gripped official Washington in 1968, the leaders in Hanoi had expected to encounter a less determined president. An editorial appearing that August in the Vatican newspaper interpreted the situation in the same terms as did Hanoi and much of the watching world: "[The McGovern nomination] certainly helps the government of Hanoi and the Viet Cong, but not the attempts of Nixon who, above all, must disengage himself from Southeast Asia without the American prestige having to suffer too much." But that was not quite the case. President Nixon had said all along he wanted out of Vietnam, but that he would exit only with honor for the United States. Which meant he would not throw South Vietnam to the wolves. He reaffirmed his support of Saigon and even increased the level of bombing. By every conceivable indicator, the American public supported the president—the polls pointed toward his reelection by a landslide. Clearly, the pressure of the forthcoming election would not stampede Washington into hasty or unfavorable action.

The politburo had surmised that President Johnson would not send American combat troops to Vietnam in 1965; it had forecast a general uprising of the South Vietnamese people in 1968; it had depended on domestic politics tying Nixon's hands in 1972. It had been wrong each time. Those miscalculations had led to the failure of all three of Hanoi's overt offensives. The first invasion had brought aerial devastation to the North, the second had resulted in the virtual elimination of the Viet Cong, and this last one had cost North Vietnam the decimation of its army and the destruction of its industry and commerce. Worse, through it all, the South had remained surprisingly strong. It was plainly time for reappraisal.

Two appointments to the politburo in August hinted at the emergence of basic changes in Hanoi's attitude.

General Van Tien Dun, chief of staff of North Vietnam's armed forces, and Tran Quoc Hoan, minister of public security, were the two selectees. Both were backers of Truong Chinh, which swung the balance to his faction. Dun's elevation appeared, in fact, to be a direct slap at Giap himself, while Hoan's seemed to indicate a new-found interest in internal affairs. Straightway, official publications began emphasizing the requirement to build socialism in the North while stating that the South "must directly fulfill the duty of liberating itself." In October, Hanoi's emissaries abruptly changed their tune and indicated a willingness to conclude the war through negotiations.

The Paris talks had been marking time ever since their beginning in the month of Nixon's inauguration, that is, for nearly four years. This was the first break, the first time Hanoi had concluded it could not win a military victory in the face of American military involvement. Hanoi's hand had been forced; unfavorable portents couldn't have been plainer. President Thieu's armed forces had proven far tougher than anticipated, the American aerial response had been heavier and more effective than even pessimists had foreseen, the politically diverse people of South Vietnam were overwhelmingly united in their preference not to be "liberated" by the North, and communist forces had been so horribly mangled that they would need at least a year or two to recover. Moreover, Moscow and Peking were showing signs of tiring of the long and largely futile war. They could not be counted upon to provide indefinitely materiel and moral support. Hanoi had to bend.

In a flurry of closed conferences in Paris and Saigon, in Hanoi and Washington, newly serious diplomats hammered out the terms of a truce. At one point when it appeared the end was near—"Peace is at hand," Henry Kissinger announced—the United States cut back on the bombing as a gesture of good will. But too many sticky points remained. Negotiators could find no mutually satisfactory way to tiptoe around them. For one thing, Saigon adamantly resisted any agreement which would leave North Vietnamese forces in control of Southern territory, poised to launch another offensive at some future date. The North, on the other hand, would not even admit that its troops were in the South. Through the waning months of 1972 both sides jockeyed for position, resupplying and fighting for control of as much territory as possible before a cease-fire might take effect. The talks dragged frustratingly on until December. Finally, convinced that Hanoi was purposefully extending the negotiations just when they were so tantalizingly close to completion, and perhaps needing to demonstrate his determination to Thieu, Nixon ordered full scale resumption of the aerial campaign.

For eleven days at the end of the year, American jets, including wave upon wave of B-52 bombers, pummelled targets across North Vietnam. They struck the Hanoi-Haiphong area repeatedly, unleashing the most concentrated and punishing attacks of the entire war. Damage was extensive and prohibitive, quite beyond anything Hanoi had previously experienced. American aircraft losses mounted as well. For the first time in the war enemy defenses began to take a significant toll of the big bombers—fifteen B-52s were shot down. But Nixon persisted. Such widespread devastation could not be endured. The politburo got the message. Hanoi quickly agreed to come to terms, and the bombing stopped abruptly. Linebacker II, as the December air finale was dubbed, provides a classic example of the overwhelming use of military might to achieve a political end quickly. Its intensive application of power carried the point with relatively few casualties to either side, especially when contrasted to Rolling Thunder, whose attrition losses were not so sudden and dramatic but ended with a much greater and more gruesome total—and which failed dismally to achieve its objectives after four years of bombing. Analysts, when they have sifted all the data, may well confirm the statement Admiral Sir John Fisher made so many years ago.

Agreement on a cease-fire for all of Vietnam was reached rapidly upon resumption of the Paris negotiations in January of 1973. Article four, by far the shortest and clearest clause in the agreement, stated flatly: "The United States will not continue its military involvement or intervene in the internal affairs of South Vietnam." For the first time since advisors began going along on operations in 1960, Americans were not fighting in Vietnam.

Actually, though upstaged by the drama in Paris and the battle scenes in Vietnam, the American exit had not been tied to the cease-fire. Even during the North Vietnamese offensive, at times right in the teeth of it, the United States withdrawal had continued according to plan. General Abrams had departed in June 1972 to succeed Westmoreland as Army Chief of Staff, being replaced in Saigon by General Fred C. Weyand, who had already spent many years in Vietnam in positions ranging from division commander to Abrams' deputy. By July fewer than 49,000 Americans had remained; by September the total had dipped to under 39,000 and was still dropping. By the end of the year, it had reached 24,000—about the strength on hand when the build-up had begun in 1965. The last combat battalion had gone home in August. It was evident to all that, regardless of the ultimate outcome of the North's 1972 invasion, the United States' military role inside South Vietnam was indeed drawing to a close. As it began. Without fanfare, slowly, inexorably, at times almost imperceptibly. (The withdrawal was, after all, in its fourth year.) To paraphrase General Douglas MacArthur, old wars never die, they just fade away.

The Vietnam War—or, to be more precise, the U.S. military commitment to it—just faded away in 1972. Of course, there were loose ends to tidy up. It had never been a neat war, so one should not have expected it to end neatly. Accounting for the missing, exchanging prisoners, negotiations in Laos, the future of Cambodia, support to Saigon, overseeing the cease-fire—those and other tough problems remained. Nevertheless, twelve long years to the month after President Kennedy had called on Americans to respond to the summons of the trumpet, the central issue of the debate in the United States was settled: direct American military involvement on the ground in Asia had ended.

There remained the nagging question of gauging results. Debate had accompanied American fighting men as they had become engaged in Vietnam, dissent had been a constant part of the scene all the while the war was being fought, and even the departure of U.S. troops failed to still the criticism. It seems a sure bet that historians a century hence will be arguing about the outcome. Did American arms suffer a defeat? What did the United States accomplish? Was it worth the price? Had the whole thing been a Greek tragedy all along, with its ending foreordained and inevitable?

Unfortunately, the long debate never produced agreed upon definitions. After twelve years, Americans still had no certain description of what the trumpet summons had meant. It remained unclear just what would have been entailed in "winning." President Nixon did not say the war had been won, he proclaimed instead that the United States had obtained "peace with honor." That didn't sound like much for so long and costly a struggle. Neither was it made clear what the American objective had been. General Westmoreland, in an open letter, commended the country's military forces for having "accomplished their mission of bringing the enemy to the conference table." That didn't sound like so much either. When the last soldier got home he couldn't tell his family whether the war had been lost or won. The most honest thing he could say was that only time would tell.

CHAPTER 30

An Indecent Interval

In the autumn of 1971, while Giap was preparing his 1972 offensive and the Allies were pursuing Vietnamization, an American historian presented a lecture on military history to cadets at the Vietnamese National Military Academy. During the discussion period afterwards, one cadet posed a thorny question.

"We have learned," he said, "that the United States has never lost a war. Now that you are withdrawing from Vietnam, will you still be able to say that?"

"To answer that, one must first look at the opposing objectives," the lecturer replied. "From the start, Hanoi's was to take over South Vietnam, while Washington's was to prevent that from happening. At this moment, then, Washington would seem to be the winner. However, the real test is in the future. The United States set itself three tasks in Vietnam which, if accomplished, would lead to success: 1) repel the North Vietnamese invaders in 1965; 2) keep them out of South Vietnam thereafter; and 3) build such a strong nation in South Vietnam that your government, with just materiel support from the United States, could stand alone against both insurgents and invaders. The first two tasks were accomplished successfully. The final test of that third one, however, is yet to come. In ten years or so ask yourself whether the government in Saigon has been overthrown by that in Hanoi. If the answer is no, the third task will have been accomplished. If the answer is yes, the United States will have lost its first war."

The answer came not in ten years, but in less than four.

The January 1973 agreement in Paris had merely acknowledged the reality of the battlefield, where a military balance between North and South had been reached. But it permitted the United States to terminate its direct involvement. South Vietnam had a proven army capable of defending the country without help so long as the balance should be maintained—and there was some reason to hope that the battlefield equilibrium would persist. The North had agreed to refrain from attacking again, and the United States had pledged to resupply the South should Hanoi renege. South Vietnam appeared no longer to need American fighting men, and would require military aid only in proportion to whatever assistance the communist side might receive. Henry Kissinger publicly announced America's promise to "continue that military aid which is permitted by the agreement" and "to gear that military aid to the actions of other countries." President Nixon personally assured President Thieu that the United States would "respond with full force should the settlement be violated by North Vietnam." The word of the United States was the foundation on which some sort of peaceful structure could eventually emerge. And that word had always been good.

In the flush of emotion over the end of hostilities and the return of captured fighting men, some of whom had languished in North Vietnamese prisons for much of a decade, Americans were initially inclined to take at face value President Nixon's assertion that the United States had achieved "peace with honor." Relieved, the country turned its attention to other matters. Or tried to. But Vietnam would not go away. Americans were no longer dying, but the fighting continued. Gradually, the combat increased in intensity. By the end of 1973, the anticipated year of peace, the war was being sustained at a level of violence practically indistinguishable from previous years. Casualties on both sides were heavy. Henry Kissinger and his Northern counterpart in the negotiations, Le Duc Tho, were awarded the Nobel Peace Prize that year. Tho pointedly declined to accept. Peace was not at hand.

Not a few observers, after reflecting on the seeming divergence between the nature of the agreements in Paris and the realities in Vietnam, expressed pessimism over the long-range prognosis for South Vietnam. One cynically suggested that the agreements had been nothing more than a subterfuge, a cover to let America get out and to postpone for a "decent interval" the inevitable fall of a South Vietnam bereft of United States military support. As it happened, the interval was shockingly indecent. South Vietnam succumbed in just over two years.

Why that happened will be the subject of bitter debate for years. There is no simple answer—and no answer at all upon which everyone will agree. Even when historians shall reach an academic consensus, at some future time free of the tug and taint of emotions, it is all but certain that a wave of revisionism will swell up to challenge it. The central issue is likely to be whether the fall of South Vietnam represents for America defeat or a default.

To attempt a reconstruction here would be neither worthwhile nor within the scope of this book. But to stop the narrative on the beaming faces of newly freed U.S. prisoners returning to American soil would be a most inappropriate way to end the tale of a woeful crusade. The final scene can be no other than that of American marines escaping from a throng of desperate South Vietnamese citizens, beating them back with tear gas and rifle butts while scrambling aboard the last helicopter taking off from the roof of the United States Embassy in downtown Ho Chi Minh City.

Although analysts will be picking over the debris of the final phase of the Vietnam War for years to come, looking for clues to complete an autopsy of the disaster, the bare-bones framework on which they will hang the bits and pieces is known now. Rhetoric aside, the facts and realities are clearly evident in the events themselves.

The first fact is that Hanoi's politburo had no intention of relinquishing its ultimate objective of acquiring South Vietnam. The Paris agreements had apparently been nothing more than a device to remove the United States' military presence from Vietnam, the negotiations nothing more than another front of the war. The only surprise involved in that attitude would be that Americans had ever believed it might be otherwise. Right away, with hardly a nod toward concealing their actions, the North Vietnamese began preparations for a future offensive. The Ho Chi Minh Trail became the Ho Chi Minh Highway as road beds were hardened and truck convoys, laden with men and munitions, streamed into staging areas in the South. A fuel pipeline paralleled the highway. Officers began refitting and retraining while the stockpiles grew. Observers calculated that in something over a year, perhaps two at the most, the NVA would be set to try again.

The second reality was that the Soviet Union and China refurbished and strengthened Hanoi's army, while the United States gradually constricted its own flow of supplies to Saigon. The reasons for the American cutback were diverse, but the results were irrefutable—major items such as tanks and airplanes were not replaced on the promised one-for-one basis as they were lost in combat; the scarcity of fuel and ammunition sharply curtailed operations; shortages of spare parts rendered much equipment inoperative. Geared to fight with American style logistical munificence, Saigon's generals had to adjust to frugally supported operations.

Closely tied to that slackening of support were undeniable signs of a burgeoning trend in the United States to dissociate this country from events in Vietnam. Despite President Nixon's "absolute assurance . . . to take swift and severe retaliatory action" should Hanoi fail to abide by the terms of the Paris agreement, the United States did nothing to stop the ominous Northern buildup. About that time, too, Washington entered a period of virtual paralysis as the Watergate scandal immersed and eventually washed out the Nixon administration. Lest anyone misread the signs, Congress spelled them out in capital letters. In August 1973 it passed a law flatly prohibiting any further military involvement in Vietnam. From that point on North Vietnam did not have to worry unduly about triggering an American response to aggression in the South—and South Vietnam was put on blunt notice that it would thereafter be wholly on its own. The makeup of the Congress elected in the fall of 1974 should have ended any lingering hopes Saigon may have harbored for a change of heart in Washington. It was manifestly against a greater involvement, and even seemed to be inclined to terminate aid altogether. President Ford would be totally unable to intervene in any way, even if he so wished.

Just how much of an impact all of this had on the morale of the South Vietnamese cannot be calculated. But it is safe to conclude that after a quarter of a century of war, the prospect of still more fighting was not especially stimulating. Nor would the fading of American support have been likely to bolster the spirit to continue resisting. Nevertheless, throughout 1973 and 1974, the Southern forces fought capably enough. Despite absorbing grievous casualties, and in the face of a worsening countrywide economic crunch which left its members with insufficient means to support their families, the ARVN remained sturdily reliable. That is what made the sudden collapse so incredible when it came.

The first real crack appeared with the fall of Phuoc Long Province, on the Cambodian border north of Saigon, in January 1975, just two years after the Paris agreement. South Vietnam, unable to pay the price in men and materiel which would have been required to retake the territory, wrote it off. If Northern leaders had any remaining doubts about U.S. intentions, they were undoubtedly relieved to see that Washington took no action. The next significant battle was at Ban Me Thuout, in the Central Highlands, where communist forces destroyed much of an ARVN division and overran the town. That forced President Thieu to rethink his strategy. Coming to the conclusion that the South was not strong enough to hold everything everywhere, he decided to withdraw from exposed positions in order to regroup and consolidate his defenses in the most crucial areas. In a meeting at Cam Ranh Bay with his top commanders in mid-March, he explained the concept of the new strategy. Six weeks later his entire country was in the hands of the North Vietnamese, who themselves could hardly believe the swiftness with which the thirty-year war had ended.

Thieu's decision to pull back the overextended forces was probably a proper one, but it carried within it the black powder of disaster. No military maneuver is more fraught with danger than a withdrawal in the face of an aggressive enemy. Requiring detailed planning and bold action, it is difficult for even the best disciplined and best led of troops to pull off smartly. The South Vietnamese had never tried anything like this before, even when American advisors had been there to help. They botched the attempt with grossly inadequate planning and abominable execution. Enormously complicating matters was the fact that the troops also had to extract their families—a situation virtually begging to become a debacle. Confusion quickly became disorder, disorder turned to chaos. Stark panic rapidly washed over the countryside, gripping soldier and civilian alike. Hundreds of thousands of terrified people jammed roads in headlong, frenzied flight to coastal cities. Attempts to form new defensive lines were futile as the calamitous human flood rolled to the sea and south. In three weeks the northern two-thirds of South Vietnam were lost. So was nearly half of the Southern army.

In the meantime, Cambodia fell to communist insurgents, requiring a helicopter evacuation of the last Americans in Phnom Penh. The rescue went off smoothly, but there were only a few dozen to be taken out. That scene focused concern on the dangerous situation in Saigon. About six thousand Americans remained in Vietnam, presenting an evacuation problem of a wholly different order.

The situation stabilized temporarily just north of Saigon as ARVN troops, not touched by the panic, dug in and North Vietnamese commanders wrestled with the two unexpected problems of occupying so much conquered territory and repositioning supplies and units for an assault of Saigon. Some sharp fighting followed, but the eventual outcome was all too evident. With his government in disarray and the situation irretrievable, Thieu resigned.

A coalition of political leaders, hoping to salvage something from the debacle, brought General Duong Van Minh out of retirement in an effort to arrange a negotiated capitulation. Minh had been the leader of the coup which had toppled President Diem a dozen years before, and had since developed something of a neutralist image. But the communists, on the outskirts of Saigon, were not about to bargain for half a loaf. They demanded and got a total surrender. On 30 April 1975 they paraded victoriously into Saigon—and renamed the city in honor of Ho Chi Minh.

Meanwhile, with the time bought by the ARVN stand above Saigon, the United States was able to evacuate most Americans and tens of thousands of South Vietnamese who were related to Americans or were marked for death because of their affiliation with various U.S. activities in South Vietnam. The last group out was extracted in a day-long helicopter shuttle started after North Vietnamese gunners began shelling the city. Two American marines were killed when a round struck the building which had once housed the MACV headquarters. The last to die in the long war, neither had been born when the United States began to back Diem with advisors in 1954.

When the final chopper lifted off, carrying the last marine guards, it signalled the humiliating end to a once bright American dream of preventing a communist takeover of South Vietnam. The trumpet was silent.

EPILOGUE:

No More Vietnams

A cry heard often in the waning years of the Vietnam War was "no more Vietnams." Evoking a kaleidoscopic image of emotions, the phrase is one difficult to explain, but one everybody understands, at least in his own terms. It expresses a hope that somehow mankind can do away with war itself, and yet at the same time says we should not make the same mistakes in our next war. It is at once a plea for peace and an entreaty to do better next time.

A cynic would say both are impossible dreams, that there will surely be another war and that we will just as surely not benefit from the lessons of the last. And history would tend to bear him out. If a study of man's record reveals anything it is that he is an inveterate warmaker and, more often than not, an egregious bungler at it.

Of the 32 years from 1941 through 1972, 22 were years of war for the United States. And many of the other ten were fraught with the threat of holocaust. Vietnam was our fourth full-scale conflict of this century (or is it five?)—there have also been dozens of "incidents" not serious enough to be labelled wars. The rest of the world's states, meanwhile, have compiled among them an incredible number of armed encounters since the First World War, "the war to end wars." A prudent nation, however sincerely it may pray for peace, must prepare for war. We may strive mightily to avoid future hostilities, but, still and all, it remains absolutely imperative to avoid repeating the errors of the past should we be unable to keep the peace.

One of the essential ingredients of preparedness, therefore, is a diligent and honest study of the past, an intellectual examination of historical successes and failures.

We did many things right in Vietnam. And many wrong. Those lessons must not be lost. The errors must not be ignored—to be repeated.

We did not heed history's admonitions before embarking on our military involvement in Vietnam. They were many and, in retrospect, obvious. One such warning came from an officer of the United States Army, penned while he was a student at the War College:

> The government, the press, and the people as a whole had no enthusiasm for the war, indeed failed to understand what the nation was fighting about. This showed in lack of spirit in the troops sent to the east and in failure of the people at home to support the war. Such support is necessary in any war . . . Unless the people are enthusiastic about war, unless they have a strong will to win it, they will become discouraged by repeated [deferments of victory] . . . [This] war shows that wars may be won or lost in the home country as well as on the battlefield and that no government can go to war with hope of success unless it is assured that the people as a whole know what the war is about, that they believe in their cause, are enthusiastic for it, and possess a determination to win. If these conditions are not present the government should take steps to create them or keep the peace.

Major G.P. Baldwin was not writing about the Vietnam War. When he set those words down in 1928, an isolationist America was hardly aware of the pres-

341

ence, much less the problems, of a place called Vietnam. He was referring to Russia's ineptitude in the Russo-Japanese War of 1904-05.

But his message is universal and timeless.

There must be no more Vietnams.

SOURCES

Attempting to write a history of any controversial event soon after its occurrence has obvious drawbacks, particularly if that event happens to have been a long and unpopular war. Foremost among them is the problem of finding adequate unclassified source material. Not that there has been any shortage of published works on the Vietnam War; to the contrary, the serious researcher is initially inundated with a flood of tracts espousing virtually every conceivable viewpoint. Many of them are unabashedly polemic, usually identifiable by the linking in their titles of the word *Vietnam* with such pejorative terms as *folly, quagmire, nightmare,* or *tragedy.* Official writings are all too often just as bad, offering a cardboard diet of limp rebuttal and defensive justification. Sorting the usable from the trash, then, is one's first task.

The works discussed below do not comprise an exhaustive or even a comprehensive listing of sources on the Vietnam War, but they are among those which I found most useful—and are titles which I would recommend to anyone interested in reading deeper into specific aspects of the war.

Not too surprisingly, the body of writings least

tainted with bias is that covering the war's background and origins. To begin with, anything by Bernard Fall is readable and reasonably accurate. *Street Without Joy* (1961) and *The Two Vietnams* (1963) are perhaps his best. Joseph Buttinger's *The Smaller Dragon* (1958) provides a political history of Vietnam, while Ellen Hammer's *The Struggle for Indochina* (1966) covers events there between 1940 and 1955. *South Vietnam: A Nation Under Stress* (1963) by Robert Scigliano, is a carefully documented and well-written account of Diem's regime. Scigliano also describes American advisory efforts and difficulties. Frances FitzGerald's *Fire in the Lake* (1972) is a widely read account of the impact of America's military involvement on Vietnamese culture, although it has been accused of sacrificing depth for glibness.

Considering the closed nature of communist societies, we have access to a remarkably large number of studies delving into the enemy side of the picture. The best known expert on the Viet Cong and the North Vietnamese is Douglas Pike. His *Viet Cong* (1966) and *War, Peace, and the Viet Cong* (1969) are musts. J.J. Zasloff did an excellent study for the RAND Corporation, *Origins of the Insurgency in South Vietnam, 1954-1960* (1968), and P.J. Honey explored *Communism in North Vietnam* (1964), though the latter focuses mainly on Hanoi's relationships with Moscow and Peking. The U.S. Department of State issued a constant stream of documents during the war which, perhaps because of their very number, were too little read. Included were special studies, translations of captured documents, and summaries of enemy activities. Some sample titles: *Viet Cong Terror Tactics in South Vietnam* (1968); *Wars of National Liberation* (1968); *Communist Directed Forces in South Vietnam* (1968). A highly readable American view of life in the enemy camp is *Five Years to Freedom* (1971) by James N. Rowe, who escaped after being a prisoner of the Viet Cong for five years.

Doctrinal works for both sides are easy to find, though not always so easy to digest. The starting point is with Mao Tse-tung; Anne Fremantle edited his works in *Mao Tse-tung* (1962). Truong Chinh's *Primer for Revolt* (1963), Bernard Fall's selections of *Ho Chi Minh on Revolution* (1967), and Vo Nguyen Giap's *People's War, People's Army* (1962) are books by high ranking North Vietnamese. The only response I know of by a South Vietnamese is Do Ngoc Nhan's *Guiding Strategy in the Vietnam War* (1970), but it had not been translated from the original Vietnamese. A spate of Western writers has addressed the post-World War II challenge posed by lower scale conflicts—limited wars, insurgencies, revolutionary war, guerrilla warfare, wars of national liberation, etc. *Limited War* (1957), written by Robert Osgood before our deep involvement in Vietnam, is an excellent version of thinking on the subject before the war itself muddied matters. Peter Paret and John Shy wrote a small but worthwhile book called *Guerrillas in the 1960s* (1962) just as Vietnam was beginning to loom so large, and Sir Robert Thompson drew on his vast experience in Malaya and South Vietnam to lay out steps for *Defeating Communist Insurgency* (1966). The most thorough discussion of the problem of combatting internal wars is *The Art of Counter-Revolutionary War* (1966) by an American army officer, John McCuen. The one book which may have influenced the United States involvement in Vietnam more than any other was the one which caught John F. Kennedy's eye—Maxwell Taylor's *The Uncertain Trumpet* (1960).

Books dealing both objectively and definitively with policy and policy-making are yet to be found. The war is still too close and too controversial. It will be decades before the entire picture emerges—if it ever does. Nonetheless, the heat of the debate itself has forced bits and parts into the light, most notably *The Pentagon Papers* (1971) by Neil Sheehan and others. Sheehan's text is quite biased and very misleading, but he did reveal many previously classified documents which, for whatever heartburn their disclosure may have caused Washington officialdom, have been a boon to historians. A more comprehensive version of the so-called "Pentagon Papers" was printed in 1971; in five volumes, it is known as the Senator Gravel Edition. *The Best and the Brightest* (1969) is an entertaining if highly acidic version of the policy-makers and their policies as seen by David Halberstam. Sir Robert Thompson, an Englishman, looked at the situation in 1969 and said that, for the United States, there was *No Exit from Vietnam* (1969). He took another look after the Paris agreements of 1973, and concluded that *Peace Is Not at Hand* (1974). The personal story of a prominent South Vietnamese, General Tran Van Don, *Our Endless War: Inside Vietnam* (1978), is especially revealing of the intrigue permeating Saigon's politics and policies from the outset to the fall. Henry Graff discussed policy-making in the Johnson administration in *The Tuesday Cabinet* (1970), while Townsend Hoopes, in *The Limits of Intervention* (1969), painted a probably less-than-objective picture of the administration's reaction to the communist offensive in early 1969. Herbert Y. Schandler's unpublished Harvard doctoral dissertation, *Making a Decision: Tet 1968* (1974), helps illuminate this key period. He expanded that into a book, *The Unmaking of a President: Lyndon Johnson and Vietnam* (1977). Unfortunately, Lyndon Johnson's *The Vantage Point* (1971), so leaves the impression of being self-serving that it carries little credibility. Maxwell Taylor probably comes as close to providing a complete picture of policy-making as is possible at this time in *Swords and Plowshares* (1972). The basis for Vietnamization is described in Richard Nixon's *U.S. Foreign Policy for the 1970's: A New Strategy for Peace* (1970).

Although no one has done a comprehensive military study of the war, numerous books trace the action in key battles and campaigns or touch on specific facets of the fighting such as the logistical build-up. Among the best is *Tet!* (1971) by Don Oberdorfer, the story of The *Tet* offensive of 1968. S.L.A. Marshall has written about combat actions at the small unit level in *Battles in the Monsoon* (1967), *West to Cambodia* (1968), and *Bird* (1968). Francis West covered several marine fights in *Small Unit Action in Vietnam* (1967) and three authors—John Albright, John Cash, Allan Sandstrom—described typical army clashes in *Seven Firefights in Vietnam* (1970). West also wrote *The Village* (1972), a book on attempts to pacify one small area. *The Grunts* (1976), by Charles Anderson is a novel-like account of men during combat and after their return to the United States. Another look at the war from the bottom is *The Advisor* (1973) by John Cook. Moyers Shore reported on *The Battle for Khe Sanh* (1969), and Lewis Walt tells how things looked to him as the top marine in *Strange War, Strange Strategy* (1970). In *Air Assault* (1969), John Galvin explored the ramifications of the vertical dimension which the helicopter added to ground fighting. Jac Weller had previously probed the wider subject of weaponry and tactics in *Fire and Movement* (1967). *Report on the War in Vietnam* (1968), an official version of the fighting to mid-1968, contains a great amount of material. General William Westmoreland prepared the account of the ground combat while Admiral U.S.G. Sharp compiled the portion dealing with the air and sea campaign against North Vietnam. General Westmoreland's *A Soldier Reports* (1976) is a must. It is a readable and balanced account of the war from his perspective. Ralph Littauer and Norman Uphoff edited *The Air War in Indochina* (1972), a very objective work considering the anti-war sentiments of most of the contributors. Finally a most significant addition to the historiography of the war is a series of monographs sponsored by the army's Center of Military History and prepared by high ranking veterans of Vietnam. Topics include battle studies, command and control arrangements, pacification, riverine operations, logistical support, air mobility, intelligence activities, and special forces utilization. The series is entitled *Vietnam Studies*.

Excluded from this listing is the host of valuable articles appearing over the years in periodicals of all persuasions. The most useful, as a general rule, were those published in journals devoted to military and diplomatic matters, such as *Military Review* and *Foreign Affairs*. Unit histories and military "after-action reports" also abound, sources not to be overlooked. *The Congressional Record,* too, contains a vast accumulation of material, as do the archives of the various military schools about the country, particularly the war colleges.

Finally, supplementing the written record would be my own experiences in Vietnam, combined with an extensive file of interviews with other participants.

INDEX

Abrams, Creighton, 267, 279, 284, 292, 295, 316, 319, 323, 330
Air Force Academy, 248
Ap Bac, Battle of, 37–51, 52, 55, 176, 289
Australia (Australians), 26, 70, 172

Baldwin, G.P., 341
Baldwin, Hanson, 33
Bao Dai, 8, 10, 12
Battles (see Ap Bac, Dalat, Cambodian Incursion, Hue, Ia Drang, Iron Triangle, Lam Son 719, Saigon)
Bay of Pigs, 28, 274
Berlin Wall, 28, 192, 274
Berry Sidney, 182
Bleier, Rocky, xvii, xxii
Bombing (see "Rolling Thunder" and "Linebacker")
Bundy, McGeorge, 198–200

Bundy, William, 96
Bunker, Ellsworth, 316

Cambodia, 6, 8, 24, 26, 54, 64, 73, 108, 116–17, 121, 126, 129, 139, 152, 168, 191, 207–08, 213, 235, 290–301, 305, 309, 312, 320, 331, 337, 338
Cambodian Incursion, 290–301
Cam Ranh Bay, 111, 113, 186, 337
Cao, Huynh Van, 39–50
Carroll, Lewis, xvii–xviii
China, 6, 7, 8, 16, 81, 88–89, 90, 99, 136, 138–39, 159, 163, 316, 321, 335
Chinh, Truong, 63, 66, 81, 88, 209–10, 302, 311, 328
Colby, William, 287
Collins, J. Lawton, 12, 56
COSVN, 295–99
Coral Sea (U.S. Navy

Aircraft Carrier), 94
Crane, Stephen, 93, 101
Cronkite, Walter, 242, 258–59

Dalat, 10, 240–41, 247–53
Dam, Bui Dinh, 39–48
Dan, Nguyen Truong, 245
Davison, Michael, 295–96, 300
De Long Pier, 112–13
Demilitarized Zone (DMZ), 8, 16, 89, 95, 117, 144, 155, 191–93, 213, 215, 296, 306, 314, 315, 316–17, 319
DePuy, William, 174
Diem, Ngo Dinh, 10–15, 19, 20, 27, 30–31, 34–35, 42, 53–59, 220, 248, 281, 338, 339
Dien Bien Phu, 7, 89, 115, 116, 163, 165, 212, 216–19, 221, 233
Domino Theory, 21, 26, 274
Don, Tran Van, 17, 56, 139
Dong, Pham Van, 96, 257, 302
Douhet, Guilio, 167
Duan, Le, 302, 311
Dun, Van Tien, 328

Eisenhower, Dwight, 7, 9, 11–12, 14, 21, 24–26, 139, 275
Erdle, Philip, 248, 252

Fall, Bernard, 33, 140
Fisher, Admiral Sir John, 99, 191, 330
Ford, Gerald, 336
France (French), 6–12, 281

Geneva Accords of 1954, 8–9, 12, 26
Giap, Vo Nguyen, 7–8, 18, 27, 63–66, 79, 87–88, 90, 102–09, 114–15, 116–19, 140, 143–44, 150, 152, 169, 207–19, 221–23, 225–29, 232–33, 236, 242, 246, 253–54, 257, 263, 266, 267, 279, 302, 307, 310–28, 332
Goldwater, Barry, 71, 96
Great Britain, 8, 35
Group Mobile, 100, 103
Gulf of Tonkin Resolution, 72, 86

Haig, Alexander, 174
Hancock (U.S. Navy Aircraft Carrier), 94
Harkins, Paul, 29, 39, 56, 71
Hinh, Nguyen Van, 12
Hoan, Tran Quoc, 328
Ho Chi Minh, 6–9, 13, 18, 54, 79–90, 97, 101, 106, 143, 153, 156, 159, 161, 195, 208, 210, 221, 225, 231, 236, 255, 264, 265, 267, 273, 285, 294, 311
    Saigon renamed in his honor, 338
Ho Chi Minh Trail, 20, 65, 75, 107, 108, 109, 119, 142, 208, 218, 302–03, 307, 312, 315, 324, 335
Hue, 53, 215, 240–41, 244–48, 252, 260, 263, 266, 296, 303, 314, 319
Humphrey, Hubert, 166
Huong, Tran Van, 61, 97

Ia Drang Campaign, 116–31, 135, 156, 181, 187, 228,

296, 313
Indonesia, 24
International Control
  Commission, 26
Iron Triangle, 168–76, 300

Johnson, Harold, 137, 190
Johnson, Lyndon, 25, 58, 70,
  71, 90, 91, 92, 94–98,
  101, 104, 106, 113, 136–
  39, 141, 149, 155, 159–
  64, 166, 186–91, 199–
  202, 207, 216, 218, 222,
  229, 257, 262, 264, 267,
  272, 275, 279, 292, 309,
  327

Kennedy, John, 3–4, 10, 23,
  25–30, 54, 56, 58, 95,
  138, 259, 271, 274, 275,
  278, 331
Kennedy, Robert, 262
Khanh, Nguyen, 60–62, 71,
  97
Khe Sanh, 194, 215–19, 223,
  228–36, 246, 258–60,
  263, 296, 303, 306, 308
Khrushchev, Nikita, 3–4, 27,
  81–82
Kim, Le Van, 56
Kingston, Bob, 298
Kinnard, Harry, 118, 121–25
Kipling, Rudyard, 43
Kissinger, Henry, 273, 276,
  328, 333, 334
Komer, Robert, 198
Korea (Koreans), xix, 7, 16,
  26, 70, 90, 113, 138, 150,
  167, 279, 313, 319
Kosygin, Alexei, 93, 201
Ky, Nguyen Cao, 61, 94, 97,
  106, 208, 282

Laird, Melvin, 267
Lam, Hoang Xuan, 304–08
Lam Son 719, 302–11, 325
Laos, 6, 8, 24, 25, 26, 54,
  64, 73, 96, 109, 139, 152,
  168, 191–94, 215, 290,
  302–09, 313, 317, 331
Larson, Stanley, 120
"Linebacker" (1972 bombing
  of North Vietnam), 321–
  22, 324, 327, 329
Loc, Vinh, 120
Lodge, Henry Cabot, 54–57,
  60–61, 70–71, 158
Lon Nol, 294, 295
Lownds, David, 217

MacArthur, Douglas, 72, 137,
  149, 167, 199, 230, 330
MACV founded, 29
Maddox (U.S. Navy
  Destroyer), 72
Malaya, 15, 35, 70, 281
Man, Chu Huy, 119, 123,
  125, 129
Mao Tse-tung, 6, 81, 138,
  267
Marshall, S.L.A., 257
McCarthy, Eugene, 262
McCone, John, 101
McConnell, J.P., 94–95
McGarr, Lionel, 22
McGovern, George, 326–27
McNamara, Robert, 36, 71,
  89, 95, 98, 100, 105,
  135–38, 141, 156, 158,
  161, 163–64, 189, 191,
  192–94, 195, 199, 201–
  02, 211, 259, 266, 267,
  283
McNaughton, John, 97, 136,
  199

Military Advisory and Assistance Group, Vietnam, founded, 13

Minh, Duong Van "Big", 56, 60, 71, 338

Minh, Ho Chi, (see Ho Chi Minh)

Montagnards, 62, 116, 131

Moore, Harold, 125–29

My Lai Massacre, 152

Nadal, Ramon, 128

National Liberation Front (NLF), 4, 30, 60, 84, 235, 256, 286, 295, 312

New Zealand, 26, 70, 172

Nhu, Madame, 55–56, 60

Nhu, Ngo Dinh, 54–58

Nhung, Captain, 58

Nixon, Richard, 23, 71, 267, 271–77, 278–84, 287, 290–92, 295, 296, 301, 309, 311, 313, 316, 321, 324–31, 333, 336

Nolting, Frederic, 54

Oberdorfer, Don, 217

O'Daniel, John, 17

Okuley, Bert, 286

Operation *Toan Thang 43*, 297–301

Parallel, 17th, (see DMZ)

Philippines, 15, 16, 70

Pike, Douglas, 60, 210, 220, 288

Quat, Phan Huy, 62, 106

Ranger (U.S. Navy Aircraft Carrier) 94

Revolution, US, 16, 37–38

Ridgway, Matthew, 279, 280

RMK (Raymond-Morrison-Knudsen), 111, 113

"Rolling Thunder", 93–101, 103, 138, 145, 148, 154–67, 168, 192, 321, 329

Ropp, Theodore, 166

Rostow, Walt, 161, 217

Rusk, Dean, 158

Russia, 3, 8, 27, 81, 159, 160, 315, 316, 335

Saigon, Tet battle of, 240–44, 263; fall of, 334–35, 338–39

Salisbury, Harrison, 189

Sharp, U.S.G., 94, 101, 155–66, 168, 191

Shoemaker, Robert, 296–98

Sihanouk, Norodom, 9, 108, 292–94

Sihanoukville (Kampong Som), 64–65, 108, 293

Smith, Scott, 298

Spellman, Francis Cardinal, 10

Starbird, Alfred, 194

Starry, Donn, 298

Strategic Hamlet Program, 34–35, 52, 54–55, 69, 281

Su, Nguyen Van, 46–48

Taylor, Maxwell, 27, 28, 29, 61–62, 67, 71, 95, 97, 98, 100, 104, 138, 155, 158, 189–90, 277

Tet Offensive (1968), 207–67, 271, 273, 276–77, 283, 285, 286, 311, 313, 322, 323, 325

Thailand, 26, 70, 74, 100

Thanh, Nguyen Chi, 142, 152–53, 207–11

Thieu, Nguyen Van, 57, 62, 106, 208, 266, 284, 303, 312, 322, 328, 337, 338

Tho, Le Duc, 334

Thompson, Sir Robert, 140, 146, 183–84, 276, 283, 285–86

Time Magazine, 131, 172, 199

Times, New York, 189, 261

Truman, Harry, 6–7, 199

Truong, Ngo Quang, 244–45, 322

Tucker, Henry, 173

Turner Joy (U.S. Navy Destroyer), 72

Units, American: 1st Cavalry Division, 114, 117–31, 213, 247, 263; 296, 297–98; 1st Infantry Division, 113–14, 173–74; 1st Marine Regiment, 263; 1st Battalion, 7th Cavalry, 125–31; 1st Squadron, 9th Cavalry, 298; 4th Infantry Division, 213; 5th Special Forces Group, 73; 11th Armored Cavalry Regiment, 173–74, 296, 298, 300; 25th Infantry Division, 173–74, 296; 35th Engineer Group, 111; 101st Airborne Division, 72, 114, 263, 306; 173d Airborne Brigade, 106, 172–74, 214

Units, ARVN: 1st Armored Cavalry Regiment, 296, 298; 1st Infantry Division, 244–45, 263, 306, 319, 322; 3rd Airborne Brigade, 296, 298; 3rd Infantry Division, 317, 319; 4th Marine Battalion, 68; 7th Infantry Division, 41–51; 11th Infantry Regiment, 44–49; 33rd Ranger Battalion, 67–68

Units, NVA: 32nd Regiment, 75, 119–31; 33rd Regiment, 119–31; 66th Regiment, 119–31; 95th Regiment, 75; 101st Regiment, 75; 304th Division, 216; 308th Division, 306; 325C Division, 216; 559th Transportation Group, 20

Units, Viet Cong: 5th Regiment, 245; 6th Regiment, 245; 9th Division, 67–68, 91, 103, 105; 145th Battalion, 251–52; 186th Battalion, 248, 251–52; 271st Regiment, 67; 272d Regiment, 67; 514th Battalion, 44–50

Van, Nguyen, 245

Vann, John, 39–49, 176, 289, 325

Vien, Cao Van, 277

Vietnamese National Military Academy, 248, 249, 332–33

"Vietnamization", 17, 278–89, 290, 301, 307, 308–09, 312–13, 313, 320, 324, 332

Walt, Lewis, 215

Weigley, Russell, 197, 201

Westmoreland, William, 71–72, 82, 92, 95, 102–11, 114–15, 117, 121, 125,

131, ("Man of the Year"),
135, 140–45, 147, 149–
50, 155, 159, 163, 166–
71, 184, 186–91, 197–99,
201, 202, 203, 207–08,
211, 214, 215, 217–19,
229–31, 233–34, 243,
246, 254, 257–58, 259–
63, 267, 282, 289, 330,
331
West Point, 71, 72, 167, 186,

228, 267
Weyand, Fred, 174, 234–35,
263, 330
Wheeler, Earle, 73, 100, 163,
191–92, 218, 259–63
Williams, Samuel, 17, 22
Williamson, Ellis, 172–73

"X-Ray", Landing Zone,
126–30
Xuan, Dao Mong, 249–52

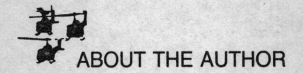

ABOUT THE AUTHOR

Dave Richard Palmer is highly qualified both as a soldier and historian. He was serving as a colonel with the 2nd Armored Division of the U.S. Army while completing SUMMONS OF THE TRUMPET. Since then he has been promoted to Major General. During the Vietnam War he served as an advisor to both the National Vietnamese Military Academy and Vietnamese armored units. He taught military history at West Point and was a staff officer in the Office of the Army Chief of Staff. He is the author of four previous books.

The confusion...
the horror...
the truth

VIETNAM

*one of the most controversial
periods of U.S. history*